ROBINSON'S GUIDE

TO BED & BREAKFASTS AND RURAL RETREATS IN VICTORIA, TASMANIA AND SOUTH AUSTRALIA

Richard & Wendy Robinson

PERIPLUS
EDITIONS

The Voucher Worth $10

MAY BE REDEEMED IN ACCORDANCE WITH THE CONDITIONS OVERLEAF AT ANY OF THE ESTABLISHMENTS WHOSE GAZETEER ENTRY SHOWS THE SYMBOL

Ⓥ

The Voucher Worth $10

MAY BE REDEEMED IN ACCORDANCE WITH THE CONDITIONS OVERLEAF AT ANY OF THE ESTABLISHMENTS WHOSE GAZETEER ENTRY SHOWS THE SYMBOL

Ⓥ

The Voucher Worth $10

MAY BE REDEEMED IN ACCORDANCE WITH THE CONDITIONS OVERLEAF AT ANY OF THE ESTABLISHMENTS WHOSE GAZETEER ENTRY SHOWS THE SYMBOL

Ⓥ

The Voucher Worth $10

MAY BE REDEEMED IN ACCORDANCE WITH THE CONDITIONS OVERLEAF AT ANY OF THE ESTABLISHMENTS WHOSE GAZETEER ENTRY SHOWS THE SYMBOL

Ⓥ

The Voucher Worth $10

MAY BE REDEEMED IN ACCORDANCE WITH THE CONDITIONS OVERLEAF AT ANY OF THE ESTABLISHMENTS WHOSE GAZETEER ENTRY SHOWS THE SYMBOL

Ⓥ

The Voucher Worth $10

MAY BE REDEEMED IN ACCORDANCE WITH THE CONDITIONS OVERLEAF AT ANY OF THE ESTABLISHMENTS WHOSE GAZETEER ENTRY SHOWS THE SYMBOL

Ⓥ

Conditions

A COPY OF ROBINSON'S GUIDE TO B & B's AND RURAL RETREATS MUST BE PRODUCED WITH THIS VOUCHER. ONLY ONE VOUCHER PER PERSON OR PARTY ACCEPTED. NOT REDEEMABLE FOR CASH. NO CHANGE GIVEN. THE VOUCHER WILL NOT BE VALID AFTER 30th JUNE 1995.
USE OF THE VOUCHER IS RESTRICTED TO WHEN PAYMENT IS MADE BEFORE LEAVING THE PREMISES. THE VOUCHER WILL ONLY BE ACCEPTED AGAINST ACCOMMODATION AT FULL TARIFF RATES.

Conditions

A COPY OF ROBINSON'S GUIDE TO B & B's AND RURAL RETREATS MUST BE PRODUCED WITH THIS VOUCHER. ONLY ONE VOUCHER PER PERSON OR PARTY ACCEPTED. NOT REDEEMABLE FOR CASH. NO CHANGE GIVEN. THE VOUCHER WILL NOT BE VALID AFTER 30th JUNE 1995.
USE OF THE VOUCHER IS RESTRICTED TO WHEN PAYMENT IS MADE BEFORE LEAVING THE PREMISES. THE VOUCHER WILL ONLY BE ACCEPTED AGAINST ACCOMMODATION AT FULL TARIFF RATES.

Conditions

A COPY OF ROBINSON'S GUIDE TO B & B's AND RURAL RETREATS MUST BE PRODUCED WITH THIS VOUCHER. ONLY ONE VOUCHER PER PERSON OR PARTY ACCEPTED. NOT REDEEMABLE FOR CASH. NO CHANGE GIVEN. THE VOUCHER WILL NOT BE VALID AFTER 30th JUNE 1995.
USE OF THE VOUCHER IS RESTRICTED TO WHEN PAYMENT IS MADE BEFORE LEAVING THE PREMISES. THE VOUCHER WILL ONLY BE ACCEPTED AGAINST ACCOMMODATION AT FULL TARIFF RATES.

Conditions

A COPY OF ROBINSON'S GUIDE TO B & B's AND RURAL RETREATS MUST BE PRODUCED WITH THIS VOUCHER. ONLY ONE VOUCHER PER PERSON OR PARTY ACCEPTED. NOT REDEEMABLE FOR CASH. NO CHANGE GIVEN. THE VOUCHER WILL NOT BE VALID AFTER 30th JUNE 1995.
USE OF THE VOUCHER IS RESTRICTED TO WHEN PAYMENT IS MADE BEFORE LEAVING THE PREMISES. THE VOUCHER WILL ONLY BE ACCEPTED AGAINST ACCOMMODATION AT FULL TARIFF RATES.

Conditions

A COPY OF ROBINSON'S GUIDE TO B & B's AND RURAL RETREATS MUST BE PRODUCED WITH THIS VOUCHER. ONLY ONE VOUCHER PER PERSON OR PARTY ACCEPTED. NOT REDEEMABLE FOR CASH. NO CHANGE GIVEN. THE VOUCHER WILL NOT BE VALID AFTER 30th JUNE 1995.
USE OF THE VOUCHER IS RESTRICTED TO WHEN PAYMENT IS MADE BEFORE LEAVING THE PREMISES. THE VOUCHER WILL ONLY BE ACCEPTED AGAINST ACCOMMODATION AT FULL TARIFF RATES.

Conditions

A COPY OF ROBINSON'S GUIDE TO B & B's AND RURAL RETREATS MUST BE PRODUCED WITH THIS VOUCHER. ONLY ONE VOUCHER PER PERSON OR PARTY ACCEPTED. NOT REDEEMABLE FOR CASH. NO CHANGE GIVEN. THE VOUCHER WILL NOT BE VALID AFTER 30th JUNE 1995.
USE OF THE VOUCHER IS RESTRICTED TO WHEN PAYMENT IS MADE BEFORE LEAVING THE PREMISES. THE VOUCHER WILL ONLY BE ACCEPTED AGAINST ACCOMMODATION AT FULL TARIFF RATES.

Robinson's Guide to Bed & Breakfasts and Rural Retreats in Victoria, Tasmania and South Australia
Richard & Wendy Robinson

Front cover painting by Hugh Sawrey
Output by Ekben Graphic Pte Ltd.
Typeset by A.V.i.
Designed by Murray Design
Printed by Singapore National Printers Ltd.

First edition published 1992
Second edition published 1994

ISBN 962-593-035-3
Published by Periplus Editions (HK) Ltd.
Printed in the Republic of Singapore

Contents

Contents

Foreword

It is a great pleasure to be asked to introduce "Robinson's Guide to Bed and Breakfast and Rural Retreats in Victoria, Tasmania and South Australia".

I am especially pleased to see that my native state of Tasmania has been included in this edition.

I think I can speak with some authority on the tourism and hospitality industries in both states, having been for three years head of Tasmania's Department of Tourism and now charged with the responsibility of running Tourism Victoria.

Wendy and Richard Robinson's first guide was really a breakthrough publication and this latest effort is even better.

While many B and B's and guest houses are being established, not all are of a high quality. Publications like this help to set a professional standard which the industry will aspire to.

They also help you, the consumer, to save time and disappointment by educating yourself about the product in advance.

This guide provides you with all the necessary information to make your decision about where you want to stay, how much it will cost and precisely how you will spend your valuable leisure time.

Wendy has had a wealth of experience in specialist accommodation, having established her own country house, The Oaks, near Alexandra in north east Victoria in 1988 and, more latterly, Robinson's By The Sea in bayside Melbourne.

I congratulate her on this outstanding publication and I confidently expect that it will be even more successful than the first edition.

It will certainly help visitors to Victoria, Tasmania and South Australia in making important decisions and therefore making their holidays and short breaks just that much more enjoyable.

Bob Annells
Chief Executive, Tourism Victoria

ATTENTION

OUR INTENTION IN WRITING THIS BOOK IS TO SAVE YOU TIME, MONEY AND DISAPPOINTMENT

Time away is more valuable than working time, there is less of it, so it must be spent wisely. The strength of alternative accommodation is its infinite variety, but it is also its greatest problem. There is a variety of experience from awful to magical.

Why do people stay in motels which offer the same experience from Ballarat to Brisbane; exactly that, they know what to expect.

No standards or regulations apply to B & B's except those applied by the R.A.C.V. The latter will downgrade a property isolated in magnificent wilderness because there are no net curtains to destroy the view, or no television to distract the visitor from an inky sky spangled with stars.

The alternative accommodation industry in Australia is the fastest growing sector of the tourism market. Most books and magazines charge operators for the exposure supplied by their publications, and cannot be objective. Warwick Randel is the notable exception, and he describes his favourite places.

Blairs & Explore Australia offer no routes and little accommodation.

The V.T.C. are pursuing a destination marketing focus and this is the structure we have embellished with our knowledge.

In this guide we have a comprehensive listing of all alternative accommodation that we could access, and have reviewed those offering the most hospitable and gratifying experience

We take the traveller to a destination, highlighting worthwhile places of interest en-route, including restaurants, and provide a choice of personally selected accommodation in the area.

Acknowledgements

This year the book had a more diverse approach in that it now covers three states and includes over 1,000 properties. Our daughter, Jo, and her friend, Julian, did painstaking research in The Dandenongs and the Goldfields.

Kendall Airlines and Tasmanian Tourism were most gracious in their assistance with our trip to Tasmania.

Thanks must go to Hugh Sawrey, Artist and Australian Living Treasure, for donating the front cover.

My thanks also to Lanta Hyde for operating Robinson's whilst I covered South Australia.

Again the diligence, patience and competence of Christine Milligan made the book possible. Thank you Christine.

Doug Booth miraculously appeared when the going got tough and helped with the final chapters.

Tourism Victoria offered support throughout the year.

But finally my warmest thanks must go to Richard for helping us establish the guide last year and encouraging me with this new edition.

I do hope that you find the book is more user-friendly and that it allows you easier access to your accommodation

KENDALL AIRLINES

The success of Kendall Airlines, Australia's largest regional carrier, which celebrates its 25th birthday this year, is due largely to the persistence and love of flying of its founder and managing director, Mr. Don Kendall.

It was on 21st June 1967 that Don Kendall and his wife, Eilish, set up Premiair Aviation with two Piper Cherokee aircraft. This was the beginning of Kendall Airlines. In 1983 the company changed its name to Kendall Airlines.

Kendall now operates six Saab aircraft, as well as eight Fairchild Metro II and two Metro 23 aircraft, to all major destinations in South Australia from Adelaide, and to major regional centres from Melbourne, including the north west coast of Tasmania, where Kendall is the main operator of services into Burnie and Devonport.

Last year Kendall was awarded the Best Regional Airline of the Year Award by the prestigious Washington-based magazine, Air Transport World.
We would like to express our gratitude to Kendall Airlines for flying us to Tasmania.

****

My wish is that this book be shared with love, lots of laughter, and that you find the accommodation of your choice in the company of good friends or your lover.
If you can do that, then the task of researching and writing this book will really have been worthwhile.
Now – watch out for Robinson's Guide to New South Wales, A.C.T. and Queensland. The Guide will go national in 1995.

WENDY ROBINSON

All business listings in this guide have been placed free of charge. We recommend them purely because of their professional and friendly approach.

VICTORIA

Best New One - B & B
Arcadia, Olinda - Geoff Simmons

Best New One - S/C
The Old Methodist Church, Buninyong - Peter Ivanoff

Most Romantic
Huntley Burn, Mt. Macedon - Penny Tate

Top Ten
Random House, Rochester
Monreale, Sassafras
The Hermitage, Narbethong
Allenvale Cottages, Lorne
Kinross, Beechworth
Gobles Mill, Port Fairy
Howqua-Dale, Mansfield
Powerscourt, Maffra
Viewly Hill, Pipers Creek
Clifftop Country House, Phillip Island

Arcadia

188-190 Falls Road, Olinda, Vic., 3788
Tel: (03) 751 1017
Contact: Geoff Simmons
Rooms: 2 & 1 Self contained cottage
Cost (B & B): From $75 - $125 double

Arcadia is a striking two storey cedar and glass home at Olinda in a quiet position away from the main road, opposite the National Rhododendron Gardens. The original cottage was built in 1932 and extensively renovated and extended in 1988. the cottage has a large country kitchen with bay windows and

2original colonial cottage furniture. The lounge features a floor to ceiling huon pine and cedar bookcase, a bay window seat and an open log fire with a spectacular 3 metre tall window overlooking the mature 2½ acre garden and trout ponds. Guests may elect to have their breakfast in front of the window and fire or in the new glass conservatory.

On entering the new section of the home from the low southside front entrance, one is struck by the height and light of the north facing two storey glass wall in the foyer with a staircase leading to the large first floor *Treetop Room*. Guests have exclusive use of the first floor, which includes an ensuite, external and internal balcony where breakfast is served overlooking the garden.

The ground floor *Garden Room* features a brass bed, picture windows, separate toilet and bathroom which has an original claw foot bath. Breakfast is served on a dropside trolley in the room.

Through the garden past beech and ash trees, rhododendrons, tennis court, in a private situation is the fully self-contained *Forest Cottage* with bedroom and ensuite, separate lounge kitchen, large sundeck and undercover parking. The cottage has a bright sunny outlook.

The house successfully integrates the old and new both in the architectural design, and the extensive use of early Australian antiques, art, pottery and artefacts collected when travelling overseas and has a comfortable and relaxing atmosphere. A substantial gourmet breakfast with local treats is provided.

The Old Methodist Church

802 Warrenheip Street, Buninyong, Vic., 3357
Tel: 053 41 3786 or 03 886 405
Contact: Peter & Lainie Ivanoff
Rooms: Self contained accommodation
Cost (B & B) $65 single

Undoubtedly in the top half dozen self contained accommodation offered in this book. A converted church, it has historic and aesthetic appeal combined with the most lavish furnishing and finishes. This renovation would grace the pages of Architectural Digest. The surroundings are pleasant in a quiet area away from the centre of the village, the large garden has mature trees, a tennis court and vegetable garden which you may freely use.

The main living area utilizes half of the ground floor and the spacious feeling is enhanced by the high vaulted ceiling. There is an ultra-modern kitchen, and large laundry, equipped with every electrical gadget. The adjacent vestry is elegantly converted to a bathroom with a huge shower servicing the two double bedrooms downstairs. A spiral staircase leads to the mezzanine floor comprising a cosy sitting area with T.V. and stereo which leads to the master bedroom with its ensuite.

Interesting works of art and antiques collected on Asian travels give a unique connected ambience to the whole interior.

Highly recommended.

TASMANIA

Best New One
Freshwater Point, Legana

Most Romantic
The Gamekeeper's Cottage, Brickendon

Top Ten
Hawley House, Hawley Beach
Franklin Manor, Strahan
Battery Point Manor, Hobart
Redlands B & B, Plenty
Meredith House, Swansea
The Old Rosary, Longford
The Pear Walk, Lalla
Crabtree House, Crabtree
York Mansions, Launceston
Alice's Cottages, Launceston

Freshwater Point

56 Nobelius Drive, Legana, Tas., 7277
Tel: (003) 30 2200
Contact: Laurie Thomas
Rooms: 2 & 3 self contained cottages

Travel north along the western side of the Tamar to Freshwater Point and my favourite house in Tasmania. A house full of sunshine and warmth. A house of style reflecting confident taste with a disregard for interior designer themes. An eclectic mix of loved objects chosen by people of natural talent with an eye for quality. Full, but not fussy. Sophisticated, but comfortable. Damask covered sofas and a comfortable cat.

Accommodation in the house is of two double rooms which share a huge bathroom.

There are three tasteful, comfortable, attractively designed cottages in the grounds. Fully self contained down to the T.V. and microwave. The Stables has a king size bed and a twin room.

Dinner, which is superb, for all accommodation is by arrangement - the view has already been arranged.

SOUTH AUSTRALIA

Best New One
The Dairy, Lyndoch

Most Romantic
The Miner's Cottage, Cockatoo Valley

Top Ten
Thorn Park Country House, Sevenhill
The Lodge, Seppeltsfield
Padthaway Estate, Padthaway
The Settlement, Kangaroo Island
Mill Park, Meningie
Apple Tree Cottage, Oakbank
Gum Tree Cottage, Oakbank
Miss Mabel's Cottage, Burra
Oliver's at Ford House, Kapunda
Warrenda Cottage, Lyndoch

The Dairy

P.O. Box 391, Lyndoch, 5351
Tel: (085) 24 4507
Owner/Contact: Tom Twopenny & Sonia Laidlaw
Cost: $95 (surcharges apply)

This romantic, delightfully converted dairy sleeps only 2 lucky people. The view from the loo must be one of the best in Australia!!
This idyllic spot should be a must for anyone feeling the stress that '93 caused – relax and enjoy The Dairy in '94.
P.S. Tom and Sonia, to complete that relaxation, can arrange for a masseuse to visit you at The Dairy.

Victoria

Victoria

Victoria offers a fabulous range of natural attractions. Beaches, rivers and lakes. High country wilderness and snowfields, rich rolling farmland and lush irrigation areas, even desert.
Evidence of our pioneering history is woven through this rural tapestry and an astonishing range of accommodation is out there if you can find it. Much of this offers more than just friendly hospitality, it provides pleasant environments where you may linger often in historic surroundings with top class facilities.
The production of food and wine has expanded enormously. Trout farms and berry farms are scattered through the state. A dozen different kinds of fungi and mushrooms are grown commercially near Mansfield, an olive grove in the western district, near Horsham, is producing olive oil, an ever increasing range of high quality hard and soft cheeses are being produced, continually improving in quality, and Melbourne bakeries produce probably the greatest variety of bread in the world. Meanwhile Victorian wine and wine making techniques are world leaders, at astonishingly reasonable prices for the quality offered.
There is a sprinkling of country house hotels of high quality throughout the state, but most establishments of quality are rare.
Unfortunately the industry often cannot provide sufficient income for the professional in our under-populated countryside so there is a large element of part-time hospitality. This can often be advantageous where the operators have made the effort to hone their skills (e.g. William Anglis College offers a food preparation course covering health and hygiene) and have the correct attitude to the customer. You may also be staying in surroundings which could not justify the business if it were purely a tourism investment with no other income support.
Amateur status, however, can be a distinct disadvantage where the host is without experience or knowledge. Such properties

give the bed & breakfast industry a bad name which reflects on the whole sector.
I have, therefore, offered a selection of venues where I can be confident your experience will be positive and enjoyable and hope this will promote the whole industry and facilitate your enjoyment of Victoria.

Melbourne

Although Greater Melbourne is a sprawling metropolis with 3 million inhabitants, the centre is compact and most of the interest and entertainment for the tourist occurs conveniently in the city and its adjacent suburbs.

The inner city areas are blessed by a concentration of fine Victorian architecture, interspersed by a large number of pleasant parks and gardens.

Melbourne is a coastal city and has a marvellous bay for recreation. In the past this bay and the Yarra River have been under-utilized resources, but recently this has changed. The new Victorian Arts Centre and the Southbank Development Southgate have been connected with walkways along the river. Restaurants like Jean-Jacques by the sea and the Stoke House enjoy the passing parade at the beach. Fitzroy Street, St. Kilda, and Bay Street, Port Melbourne, have become busy with late night eating venues.

Melbourne is the shopping and arts centre of Australia and is noted for its night-life and the quality and variety of its restaurants.

Live entertainment is enthusiastically supported, whether it be bands in pubs; comedy at theatre restaurants; concerts and opera; theatre or lavish productions like Phantom of the Opera, all are of high standard and available year round. Melbourne also hosts world class events; The Arts Festival, Comedy Festival, Spring Racing Carnival, the Tennis Open, the Nissan Regatta and later in the 1990's Melbourne will host the Australian Grand Prix.

SOUTHGATE ON SOUTHBANK

Developers can be bean counters or philistine money grabbers, but when competition or recession bite can come through with vision.

Southgate is an enormously successful concept - architecturally and in fulfilling a demand. Sadly the restaurants, generally, except for Walter's Wine Bar and Blakes, at each end of the complex are disappointing. Posing as sophisticated dining venues, they rely on the position and reputation of the complex and its entertaining passing parade, and augment their mediocre expensive food with sullen service.

The observation has been made in conversation with hospitality entrepreneurs that these 'concept venues' attract the kind of restaurateurs who care more for turning over a restaurant for a quick capital gain than in building a consistent reputation for the long haul. The notable exception is The Blue Train.

An optimistic note is that the talented guys responsible for Cerebonas in Carlton and Flinders Lane have been invited to take over a huge space in the centre of the first floor. Three espresso machines, wines by the glass, no food over $10.50, designer pizzas and a lot of clatter and buzz, will be fun.

PARKS

- Albert Park & Lake - South Melbourne
- The King's Domain & Botanic Gardens - South Yarra
- Fawkner Park - South Yarra
- Fitzroy Gardens & Treasury Gardens - East Melbourne
- Flagstaff Gardens - West Melbourne
- Royal Park & Zoological Gardens - Carlton
  The Zoo has many fine exhibits - especially pleasant is the 'free range' butterfly house

VICTORIAN ARCHITECTURE

- East Melbourne, Fitzroy & Carlton for fine terraces
- South Melbourne, Albert Park & Middle Park - cottages and less ostentatious Victorian houses, except:
  St. Vincent Place - a fine circle of top drawer Victorian houses

SHOPPING

- The City - Bourke Street & Collins Street, plus the Victorian Block Arcade and Royal Arcade
- Richmond - Bridge Road for clothes and 1A Somerset Street for fashion bargains at 'First-In-Best Dressed'
- Prahran - Chapel Street; young shopping
- Greville Street - Grunge shopping
- Armadale - High Street; designer labels and antiques
- Toorak - Toorak Road; designer labels
- Victoria Market - A brilliant view of the cosmopolitan nature of Melbourne, its enormous range and quality. Everything you could imagine in meat, fish, cheese, vegetables, plus shoes, fabrics, pots & pans, even pets. A wonderful place to buy or browse. Victoria's No. 1 tourist attraction.

FOOD

Lunch

- Café Kanis - Bridge Road, Richmond
- Pieroni - Toorak Road
- Campari - Hardware Street, City
- Harry's Bar - Wellington Parade, East Melbourne
- The George - Fitzroy Street, St. Kilda
- Café Sweethearts - Coventry Street, South Melbourne
- Rosati - Little Flinders Lane, City

Sample Menu - Harry's Bar

Entrée

Antipasto Varies
Sandcrab soup with toast & rouille
Croque Monsieur
Homemade gnocchi in a rich beef ragout

Main

Crumbed blue eye cod filled with herb butter and served on a bed of creamy garlic mashed potato
Chargrilled tuna steak with olive oil and a dash of balsamic
Panfried breast of chicken with red wine sauce and braised beans
Strips of calf's liver sautéed with onions in a white wine sauce

Desserts

Chocolate and pineapple parfait with coconut cream
Mascarpone chiboust with orange segments & caramel sauce
Selection of cakes on display
Selection of cheeses

Evenings - I don't 'fine' dine anymore.
- Tolarno's Bar - Fitzroy Street
- Catani's - Fitzroy Street
- France Soir - Toorak Road
- Blake's - Southgate
- Walter's - Southgate
- Brunetti's - Brunswick Street
- Madame Joe Joe - Fitzroy Street
- Ristorante Roberto - Exhibition Street

Fish & Chips
- Thy Thy 1 - Swan Street
- A Fish Out of Water - Richardson/Armstrong Street

Hamburgers
- Fats Domino - Toorak Road

Pubs
- Horse & Hound - Queen Street
- Grace Darling - Smith Street

- P.J.'s - Chapel Street
- Fitzroy Club - Chartis Street, Northcote

Robert Ledingham's Top Ten

For those of you who didn't meet Robert at The Latin, he is now at Brunetti's.

1. Caffe & Cucina - Chapel Street
2. The Globe - back room, but check out the toilets
3. Blakes - Southgate
4. Walters - Southgate
5. Iguana - Chapel Street
6. Catsni's - Fitzroy Street
7. Dog's Bar - Ackland Street
8. Calmini's - Toorak Road
9. Pelligrinis - Bourke Road
10. The George Hotel - Fitzroy Street

SPORT

- Tennis Centre - tournaments or hire a court
- M.C.G. - Winter, A.F.L. Football; Summer, Cricket
- Albert Park - Golf in the City
- Kerford Road - Windsurfing & sunbathing

BEACHES

From Port Melbourne to Elwood, especially the Pier at St. Kilda, the Marina between St. Kilda & Elwood, Kerford Road Beach, Albert Park - best bodies.

ACCOMMODATION

Robinson's By The Sea

335 Beaconsfield Parade, St. Kilda West, 3182
Tel: (03) 534 2683 Fax: (03) 534 2683
Contact: Wendy Robinson
Rooms: 3
Cost (B & B): $85 - $175

Rooms with a view.
Beautiful ocean views, magnificent architecture and sumptuous food to make your day begin with a zing.
The South of France, Malibu, the Bahamas, perhaps?
No! St. Kilda, just a stone's throw from the heart of Melbourne, one of Australia's busiest and liveliest cities. That's the sort of five-star treatment you receive at Robinson's By The Sea. It's the ideal place for that relaxing wekend break, but close enough to nightlife and restaurants for those eager to indulge.
The house is a grand triple-fronted masterpiece. There are only three luxurious double bedrooms, each with their own private bathroom, one with spa. Downstairs, relax in the chandelier-lit drawing room with a nightcap or read a book from the extensive library.

A late night romantic stroll along the beach may be the ideal way to end the day. It's also a good way to whet the appetite for the delicious breakfast the next morning.
If luxury and relaxation are two of your favourite pastimes, then take a break at this special place on Beaconsfield Parade. Host Wendy Robinson will make you feel at home.

The Avoca

98 Victoria Avenue, Albert Park, 3206
Tel: (03) 696 1661 Fax: (03) 690 6427
Contact: David Hunt
Rooms: 3
Cost (B & B): From $85 double

The Avoca, a comfortable bed and breakfast house built in the 1800's, is opening in April 1994.
There are only three guest rooms, all furnished and decorated in the Victorian period and each with separate facilities, including a full bath. A continental breakfast is available, but most visitors will prefer the full breakfast served downstairs in the guests' sitting room, which also provides writing facilities, TV/VCR and old fashioned wood fires in winter time.
The Avoca is within easy walking distance of the beach, extensive parklands and a score of eating houses which range from humble pizza bars to smart Italian bistros, a lively Greek Taverna and more subdued and gracious licensed restaurants. You might even like to try an Aussie pub!
If you wish to be more adventurous, a short tram ride or a $5 cab fare gives you the choice of cosmopolitan St. Kilda, upmarket Toorak Road, the city, or elegant Southbank with its galleries, theatres, shopping arcades and yes, more lovely restaurants.
Fax and secretarial services are available for the business traveller.

Malford

24 Sunnyside Avenue, Camberwell, 3124
Tel: (03) 882 3289
Contact: Gay and Alan Taylor
Rooms:1 ensuite & 1 s/c unit, ensuite
Cost (B & B): $90 single, $100 double, $20 extra person

This elegant Edwardian home in historic Camberwell has a large, quality suite comprising lounge/dining room, colour T.V., full kitchen, bathroom, washing machine and dryer. By combining the suite with the separate double ensuite bedroom, accommodation is available for up to five people travelling together.

This is an ideal base for the discerning traveller or business person, providing attention to detail and the friendly atmosphere that only a home environment can provide.

The Tilba

Toorak Road & Domain Street, South Yarra
Tel: (03) 267 8844 Fax: (03) 267 7567
Contact: The MacGregors
Rooms: 15 ensuite

The Tilba has a magnificent position on Toorak Road, at the city end, opposite the 100 acre Fawkner Park. A short walk to the Botanic Gardens and 5 minutes by train to the city.

A gracious small hotel with 15 double rooms all ensuite. all of them are individual in shape, design and ambience, with meticulous detail in furnishings, fabrics and the provisioning of the bathrooms. Dinner is not provided, but here on Toorak Road you have choice of price and style. Breakfast, continental in style and substance, is served in the atrium amongst a profusion of palms or in your room.

The front rooms are of magnificent proportions and appointments, the only problem being that these, the largest rooms, are a little noisy since they look out onto Toorak Road, which buzzes all night. The side and back rooms are entirely peaceful.

Kingsgrove Apartments

44 Fitzroy Street, St. Kilda
Tel: (03) 536 3000 Fax: (03) 525 4571
Reservations: (008) 033 786
Contact: Allan & Carol Essery
Rooms: 24
Cost: $95 - $210 per night, $480 - $1,050 per week

The old-world charm of this heritage building will take you back to the spacious luxury of a bygone era. Each tastefully appointed apartment is fully self-contained with all modern conveniences, including a full kitchen.

A choice of both Deluxe and standard 4 star accommodation makes the Kingsgrove Serviced Apartments an ideal setting for that weekend away, a family holiday or for those business people who need to be close to the Central Business District.

Set in the heart of St. Kilda, with quality restaurants just a short walk away, the Kingsgrove is only a fifteen minute tram ride from the front door to city shopping, theatres and a host of tourist venues.

Treetops

16 Linum Street, Blackburn
Tel: (03) 877 2737 Fax: (03) 894 3279
Contact: Sue & Jim Chambers
Rooms: 2

There are not many B & B's in Melbourne, and Treetops in Blackburn is certainly one of the best. Sue & Jim Chambers have 2 large, comfortable rooms decorated in a cottage style. each room has its own ensuite, lounge area, T.V., fridge, tea and coffee making facilities - opening out onto wide verandahs, large pretty trees and an attractive garden.

Linum Street is classified by the National Trust, and with the personal attentive care of Sue Chambers you are assured of a most enjoyable stay.

Castlefield Cottage

13 Earlsfield Road, Hampton, 3188
Tel: (03) 597 0896 Fax: (03) 521 0573
Contact: Jan & Laurie Begg
Cost (B & B): $65 double, $50 single

Castlefield Cottage is situated just 20 minutes from the heart of Melbourne. Guests will be able to enjoy the warm and friendly atmosphere of Jan and Laurie's faithfully restored brick 30's style home.

The area offers golf, bowls, tennis and, of course, swimming. Hampton Street is a shopping paradise. It also offers a wide variety of restaurants.

One double or twin with electric blankets, sitting room with T.V. and open fireplace

Lord Lodge

30 Booran Road, Caulfield, 3162
Tel: (03) 571 5315 Fax: (03) 571 5310
Contact: Jackie Little

This wonderful old house is being renovated to its former glory by Jackie Little. It is an impressive house by any standards, but sitting on the edge of the Caulfield Racing Track with Colin Little's stable complex directly outside the back door makes this B & B more than special.

The barn was built in 1870 and has stabled such famous horses as Lord, Havelock, Proud, Sobar and Future.

The day will start at 6.00 a.m., when you will go out onto the track to watch some of Victoria's top thoroughbreds go through their paces in the exercise ring, in the swimming pool and on the track. Then there will be an opportunity to talk to a trainer or two and the jockeys.

Back inside for a full cooked breakfast before perhaps heading off to the races or a visit to the Victorian Racing Museum.

Sunday is Owners Day, so again there is the opportunity to mingle with the racing fraternity.

Harry Courtney, Angus Armanassco, Richard Freedman, Russell Cleeland and Mark Riley are all within walking distance. Arrangements can be made for visits to other training complexes during your stay.
Celebrity Dinners are planned throughout the year.
This B & B is a real opportunity to be part of the Victorian Racing History.

Bettina Cottage

Cora Lynn, P.O. Box 253, Lilydale, 3140
Tel: (03) 739 1754
Contact: Mrs. B. Harman
Rooms: s/c cottage
Cost: $100 per night

This delightful double storey cottage was built in 1848 and nestles in the beautiful garden of Cora Lynn - the home of the Harmans.
Upstairs there is a double and a single bedroom. Downstairs a sitting room with fireplace and a fully equipped kitchen. Wonderful breakfast provisions, including champagne and orange juice are there for you to enjoy, plus homemade soups, rolled chicken, smoked salmon - just in case you get hungry by lunchtime.
A real add-on here is the stabling facility and the opportunity to be a guest of the Yarra & Lilydale Hunt Club.
Reservations essential during the hunting season.

"Ildemere"

10 Motherwell Street, South Yarra, 3141
Tel/Fax: (03) 826 2921
Owner/Contact: Kerry Hiddlestone
Rooms: s/c Suite
Cost: $110 per night, $500 per week

Conveniently situated near the heart of Melbourne's top drawer district Toorak–South Yarra, "Ildemere", behind its high exclusive wall, offers a secluded, central retreat. A single suite is offered with its own adjacent sittingroom, furnished in

perfect antique style. It has a warm and cosy ambience, and your hostess, Kerry, is charming and knowledgeable.
"Ildemere" is close to both Toorak Road and Chapel Street's top restaurants, entertainment and shops. The city is 10 minutes away, train and tram services are within 5 minutes walk.
Conveniently close by are tennis courts and gymnasium, for which Kerry can arrange introductions.
Tea, coffee and fresh fruit baskets are available ad lib. Gourmet dinners are available by prior arrangement.
Breakfast may be taken Al Fresco or in the sittingroom.

Horse & Hound Tavern

Basement, 221 Queen Street, Melbourne
Tel: (03) 670 8488

Located in the Legal & Banking Precinct, in this basement pub you'd be forgiven for thinking you're in old London town or Boston. Frequented by Melbourne's own Rumpoles, it's a cheerful place to partake in conversation while downing the choice of your favourite beverage.
Prop yourself at the American oak-topped bar amongst all the brass, dobois bricks, old stable doors, prints and trophies.
Big thick timber beams and posts hold up the low ceiling. Quite intricate, the structure, and it's no wonder as the co-owner is an architect who enjoys restoration work.
For quick lunches, select from the bar, or if you have more time there's full table service from the à la carte menu or daily specials. There's an extensive selection of wines and beers to choose from.
No evening meals are served, but there are always complimentary snacks on offer with your after work drinks.

Prince of Wales Hotel

1 Nelson Place, Williamstown, 3016
Tel: (03) 397 5101

Tucked away in Williamstown, 15 minutes across the Westgate Bridge from the city, this superb bluestone pub with an iron corner balcony supported by scrolled wrought iron corbels, is a discovery of restoration and decoration.

Flagpole masts, gangwalk, bollards and all things nautical lead to an entry filled with model ships, brass bells, lanterns and greetings by white starch jacketed "Capt'n" Andrew Singer, the hospitable Hungarian. From the most ornate carved bar at the entry, you're led to a wonderful dining room, all starched table cloths, but the real surprise awaits you in the "Titanic" room.

A truly beautiful upright piano in the corner of the bar is used to entertain the patrons.

An extensive range of wines and a menu worthy of an ocean cruise without leaving shore.

Melbourne

ALBERT PARK VIC. 3206

The Avoca, 98 Victoria Avenue
Tel: (03) 696 1661 Fax: (03) 690 6427
Owner/contact: David Hunt
Rooms: 3 Ⓥ
Cost: From $85 double

BEAUMARIS VIC. 3193

Grantlew Hospitality, 13 Holding Street
Tel: (03) 589 3846
Owner/contact: Celina Grant
Rooms: 2
Swimming pool

BLACKBURN VIC. 3130

Treetops, 16 Linum Street
Tel: (03) 877 2737 Fax: (03) 894 3279
Owner/contact: Sue and Jim Chambers
Rooms: 2 Ⓥ
Children welcome

BORONIA VIC. 3155

Rosbar House, 1 Lachlan Road
Tel: (03) 762 5513 (after 4 p.m.)
Owner/contact: Catherine Wood
Rooms: 2
Cost: $45 single, $70 double; Dinner approx. $15 single
Dinner by arrangement ◆ *No pets* ◆ *No children under 12*

BUNDOORA VIC. 3083

6 Amber Court
Tel: (03) 467 1335 Fax: (03) 467 8488
Owner/contact: Mrs. J. Cantrill
Rooms: 1
Cost: Bed & Breakfast - P.O.A.; Dinner $12

Melbourne

CAMBERWELL VIC. 3124

Malford, 24 Sunnyside Avenue
Tel: (03) 882 3289 Fax: (03) 882 8258
Owner/contact: Gay and Alan Taylor
Rooms: 1 and 1 s/c unit, both ensuite (V)
Cost: $90 single, $100 double, $20 extra person

Toad Hall, 34 Fordham Avenue
Tel: (03) 830 5620
Owner/contact: Patrick Poppins
Rooms: 1
Meals by arrangement ◆ *No smoking*

CAULFIELD VIC. 3162

Lord Lodge, 30 Booran Road
Tel: (03) 571 5315 Fax: (03) 571 5310
Owner/contact: Jackie Little (V)

CHELTENHAM VIC. 3192

Number Nineteen, 19 Olympic Avenue
Tel: (03) 584 4403
Owner/contact: Jan Jerman
Rooms: 3

CHIRNSIDE PARK VIC. 3116

Hillview Lodge, 39 St. Andrews Drive
Tel: (03) 739 5163
Owner/contact: Penelope & Des Moxey
Cost: From $85 double
Rooms: s/c suite

Melbourne

CROYDON VIC. 3136

Mountain View, 15 Janson Court
Tel: (03) 722 1038
Owner/contact: Mary Mustafa
Rooms: 2
Meals by arrangement • No smoking

DONCASTER VIC. 3108

8 Tiffany, 8 Tiffany Court
Tel: (03) 848 7960
Owner/contact: Marion Johanson
Rooms: 1
Meals by arrangement • No smoking • No children

EAST MELBOURNE VIC. 3002

Georgian Court Guest House, 21 George Street
Tel: (03) 419 6353
Owner/contact: Greg Chivers
Rooms: 30
Meals Sunday to Thursday only

Magnolia Court, Powlett Street
Tel: (03) 419 4222
Contact: Helen Doherty

FITZROY VIC. 3065

The Nunnery, 116 Nicholson Street
Tel: (03) 419 8637 Fax: (03) 417736

FOREST HILL VIC. 3131

Glenmore Homestyle Accommodation, 46 Husband Road
Tel: (03) 877 7416
Owner/contact: Katie & Tony Dear
Rooms: 2
Cost: $45 single, $60 double; Dinner $14 single
Children half price

HAMPTON VIC. 3188

Castlefield Cottage, 13 Earlsfield Road
Tel: (03) 597 0896 Fax: (03) 521 0573
Owner/contact: Jan & Laurie Begg Ⓥ
Cost: $50 single, $65 double

HARKAWAY VIC. 3806

Glenogil, 76 Baker Road
Tel: (03) 707 1646
Owner/contact: Judy Wallace
Rooms: 2
Cost: $50 single, $80 double; Dinner $20-$25 per person
No smoking

LILYDALE VIC. 3140

Bettina Cottage, Cora Lynn, P.O. Box 253
Tel: (03) 739 1754
Owner/contact: Mrs. B. Harman
Rooms: s/c cottage Ⓥ
Cost: $100 double

MALVERN VIC. 3145

Nesbits, 187 Darling Road, East Malvern
Tel: (03) 571 8979
Owner/contact: Joan Nesbit
Rooms: 2
Meals By Arrangement

MELBOURNE VIC. 3000

Lochend, Spencer Street
Tel: (054) 46 8204
Owner/contact: Patricia & Hugh Sayle
Cost: $70 single, $110 double

NOTTING HILL VIC. 3150

Cameo House B & B, 78 Westerfield Drive (P.O. Box 947), Glen Waverley)
Tel: (03) 560 4675
Owner/contact: Jo & George Murray
Rooms: 2 ensuite
Cost: $60 single, $70 double
No Children ◆ No Smoking

PARK ORCHARDS VIC. 3114

The Willow Tree, 32-34 Arundel Road
Tel: (03) 876 1907
Owner/contact: Margaret & Alistair Mackie
Rooms: s/c suite
Cost: From $85

PARKDALE VIC. 3194

The Banksias, 7A Monaco Street
Tel: (03) 580 5219
Owner/contact: Graham & Helen Jones
Rooms: 1 ensuite
Cost: $55 single, $65 double
No smoking

PORT MELBOURNE VIC. 3207

Ross Street Bed & Breakfast, 52 Ross Street
Tel: (03) 645 3205 or (018) 537 446 Fax: (03) 645 3808
Owner/contact: Henry & Simone
Cost: Per person - $42 twin share, $60 single
Dinner by arrangement

PRESTON VIC. 3072

The Terrace, 418 Murray Road
Tel: (03) 470 1006
Cost: From $12 room only

SOUTH YARRA VIC. 3141

"Ildemere", 10 Motherwell Street
Tel/Fax: (03) 826 2921
Owner/contact: Kerry Hiddlestone
Rooms: s/c suite
Cost: $110 night, $500 week
Dinner by arrangement

Ⓥ

The Tilba, Toorak Road & Domain Street
Tel: (03) 267 8844 Fax: (03) 267 7567
Owner/contact: The MacGregors
Rooms: 15 ensuite
Cost: From $125

Ⓥ

ST. KILDA VIC. 3182

Kingsgrove Apartments, 44 Fitzroy Street
Tel: (03) 536 3000 Fax: (03) 525 4571
Reservations: (008) 033 786
Owner/contact: Mrs. Anne Geroe
Rooms: 24
Cost: $95-$210 per night, $480-$1050 per week

Ⓥ

Robinsons By The Sea, 335 Beaconsfield Parade, St. Kilda West
Tel/Fax: (03) 534 2683
Owner/contact: Wendy Robinson
Rooms: 3
Cost: $85 - $175

Ⓥ

Victoria House, 47 Mary Street, St. Kilda West
Owner/contact: Marcia McKay
Rooms: 2
Cost: $45 single, $85 double
No children ◆ No smoking

TOORAK VIC. 3142

Toorak Manor Hotel, 220 Williams Road
Tel: (03) 827 2689 Fax: (03) 824 2830
Owner/contact: Nola Higgins
Rooms: 4 (3 ensuite)
Cost: $125 inclusive of continental breakfast

WHEELERS HILL VIC. 3170

Sunnybrook, 41 Sunnybrook Drive
Tel: (03) 560 2748
Owner/contact: Terence & Gloria Moore
Rooms: s/c suite
Cost: $40-$50 single, $75-$80 double
Gourmet meals by arrangement ◆ *No smoking* ◆ *No children*

Nepean Highway Mornington Peninsula

Drive south through the sprawling suburbs of Melbourne and realise a dream of picturesque bay beaches, rough and exciting back beaches and limitless wonders in between.

The Mornington Peninsula, accessed from Melbourne by the Nepean Highway, is bordered by Port Philip Bay from Frankston through to Portsea and Point Nepean.

From Mount Eliza to Mount Martha, the coastal suburban density thins and patches of countryside, charming beaches and sweeping views back across the bay are visible. While Mount Martha can be described as a quiet cul-de-sac, the Mornington Peninsula from Dromana to Sorrento abounds with holiday motels and caravan parks. Here the towns run into each other with little architectural distinction.

Your oasis of charm is Sorrento. Blessed with a pretty main street, most of Sorrento's quaint, stone buildings date from 1870. at Sullivan's Bay, visit the site of Victoria's first European settlement and, in the summer, catch a ferry across the bay to Queenscliff.

Travel another four kilometres to Portsea, the up-market end of the Peninsula's bay side. For most travellers, the Portsea Pub with its spectacular views and the bay and back beaches are the main attractions.

Nepean Highway, Mornington

Venture inland, where the Peninsula becomes hilly and scenic, with a scattering of small towns. Red Hill is a focal point and the site of a wonderful and well attended monthly Sunday market. People come from all over Victoria to browse through art and craft stalls and sample delicious homemade produce.
Hastings, the Peninsula's premier fishing port, and Flinders, the most southern town on the western side of the Peninsula, are both worthy of a visit. Or, for something different, stop at the Ashcombe Maze, a true maze of green hedges with an adjoining rose maze.
The Mornington Peninsula is well served with wineries (30), restaurants, arts and crafts and antique shops. The emphasis is on outdoor activities with the wonderful beaches; tranquil on the bay side or booming with Bass Strait surf, appealing to holiday makers of all ages.

ATTRACTIONS

National Parks

- Point Nepean National Park. From Point Nepean, fronting the Bass Strait and the surf beaches to Cape Schanck. Access is from Portsea or at Cape Schanck, and is sensational. There is a boarded walk to the old lighthouse.
- Arthur's Seat. Worth the trip for the Bay views.
- Hastings foreshore - Wetlands.
- Devilbend reservoir.
- Seawinds National Park Near Mornington - just 34 ha. of natural bush and exotic gardens, with William Ricketts' sculptures

Ferry Rides

- To Queenscliff from Portsea or Sorrento.
- From Stoney Point to Cowes, Seal Rocks or French Island.

Homesteads

- McCrae Homestead, McCrae. A simple drop slab cottage.
- Coolart, Somers. Century-old mansion. Landscaped gardens. Woodland and superb wetlands sanctuary, with bird viewing hides.

- The Briars, Mt. Martha. Stately homestead. Classified by the National Trust. Bird hides on wetlands and walks.
- Heronswood, Dromana. Gothic revival homestead, classified by the National Trust. Sensational gardens.
- Sages Cottage, Baxter. A rural cottage with 33 acres farm. A shingle and slab building with high quality restaurant and animal sanctuary.

Other Attractions

- Antiques at Moorooduc and Tyabb.
- Ashcombe Maze, Shoreham.

Tuerong Estate Vineyard and Restaurant

Mornington - Flinders Road, Red Hill, 3937
Tel: (059) 89 2129
Owner/contact: Gennaro Mazzella

A welcome addition to Gennaro's hospitality for the casual visitor is the opportunity for alfresco dining, weather permitting. Pizza, antipasto and other light offerings with wine in the garden. The first vintage of Tuerong Estate sparkling wine is now on offer.

Sample Menu

Antipasto
Spaghetti with Calamari
Salad
Cheese
Coffee

$38 per person
There is also a garden menu available now with dishes starting at $5

ACCOMMODATION

Willowmee Red Hill

Lot 2 Eatons Cutting, Red Hill, 3939
Tel: 059 89 2191 Fax: 059 89 2234
Contact: Loris and Roy Harper
Rooms: Self contained accommodation
Cost: From $95 double

This modern home is set on 4 acres of glorious gardens with a view across the bay to Melbourne. The Harpers delight in people sharing their environment.

Your comfortable accommodation is separate to the main house - 2 bedrooms, 1 double and 1 twin, with a large lounge upstairs, and a kitchen/dining room and bathroom downstairs. Easy access to the solar heated swimming pool and meditation pavilion.

This is a caring, nurturing spot to really unwind.

They also own a 'Golden'!

Warrawee

87 Warrawee Road, Balnarring, 3926
Tel: (059) 83 1729
Contact: Jane & Keiran Scott
Rooms: 4 ensuite
Cost (B & B): $145 double

Built circa 1860 by Paul Van Suylen, a sail and tent maker and obviously a very successful one. The publicity brochure mentions that history does not record the architect or builder responsible for the homestead. If he existed I am tempted to suggest that he was either irresponsible or a committee. The house creaks and I am sure grew like couch grass, and was occasionally chopped back.

The approach features a wonderful tall century-old yew hedge, pleasant perennial border and cool wide verandah. Inside the passageway is pretty dark because the verandah ensures little sunlight. The decor, though, is imaginative with fine stencilled borders, and recalls the period. Old furniture, photographs and paintings fill the house and create a pleasant jumble. The bedrooms, all ensuite, are comfortable and very romantically furnished.

Warrawee is also a restaurant with open fires and a good reputation, and its position deep in the Mornington Peninsula is excellent for the local attractions and activities. Close by are many excellent golf courses and wineries.

Sample Menu

Entrée

Homegrown Tomato & Herb Soup
Tasmanian Oysters - Natural, Mornay, Garlic or Kilpatrick
Trout mousseline garnished with smoked Atlantic Salmon

Main Course

Seafood Mille feuille - fish and shellfish in a lemon cream layered with puff pastry
Choice Steak - Porterhouse or Eyefillet with your choice of sauce - Pepper, Garlic, Horseradish or Bearnaise

Dessert

Homemade Ice creams - nougat, passionfruit, mocha, garnished with spun toffee

Rich Chocolate Mousse Dessert Cake

Fruit & Cheese Platter

Tea or Coffee with petit fours

Le Pavillon

1 Pine Grove, Shoreham, 3916
Tel: (059) 89 8433
Contact: Colline & Malcolm Nicolson
Rooms: 3
Cost: $105

A new sophisticated adornment to B & B on the Mornington Peninsular. It is advertised, correctly in my view, as a little piece of Provence on the outskirts of Shoreham.

The mud-brick and stone villa accommodates six people in 2 double rooms and a twin in a unique atmosphere, rustic yet sophisticated. A large 'Morso' wood heater provides winter warmth, whilst in the summer the house may be 'opened-up' so that the paved courtyard becomes part of the living area. Breakfast provisions are supplied and include homemade breads and preserves, chipolata sausages, bacon, tomatoes, fresh orange juice, ground coffee and tea, along with a fresh fruit bowl.

The Black Rabbit

Hillcrest Road, Shoreham, 3916
Tel: (059) 89 8500 or B.H. (03) 696 1011
Contact: Ann & Ian Russell
Rooms: s/c apartment and house
Cost: Apartment $100 per couple, House $135 per couple

The Black Rabbit is a delightful limestone villa nestling in the heart of the glorious Mornington Peninsula, just 75 minutes from Melbourne.

Accommodating up to 6 people, the main house and adjoining separate apartment combine all the charm of a traditional Mediterranean villa with the comforts of a modern Australian home. Exquisite touches include Italian tiles and slate flooring in the bathrooms and kitchen.

French doors in each of the beautifully appointed bedrooms lead out onto a wide verandah and spectacular views of Western Port Bay and the lush, green hills of the Peninsula's Hinterland.

The house is well stocked with breakfast goodies - including local eggs, sausages and bacon; and fresh baked breads from the local baker.

Picnic in the property's 6 acres of native forest, where wombats and wallabies can be seen, or play tennis on a mod-grass court. The Black Rabbit is also ideally placed for the Peninsula's rich variety of pursuits - from wineries and historic homesteads to superb wildlife, golf courses, beaches and panoramic walks.

Willandra Estate

P.O. Box 4, Balnarring Road, Merricks North, 3926
Tel: (059) 89 7300 Fax: (059) 89 7450
Contact: Lyn Peart
Rooms: 2
Cost (B & B): $85

Willandra Estate is centrally located on Victoria's picturesque Mornington Peninsula and consists of 22 acres of farmland overlooking a secluded valley with magnificent rural and wetland views.

This unique architect designed private hideaway is only minutes from Western Port and Port Phillip Bay beaches.

Willandra Estate provides a perfect base from which to explore the fine local wineries, restaurants, galleries and markets, or enjoy water sports, country walks, fishing and golf.

Guest accommodation is separated from the main house by an enclosed glazed atrium. A private sitting room area is available in addition to the bedroom and bathroom facilities.

Refrigerator, television, electric blankets, heating, tea/coffee making facilities are available. Fresh rainwater and a selection of seasonal fruits are provided.

Rumdoodle Retreat

26 Horners Lane, Rye, 3941
Tel: (059) 85 1114
Contact: Sandra & Ray McMahon
Rooms: s/c suite
Cost (B & B): $75 single, $80 - $95 double

Rumdoodle Retreat is a uniquely designed home, very modern, open and lots of glass, with all the living rooms opening out onto a large decked area which is situated at treetop level. The home is built on an acre of wooded land on Whitecliffs Ridge, and from the first floor balcony there is a wonderful view of the Southern end of Port Phillip Bay overlooking Sorrento and Queenscliff.

Rumdoodle Retreat is quiet and secluded within its wooded environment, yet it is only a 5 minute stroll to the foreshore beach and another 5 minutes walk in to the village of Rye.

BALNARRING VIC. 3926

Warrawee, 87 Warrawee Road
Tel: (059) 83 1729
Contact: Jane & Keiran Scott
Rooms: 4 ensuite Ⓥ
Cost: $145 double
Restaurant, à la carte, b.y.o. & licensed • *No children* • *No smoking*

FRANKSTON VIC. 3199

Long Island Bed & Breakfast, 98a Gould Street
Tel/Fax: (03) 783 2355
Owner/contact: Cathy & Terry Hope
Rooms: 2
Cost: $50-$70 single, $80-$100 double, $30 child

LANGWARRIN VIC. 3910

Hemerton Homestead, 4 Nirvana Close
Tel: (03) 789 9318
Owner/contact: Kevan & Jenny Smith

MAIN RIDGE VIC. 3938

Bellingham Lodge, Arthurs Seat Road (P.O. Box 90, Red Hill South, 3937)
Tel: (059) 89 6170 Fax: (059) 89 2234
Rooms: Self contained
Cost: $350-$450 weekend
Various packages available

Greenwood Lee, Purves Road, Arthurs Seat (P.O. Box 169, Dromana, 3936)
Tel: (059) 81 0254
Owner/contact: Betty & Roy Barclay
Rooms: 2
Cost: $65 single, $75-$85 double
No children • *No smoking* • *Dinner by arrangement*

Pines Ridge Retreat, Main Creek Road (P.O. Box 90, Red Hill South, 3937
Tel: (059) 89 6170 Fax: (059) 89 2234
Owner/contact: Joan & Bernard Joyce
Rooms: 4
Cost: $95-$105 double
No smoking indoors • Dinner by arrangement

Summerhill Farm, R.M.B. 7546 Barkers Road
Tel: (059) 86 2089

McCRAE VIC. 3938

Stay A While Lodge, 25 Bartels Street
Tel: (059) 86 4558
Owner/contact: Mona
Rooms: 3
Cost: Bed & Breakfast $35 single, Full Board $55 single

MERRICKS NORTH VIC. 3926

Willandra Estate, 158 Balnarring Road (P.O. Box 4, Balnarring)
Tel: (059) 89 7300 Fax: (059) 89 7450
Owner/contact: Lyn Peart
Rooms: 2 Ⓥ
Cost: $85
Smoking outside only

MORNINGTON VIC. 3931

Balaka, 176 Barkly Street
Tel: (059) 75 3398
Owner/contact: Nallis Kelly
Rooms: s/c cottage
Cost: $95
Dinner by arrangement

MOUNT ELIZA VIC. 3930

Streathern, 6 Mooring Court
Tel: (03) 787 1430
Owner/contact: Marjorie & Eddy Pearson
Rooms: 2

View of the Bay, 47 Kunyung Road
Tel: (03) 787 8652
Owner/contact: Fred & Aileen Rolfe
Rooms: 1 s/c suite
Cost: $55 single, $75 double, $15 extra person
No children • No smoking • Dinner on request when booking

Yamil, 55 Williams Road
Tel: (03) 787 1119

MOUNT MARTHA VIC. 3943

Kacey-El, 54 Glamorgan Crescent
Tel: (059) 74 1208 or (03) 889 3119

Tillabudgery, 10 Stiles Street
Tel: (059) 74 3404
Owner/contact: Dick & Lee Wines
Rooms: 1 and 1 s/c suite
Cost: $65 single, $85-$95 double
Dinner by arrangement • No smoking • Children by arrangement

PORTSEA VIC. 3944

Delgany, Nepean Highway
Tel: (059) 84 4000 Fax: (059) 84 4022
Lunch And Dinner Available

RED HILL VIC. 3937

Red Hill Retreat, Lot 21 William Road
Tel: (059) 89 2035
Owner/contact: Jan & Trevor Brandon
Rooms: 2
No smoking ◆ *Dinner by arrangement* ◆ *Weekend packages*

Willomee, Lot 2 Eatons Cutting
Tel: (059) 89 2191 Fax: (059) 89 2234
Owner/contact: Loris & Roy Harper
Rooms: 2
Cost: From $95 double
No smoking ◆ *Dinner by arrangement* ◆ *Children by arrangement* Ⓥ

ROSEBUD VIC. 3939

Inglewood, 268 Jetty road
Tel: (059) 86 1552
Owner/contact: Janet & Keith Jackson
Rooms: 3
Cost: $45 single, $65 double

RYE VIC. 3941

Rumdoodle Retreat, 26 Horners Lane
Tel: (059) 85 1114
Owner/contact: Sandra & Ray McMahon
Rooms: s/c suite Ⓥ
Cost: $75 single, $80-$95 double

SHOREHAM VIC. 3916

Le Pavillon, 1 Pine Grove
Tel: (059) 89 8433
Owner/contact: Colline & Malcolm Nicolson
Rooms: 3 Ⓥ
Cost: $105

The Black Rabbit, 30 Hillcrest Road
Tel: (059) 89 8500
Rooms: s/c apartment and s/c house (V)
Cost: Apartment $100 couple/night; House $135 couple/night, $30 extra person; Seven day package $650 couple

The Outlook, Lot 9 Nelson Street
Tel: (059) 89 8532 Fax: (059) 89 8326
Owner/contact: Meg & Barry Merton
Rooms: 2 ensuite
Cost: From $75 single, $105 double
No children • No smoking inside • Dinner by arrangement

SORRENTO VIC. 3943

'Carmel', 142 Ocean Beach Road
Tel: (059) 84 3512
Owner/contact: Bill & Louise White
Rooms: 4 and s/c unit
Cost: Bed & Breakfast $55 single, $80 double; Unit $450 week, $80 double overnight, $10 extra person
No smoking • Dinner by arrangement

Whitehall, 231 Ocean Beach Road
Tel: (059) 84 4166
Manager/contact: David Croucher
Rooms: 35
Cost: From $55 double, From $15 child
Restaurant for dinner on Friday & Saturday

WHAT ABOUT OPERATING STANDARDS?

The Bed & Breakfast industry has sometimes been described as "borderline" in relation to health and food standards because of the number of guests accommodated, and the different types of accommodation at each property.

Reg Holland of Health & Hospitality Services offers a complete assessment of the current operations of Bed and Breakfasts and can advise on standards as they relate to the particular business. Reg is a qualified health officer with more than 20 years experience in health inspection and building construction. He also provides personal advice and training in food handling on the premises so that the inconvenience of travelling to some distant venue is avoided.

This service is unique in its concept, and certification of the achievement of appropriate standards is provided on completion of the assessment.

An Information Kit is also provided to the operators.

Reg may be contacted for further information by telephoning (059) 85 1070, or writing to him at 24 Burdett Street, Tootgarook, 3941.

South Gippsland Highway Bass Highway Phillip Island and Wilsons Promontory

From Dandenong take the South Gippsland Highway to Cranbourne and on to Western Port Bay following the bay as it curves east, passing Koo-wee-rup and Lang Lang on to San Remo and Phillip Island.

PHILLIP ISLAND

Commanding the entrance to Westernport Bay this island, 140 km. from Melbourne, is flat and largely cleared of trees. The coastline looking out to Bass Strait varies from rocky in the west at the Nobbies to the large sand dunes and famous surf beaches at Woolamai in the east. Facing San Remo the mainland side of the Woolamai peninsula has a pleasant safety beach.

Bass Highway, Phillip Island

The principal town is Cowes on the northern coast, which is sheltered and offers safe swimming and water sports and the Ferry Terminal to French Island and Seal Rocks. Cowes is a pleasant town, lively in the summer season or on the Grand Prix weekend, but otherwise quiet and devoid of 'tourist attractions'. The main centres of interest are Woolamai beach for the surfers and the Nobbies for walks and its viewing areas of the seal colonies at Seal Rocks. The premiere tourist attraction, the famous Penguin Parade, is also here - watching these serious little guys commuting up the beach home from the ocean is a surprisingly touching event, even when shared with 300 people.

ATTRACTIONS

- Koala Reserve
- Phillip Island Wildlife Park
- Churchill Island Historic Homestead
- Grand Prix Circuit
- Penguins, seals and Mutton birds
- The view from Cape Woolamai
- A Maze 'n' Things for Kids

ON TO WILSON'S PROMONTORY

Leaving Phillip Island and San Remo, the Bass Highway turns south along the coast. Inverloch and Tarwin Lower are idyllic little settlements at either end of the pretty Anderson Inlet. It says a lot for the egalitarian native of Australian Society that every beautiful place from Inverloch to Mallacoota has a caravan park as its centre piece. With our tiny population I am at a loss to understand where all these people come from - but they are very fortunate in their choice of beautiful surroundings.

The South Gippsland Highway approaches Wilsons Promontory inland from Lang Lang to Leongatha (where it is joined again by the Bass Highway) to Foster.

The whole area from San Remo to the Promontory and Port Welshpool, the Catamaran ferry terminal to Tasmania, and on to Yarram is very thinly supplied with accommodation other than very simple motels, self-contained cottages and a few host farms.

Wilsons Promontory is a fabulous wilderness. A combination of Halls Gap and Mallacoota Inlet. It is a bit like entering a game park in Kenya but with emu and kangaroos everywhere instead of Zebra. The beaches are magnificent, as are the forest walks, and not a caravan park in sight; they are hidden in the trees

ACCOMMODATION

Narrabeen Cottage

16 Steele Street, Cowes, Phillip Island, 3922
Tel: (059) 52 2062
Contact: Marlene Forrester and Peter Berry
Rooms: 5 double (2 ensuite), 1 single
Cost (B & B): $110 - $134 double, $60 single, Dinner $42

Phillip Island to some is Fairy Penguins and summer holidays, but Phillip Island in winter, staying at Narrabeen Cottage, is wonderful. Sink into a large, comfortable chair by the roaring fire with a good book, knowing that dinner will be superb.

We went for a Christmas dinner in June, and they put up streamers, had crackers, candles - and the most super hot trout soufflé as an entrée.

Sample Menu - Narrabeen

Hors d'oevre

Olive & Anchove Tapenade

Bread

Homemade walnut and onion bread

Entrée

Smoked eel soufflé with a fresh dill and lemon Hollandaise sauce

Main

Baked eye fillet of beef with Bordelaise sauce, maced pumpkin, parsley potatoes and green beans & bay leaf

Dessert

Tiramisu, strawberry coulis and mint ice cream

Tea or Coffee and homemade chocolates

Everton Cottage

Berrys Beach Road, Ventnor, Phillip Island, 3922

Tel: (059) 56 8230

Contact: Greg & Lisa Price

Rooms: Self contained cottage

In the open centre of the island, this stone cottage stands on a rise adjacent to the main house. It is spacious, comprising an open plan living room, kitchen and a double bedroom with bathroom. The views are terrific, cottage plants and creepers soften the exterior. It conveys a well established feeling with old doors, etched glass and half panelled walls.

Greg and Lisa Price have created a friendly comfortable environment and thoughtfully provided many extras. Port, chocolate, biscuits and a roaring fire await your arrival. In season, fresh herbs, fruit and vegetables are supplied from the garden. The breakfast basket has home-made bread and conserves, cereals, free range eggs and fresh ground coffee. All modern conveniences, including television.

The Gatehouse Cottage

34 Walton Street
Tel: (059) 56 9406 or (03) 625 9083
Owner/contact: Vikki Driscoll
Rooms: 1 s/c, ensuite
Cost: Bed & Breakfast hamper - $130

Vikki Driscoll has created the most delightful self-contained cottage in the sleepy seaside village of Rhyll. The interior has polished Baltic pine floors, cathedral ceilings, a pot belly stove, books, music and generous breakfast provisions. Vikki is also happy to provide any special dietary food upon request.
The french doors open out onto a brick paved terrace overlooking the attractive garden. But it is Vikki's presence that makes The Gatehouse special.
Do book early here - it is always busy.
Another cottage is planned:

34 Walton Street, Rhyll
Tel: (059) 56 9406

The Windrush

41 Maroubra Drive, Cape Woolamai, Phillip Island, 3925
Tel: (059) 56 7937
Contact: Heather & John Marshall
Rooms: 2
Cost: $50

This is a comfortable mud-brick home of unusual design, but no airs and graces, on a suburban street. Owned by a delightfully open Scottish gentleman, John Marshall, and his wife Heather.

Fantastic value in the double room with ensuite, a twin is also available, share bathroom. Have the run of the house, and have the safety beach at Woolamai only 50 metres away. God bless them! This is an English-style B & B

'Rothsaye' on Lovers Walk

2 Roy Court, Cowes, Phillip Island, 3922
Tel: (059) 52 2057
Contact: Jenny & Robert Hudson
Rooms: 2 s/c suites
Cost: $65 - $80 double

Jenny and Robert Hudson are an interesting couple who opened a Bed & Breakfast in January 1991. By extending their home they have created 2 delightful suites, with private courtyards and direct access to a lovely strip of beach. 'The Iris' and 'The Hydrangea' suites both have kingsized posturepaedic beds, cane or pine furniture, pretty fabrics, fully equipped kitchens, laundries and gas B.B.Q. facilities. This is a charming little haven, just a short stroll from the main street in Cowes and a stone's throw from the wonderful restaurant at Narrabeen Cottage.

Clifftop Country House

1 Marlin Street, Smiths Beach, Cowes, Phillip Island, 3922
Tel: (059) 52 1033
Contact: Pamela Lloyd
Cost: $80 - $140

Nestled amid a peaceful 9 acres, 'Clifftop' overlooks rugged coastline with access to beautiful beaches.
This stylish cedar house offers luxurious comfort with many personalised touches to pamper you and make you feel welcome.
Enjoy breakfast at your leisure, then do as little or as much as you like before an optional candlelit dinner.
Guest accommodation is provided in double bed/sitting rooms decorated in provincial style, all with ensuite.
This is definitely an environment for those who enjoy comfort with style, who enjoy a real beach house feel - who just enjoy!!
Highly recommended.

Trenavin Park Country House

R.M.B. 1090 Ventnor Road, Cowes, Phillip Island, 3922
Tel: (059) 56 8230 Fax: (059) 56 8612
Contact: Mari Gillingham
Rooms: 5
Cost (Single): $55 Sun - Fri B & B,
$105 Sat, includes dinner

I drove down a kilometre long avenue of magnificent old cypress trees leading from the main road to the homestead and stopped half way to admire the spectacular view. Trenavin Park Country House, built late last century, is the outstanding historic property of Phillip Island. The imposing two storey grey stone building, with its gables, slate tiled roof, chimney-pots, mullioned windows and bevelled glass doors is a picture straight out of an English countryside.

The sitting room and dining room are comfortable and welcoming with a profusion of flowers, books and artefacts collected over many years of travelling, and reflect the host's wide-ranging taste and interests.

Accompanied by 'Delishus Delilah', I walked around the extensive garden with its sweeping lawns and magnificent vistas. I came upon an enchanting little white, red-roofed wooden chapel, perched high on the headland overlooking the Bay. Brought to the property in 1988, the small wood panelled building is used for regular church services, as well as innumerable weddings throughout the year.

Pre-dinner drinks in front of an open fire, an elegant dinner including smoked salmon roulade and duckling in plum sauce was the perfect way to end the day.

The house is centrally heated and all the bedrooms have different views of ocean, garden or lagoon, depending on their location. Some have attic ceilings, others are pine lined; each has an individual appeal.

Jindalee Lodge

Cape Liptrap Road, Walkerville, 3959
Tel: (056) 63 2336 or (03) 696 5400
Contact: Marcella & Graham Brennan
Rooms: 4 ensuite, s/c summerhouse

This is a modern timber house in a stunning position looking over Waratah Bay to Wilsons Promontory.

The house is open plan, having a huge living room with sofa's, dining area, pool table and kitchen. Guest accommodation is four double ensuite rooms, each opening onto a verandah which connects this accommodation to the house. Meals may be provided for you in the house and include wine, or self catering is possible by using the separate summer house which has full kitchen facilities (except washing up), indoor and outdoor eating areas.

A free and easy atmosphere with sophistication if you wish.

CAPE WOOLAMAI VIC. 3925

The Windrush, 41 Maroubra Drive
Tel: (059) 56 7937
Owner/contact: John & Heather Marshall Ⓥ
Rooms: 2 double/twin ensuite
Cost: $50 single

COWES (PHILLIP ISLAND) VIC. 3922

Clifftop Country House, 1 Marlin Street, Smiths Beach
Tel: (059) 52 1033
Owner/contact: Pamela Lloyd Ⓥ
Cost: $80 - $140

Narrabeen Cottage Gourmet Getaway, 16 Steele Street
Tel: (059) 52 2062
Owner/contact: Peter Berry & Marlene Forrester Ⓥ
Rooms: 5 double/single
Cost: $60 single, $110 - $134 double; Dinner $42
No children • Smoking outside • Guest lounge, library

Rhylston Park Historic Homestead, 190 Thompson Avenue
Tel: (059) 52 2730
Owner/contact: Kris Klabis & Mary Chester
Rooms: 4 (all sleep 3)
Cost: Bed & Breakfast - $70-$75 double, $15-$20 extra person, Cooked breakfast $7
105 Year old homestead • T-bar facilities • Children by arrangement

Rothsaye on Lovers Walk, 2 Roy Court
Tel: (059) 52 2057
Owner/contact: Robert & Jenny Hudson Ⓥ
Rooms: 2 s/c
Cost: $65-$80 double, 10% discount for weekly
Dinner by arrangement • No children • No smoking in rooms

Trenavin Park Country House, R.M.B.1090 Ventnor Road
Tel: (059) 56 8230 Fax: (059) 56 8612
Owner/contact: Mari Gillingham
Rooms: 4
Cost: Single - $55 Bed & Breakfast. Saturday dinner, bed & breakfast $105 (V)
Other meals by arrangement

FISH CREEK VIC. 3959

Maranatha, Waratah Road
Tel: (056) 83 2464
Owner/contact: Dick & Judy Edwards
Rooms: Self-contained cottage (6 guests)
Cost: Self-catering - $125 weekend, $250 week
Host farm

Taigh Na Mara, Cnr. Waratah & Savages Roads
Tel: (056) 83 2408
Owner/contact: Marie & Neil McIntosh
Cost: $70 double

FOSTER VIC. 3960

Kutuderi
Tel: (056) 82 2384
Owner/contact: Maureen & Adrian Jones
Rooms: 2 (double/twin)
Host farm

FRENCH ISLAND VIC. 3921

Tortoise Head - French Island, Lot 10, Tankerton Road, Tankerton
Tel: (059) 80 1234 or (059) 80 1222
Owner/contact: Sue O'Brien & Peter James
Rooms: 10
Cost: Full Board (1993) - $90 single, $170 double, $190 double cabin, $70 children; Murder Mystery Weekend $135 single

KOONWARRA VIC. 3954

Koonwarra House, Kookaburra Drive
Tel: (056) 64 2250
Owner/contact: Gael Knepfer

KORUMBURRA VIC. 3950

Pindari, South Gippsland Highway, Ruby
Tel: (056) 62 2005
Owner/contact: Val Brown
Rooms: 3
Cost: $60 single, $95 double
Meals by arrangement ◆ *No children*

LEONGATHA VIC. 3953

Tarrawatta Homestead, R.M.B. 7310 Nerrena-Dumbalk Road, Nerrena
Tel: (056) 64 9242
Owner/contact: Melinda & Herb Wildes
Rooms: 1 twin

OUTTRIM VIC. 3950

Down on the Farm, Inverloch Road
Tel: (056) 57 3206 or (056) 57 3212
Owner/contact: Sylvia Olden
Rooms: (single/double/twin)

RHYLL (PHILLIP ISLAND) VIC. 3923

Pen Y Mel, 4 Underdown Court
Tel: (059) 56 9302
Owner/contact: Ann Melville
Rooms: 2 double/twin ensuite
Cost: $90-$120 double

The Gatehouse Cottage, 34 Walton Street
Tel: (059) 56 9406 or (03) 625 9083
Owner/contact: Vikki Driscoll
Rooms: 1 s/c, ensuite Ⓥ
Cost: Bed & Breakfast hamper - $130
No smoking ◆ No children

TARWIN LOWER VIC. 3956

Jindalee Lodge, Cape Liptrap Road
Tel: (056) 63 2336 or (03) 696 5400
Owner/contact: Marcella Brennan
Rooms: 4 double/twin ensuite Ⓥ
Cost: Double - $85 B & B, $165 D, B & B

TOORA VIC. 3962

Ambleside Guest House Toora, R.M.B. 1130 Grip Road
Tel: (056) 82 2365 (B.H. 056 82 2822)
Owner/contact: Loretta Crichton
Rooms: 3
Cost: $130 double/night
No children ◆ No smoking

VENTNOR (PHILLIP ISLAND) VIC. 3922

Everton Cottage, "Everton Hill", R.M.B. 1160
Tel: (059) 56 8636
Owner/contact: Greg & Lisa Price
Rooms: s/c cottage Ⓥ
Cost: Double - $80 night, $350-$500 week

First Class Bed & Breakfast, Nobbies Road
Tel: (059) 56 8239 or (018) 38 9284
Owner/contact: Graeme & Margot Wells
Rooms: 3
Cost: $60 double

Manildra, Cnr. The Esplanade & Shalfleet Ave. (P.O. Box 189, Cowes, 3922)
Tel: (059) 56 8400
Contact: Dawn & Iain Raff
Rooms: 2 double
Cost: $65 double, $50 single
No smoking

Nyleeta, R.M.B. 1129, Watts Road
Tel: (059) 56 8570 Fax: (059) 56 8549
Owner/contact: Ian & Marnie Cairns
Rooms: 2 double/twin
Cost: From $45 single and $75 double

WARATAH BAY VIC. 3959

Sabrelyn Park, Waratah North
Tel: (056) 83 2298
Owner/contact: Geraldine & Don Wogan-Browne
Rooms: 4
Cost: $35 single, $65 double; Dinner $20 single
Other meals by arrangement ◆ Child concession

Waratah Park Country House, Thomsons Road
Tel: (056) 83 2575 Fax: (056) 83 2275
Owner/contact: Bill & Paula Thomson
Rooms: 6 ensuite
Cost: Single - $75 B & B; $120 D, B & B

YANAKIE VIC. 3960

Girriwana, R.M.B. 3733
Tel: (056) 87 1262 Fax: (056) 87 1409
Owner/contact: Lionel & Sue Rockman
Rooms: Self-contained cottage
Cost: $60 per night

The South East Gippsland

Take the Dandenong Road out of Melbourne to Dandenong. From Dandenong (do not confuse with the Dandenongs a few miles to the North East) keep on the Princes Highway to Drouin and Warragul, ignoring the temptation to follow the signs to the South Gippsland Highway. Warragul is a convenient stop at the centre of the widely promoted West Gippsland Gourmet Deli Trail. In itself Warragul offers little besides the remarkable Flamin Bull.

FOOD

Flamin Bull (Warragul)

This is an Australian Bush Architecture 'Theme Park' in a restaurant. The menus are on pieces of laminated corrugated iron, and the tables and chairs are hand made by the owners. There are rough, hewn timber beams and the walls are adorned with the paraphernalia of a country junk yard. Don't let this sap your confidence in the food; besides the lack of choice between here and Sale, the food here is excellent and generous. Well aged beef in huge steaks, well presented with interesting use of sea food and yabbies. Matilda, your hostess, is a charming dynamo - Gippsland tourism needs more like her.

Gourmet Deli Trail

This is a good marketing tool to promote the Warragul area which has the stunning rural mix of farms, rolling hills and forest.

- The Grand Ridge Brewery continues to manufacture some of the best boutique beers in Australia and the range is fabulous. From the immoral moonshine at 8.5% alcohol to the tasty moonlight - what a good name, at 3.3% alcohol. Variety is further enhanced by a Pilsner Lager and the malt, Gippsland Gold. Staff continue to be motivated and caring and, with luck and money, the restaurant will be refurnished to give an ambience commensurate with the good quality food. Support them please. Brewery tours and cosy bar.
- Also in the south, Casalare Pasta next door to the brewery. Tel: (056) 68 1746.
- Sunny Creek Fruit & Berry Farm (organic). Top Paddock Cheeses - with great variety, including our favourite washed rind cheeses and two blues.
- North of Warragul, Trout at Noojee, the Alpine Trout Farm.
- Pimpernel Restaurant & Hursehberg Deer Farm, with classic Teutonic hospitality and fantastic quality at good prices.
- Jindivick Smokehouse - more great quality and even more competitive prices.
- Tarago River Cheese Co. - A class act inspired by Lory Jansen and the legendary Richard Thomas. They offer Gippsland Blue, Royal Victorian with wonderful rich colour and depth of flavour and Blue Orchid, a convincing Gorganzola. Also Lavender cheese (UGH), French Curd, mature and tasty Cheddar, French cream and yogurt. White cheeses include Brie, a triple cream, mini Brie and a Camembert; these overseen by a great character, Frank Mauro, proprietor of the Old Bakery Restaurant.
- Note: Also The Herbal Harvest, Jackson Track, Jindivick, 3818 (Tel: 056-285398). A wide variety of culinary and medicinal herbs.

The South East, Gippsland

The Trail north of Warragul winds up into the dividing range with its mountains, valleys and rainforest. It is worthwhile just for the scenery, especially around Noojee, home to the Alpine Trout Farm. Try Gippsland Blue Cheese between Neerim and Neerim South, Jindwick for Brie and smoked meats, deer and fruit & berry farms in season.

Moe to Sale is the heart of the LaTrobe valley notable for the river and the brown coal and power stations in its heart. The road passes through rich grazing land with the dividing range close by in the north.

Due north of Morwell is Walhalla, an old gold town, whose proud population has dwindled from 5,000 to just 20. For proper hikers this is the start of the Alpine Walking Track. For walkers, take the old timber tramway to the cricket ground or Thompsons Bridge. For a stroll, take a turn around town with its historic buildings and fine trees.

The south of the LaTrobe valley is bounded by the exceptionally pretty Strzelecki Range. Note that the Midland Highway south from Morwell via Churchill to Welshpool on the coast is exceptionally scenic, but for a large part unsealed and tortuous, and therefore time consuming.

Note also the Tarra Bulga National Park Mountain Ash and Myrtle Beech Forest.

SALE

Sale is a relief after the freeway and mining towns of the valley.

ATTRACTIONS

The city has some pleasant avenues, King George V and Jubilee Avenue, and historic buildings like the Criterion Hotel with pleasant lacework and verandahs (offers ensuite accommodation). Sale is the gateway to the lakes at Marlay Point on Lake Wellington.

Sale Common and the State Game Refuge are extensive wetlands offering varied birdlife.

VINEYARDS

- Briagolong Estate
- Wa-de-Lock Vineyards
- McAlister Vineyards

BAIRNSDALE

A holiday town on Lake King at the mouth of the Mitchell River. It is an excellent place from which to explore the hills north to Omeo or the lakes to the south.

ATTRACTIONS

- Eagle Point Bluff - the site of the world's 2nd longest silt jetty
- Den of Nargun - in a gorge on the Mitchell River to the north

VINEYARDS

- Golwinda
- Nicholson River

LAKES ENTRANCE

Pause on the hillside overlooking The Entrance for one of the best views in Victoria. The colour of the water, the bar and surf beyond the narrow entrance to the lakes, make a picture full of movement. The thin wall of sand dunes in front of you forms the eastern end of ninety mile beach. The port to your left is home to a huge collection of boats, including a large fishing fleet. The Highway passes the length of these moorings and if you look to the water, Lakes Entrance becomes a beautiful place. Unfortunately the small town is architecturally unremarkable except for the incredible concentration of cheap motel accommodation.

- The Lakes

ATTRACTIONS

- The Harbour
- Ninety Mile Beach
- Lake Tyers Forest Park

- Nyerimilang Park Historical Homestead (with gardens, walking tracks and a bird hide)
- North to Buchan - a beautiful township and:
  - Buchan Limestone Caves
  - Wyanga Park Winery

The Lakes may also be enjoyed at Metung and Paynesville. These towns face each other across Lake King and are important leisure boating centres.

METUNG

- The lake and jetty outside the Metung Pub is the centre of

activity. Next to the pub is a restaurant, Morcombe's of Metung
- Bulls - motor cruisers for hire (Tel: (051) 56 2208)
- Riviera Nautica - yachts for hire (Tel: (051) 56 2243)

PAYNESVILLE

The approach to the town through a flat suburban streetscape is disappointing, but the foreshore, with its boat moorings, is pleasant in the winter and a hive of bustle and activity in the summer.

- Raymond Island - Koalas outnumber the human population
- Rotoman Island - emu, hog deer, tame kangaroos and a bird observatory - accommodation here by National Parks (take your own sleeping bag).
- M.V. Lakes Odyssey - Cruises

ORBOST

A long wooden tressle bridge and the Snowy River welcome you to Orbost. The most important building in town is Marshalls Commonwealth Hotel whether or not you need a drink.

South to the coast and Marlo and the Cape Conran Foreshore Reserve. Cabins (B.Y.O. sleeping bag) are available from Conservation Forests and Lands, c/o Post Office, Marlo, 3888 (Tel: (051) 54 8438)

Note that scrub ticks are found along this south-eastern coastline - remove as soon as possible.

GENOA

Genoa Peak and Genoa Falls (the last few feet to the top of the peak is by a metal ladder).

MALLACOOTA

Mallacoota is situated at the mouth of the Mallacoota inlet, a truly beautiful place. The inlet viewed from the foreshore caravan park is pure perfection. This must be one of the most scenic caravan parks in the country. The town is in the heart of the Croajingolong National Park, a sensational fishing and bird watching paradise.
M.V. Loch Ard is available for cruises around the inlet, including twilight trips.
Ask where the fresh water falls into the sea and seals bathe.

GIPSY POINT

A few houses, a pub and a guest house at the head of the inlet. Another piece of paradise - without caravans. This is a tiny remote settlement peacefully nestled against the water.
It must be reiterated that Croajingolong is of international importance for its beauty and unique variety of flora and fauna. This is a major Victorian tourist attraction.

ACCOMMODATION

Bon Accord

153-155 Dawson Street, Sale, 3850
Tel: (051) 44 5555 Fax: (051) 44 5555
Contact: Michelle Pugsley
Rooms: 2

This delightful B & B, reminiscent of early century homestead living, is an enchanting discovery in the midst of Sale. carefully tended gardens add to its olde world charm.

Sale, located at the junction of the Princes and South Gippsland Highways, is 214 kms. east of Melbourne. With a population of approximately 15,000, the area lends itself readily to a variety of activities, which include golf, croquet, fishing, horse racing, sailing, bush walks, scenic drives, tennis, water skiing and bowls.

Bon Accord has two beautifully turned out double rooms, which exhibit an attention to detail found in the best B & B accommodation. Dried rose petals delicately fragrance the rooms, whilst fluffy white bath robes hang thoughtfully from the doors. The beds are a delight, the sort that a person can disappear into, that almost guarantee an excellent night's sleep.

Dinner can be arranged on request either in the dining room or in the open kitchen area (a particularly good idea for lone people if they wish company). Your hosts can also recommend the fine fare of a few local restaurants, should you choose to dine out.
Breakfast can either be a cooked affair or light. This includes a choice of home made preserves, which also adorn the tables as part of the afternoon teas served to both guests and anyone else who wishes to enjoy the beautiful surrounds of Bon Accord.

Bunurong

Stolls Road, Buln Buln East, 3821
Tel: (056) 26 6289
Contact: Rob Devling & Wendy McKeown
Rooms: 2 ensuite
Cost (B & B): $90 double, $55 single

Central to the northern section of the gourmet Deli Trail, Buln Buln is a convenient one and a half hours drive from Melbourne, as long as you do not get lost on the last leg.
This modern home with its extensive pretty garden has two comfortable double rooms with ensuite, a private sitting room and dining room. Rob and Wendy are warm, hospitable people who go out of their way to ensure you enjoy your visit.

Powerscourt Country House

R.M.B. 6095, Maffra, 3860
Tel: (051) 47 1897 Fax: (051) 47 1431
Contact: Martin Van Ooyen
Rooms: 5

The best dining and accommodation of the district is near Maffra 20 km. north of Sale.

A country house dating from 1850 in a pleasant garden setting with a croquet lawn. The ballroom, resplendent with chandeliers and stained glass, is now a restaurant which accommodates outside diners as well as house guests.

The owner, Martin Van Ooyen, has been awarded a distinction in the Fine Dining category of the annual V.T.C. awards and also an award for excellence for the accommodation offered in the seven bedroom suites. The rooms in-house are particularly stylish, with four poster beds and huge original tiled bathrooms. Sitting areas are provided in the drawing room and bar room, and open fires crackle everywhere, even in some of the bedrooms. A very elegant period house with an enviable reputation.

There are 4 double rooms, one twin and one family, and there is disabled access.

Riversleigh

1 Nicholson Street, Bairnsdale, 3875
Tel: (051) 52 6966
Contact: Melinda Waters
Rooms: 22
Cost: $69 single, $78-$150 double/twin

Gippsland is fortunate to have two of the best small country house hotels in Victoria. Powerscourt offers opulence and period charm, allowing the feeling of being a guest in an Australian Homestead, in rolling countryside. Riversleigh has a different atmosphere and is somewhat larger.

This is a small European style hotel on the edge of town in a lovely position overlooking the Mitchell River. Offering 22 rooms, all with modern ensuite facilities, two with spas, it is furnished in sympathy with the period of the original buildings, two large Victorian Villas.

The architectural flare of the owner, Melinda Waters, is evident in the modern link to these lovely buildings which manages to retain a period feeling. The garden and balconies offer pretty aspects and peaceful environments.

The most famous facet of Riversleigh is the hotel restaurant, 'Waters at Riversleigh'. French in style, local in ingredients and wine, the restaurant has been a winner of the country dining section of the annual V.T.C. awards. Melinda now only cooks on Monday, giving responsibility for the rest of the week to a prodigée who she assures me is even better than she!

Riversleigh also offers an elegant lounge overlooking the garden, a swimming pool and a large cruiser, 'The Gull', for river excursions for up to 25 people.

Wattle Point Holiday Retreat

R.M.B. 7524, 11 Wattle Point Road, Wattle Point, via Bairnsdale, 3875
Tel: (051) 57 7517 Fax: (051) 57 7517
Contact: Wayne Miller
Rooms: 15 double bedrooms, 93 s/c lodges
Cost: From $59 double, from $89 four people

Pleasant modern units blend into 20 acres of Banksia, Wattle and Eucalyptus. Every attempt has been made to keep the accommodation in harmony with the environment and preserve the natural surroundings. The owner, Wayne Miller, has thrown away his lawn mower, the grass is so efficiently cropped by the local wildlife.

The units are tastefully designed, private and allow intimacy with the bush setting and its bird and animal life. Wayne is at pains to retain this environment, which is the draw-card of this retreat. The units have all modern appliances, a log fire, one double and one twin room, private barbecue and a deck. Bird feeding boards are placed close to this deck to bring the exceptional bird life to the door of each lodge, and occasionally the tame wombat.

A jetty and boat facilities are supplied. The retreat is adjacent to a 10,000 acre National Park, home to sea eagles, hog deer, kangaroos and emu.

Bicycles are provided free of charge, children are welcome and it is extremely good value.

The Slipway Holiday Village

P.O. Box 82, Metung, 3904
Tel: (051) 56 2469

New, good looking 3 bedroom town houses, each with a private mooring. Good value, with a waterfront position 50m. from the famous Metung Pub.

McMillans of Metung

155 Main Road, Metung, 3904 (P.O. Box 66)
Tel: (051) 56 2283
Contact: John & Kaye McMillan
Rooms: 12 s/c cottages
Cost:$75 double midweek, $95 double weekends

This old family property of 8 acres of established grounds with a gracious old homestead is where the McMillans entertain their guests.

Your accommodation is in one of the 12 self contained cottages. They are simple and spacious, with all the electrical appliances you might need, including dishwashers and microwaves. There is a private jetty, tennis court and 2 solar heated pools. There is also a library and a video room for children.

But, it is the attention to detail and caring nature of John and Kaye that makes you realise why McMillans win awards year after year.

Mariners Cove Resort

The Esplanade, Paynesville, 3880
Tel: (051) 56 7444 Fax: (051) 56 7069
Contact: Tony Spiekman
Rooms: 15
Cost (Room only): $60 - $108, $10 each extra person

If you wish to be at the centre of the activity, surrounded by boats and feel a little exclusive, stay at the excellent Mariners Cove Resort. This motel has a great position at the centre of the Paynesville Marina.

The apartments are larger and better furnished than many city hotels. Each looks out to its own mooring and has a pleasant terrace with table and chairs. The motel is exceptionally neat, clean and well run. My unit, besides a large bathroom, had a spa in the corner of the bedroom.

Kuna Kuna Farmhouse

Buchan Road, Orbost, 3888
Tel: (051) 54 1825
Contact: Ginger & Helen Johnstone
Rooms: 2
Cost (single): $35 B & B, $60 D, B & B

Experience real Snowy River country.

This property might be out of the way, but that is one of the many reasons that a detour to this niche in the beautiful Snowy River valley is so sensational. Immerse yourself in Australia.

This river is magnificent, white boulders and white water alternate with deep still stretches of slowly moving water. Kuna Kuna, nestled in its mature garden, is a stone's throw from the banks of the Snowy.

The homestead is eighty years old, but fully refurbished whilst retaining the period features such as direct access to the verandah from your bedroom. Two twin rooms are offered and these share a bathroom.

Dinner is en famille and may be in the dining room or the kitchen on request. The food is much better than farmhouse cooking - you have to eat in anyway or you would not be back in time for breakfast.

The conviviality of the hosts reflects a real pleasure in the entertaining of visitors.

Gipsy Point Lodge

Gipsy Point, 3891
Tel: (051) 58 8205 Fax: (051) 58 8205
Contact: Alan Robertson & Susan Webb
Rooms: 8 ensuite, s/c cottages
Cost (Single): $85 D, B & B, $95 Full

Gipsy Point Lodge is 6 hours from Melbourne and less than 4 hours from Canberra in one of the beautiful locations in the state.

This is a special environment. You have the choice of full accommodation in the guest house, or renting the self-contained cottages. These are spacious and well appointed, but guests need to bring their own bed linen, towels and food.

But it is the environment and what it offers that makes people return again and again. Alan organises special 'Bird Weeks' throughout the year. There is a field naturalists' week, and a Pelagic bird and whale watching trip. Also this year Alan has organised a two week intensive permaculture design course.

But, of course, you don't have to do anything, except maybe fish for bream, read a book - and relax.

BAIRNSDALE VIC. 3875

Riversleigh Country Hotel & Restaurant, 1 Nicholson Street
Tel: (051) 52 6966 or (051) 52 4336
Owner/contact: Melinda Waters
Rooms: 22 (single/double/twin/family) Ⓥ
Cost: $69 single, $78-$150 double/twin
Dinner available

BALOOK VIC. 3971

Fern Valley, Grand Ridge Road
Tel: (051) 96 6141
Rooms: 11 (double/twin)
Dinner available

Tarra-Bulga, Grand Ridge Road
Tel: (051) 96 6141
Owner/contact: Des Davison
Rooms: 11
Cost: Dinner bed & breakfast - $55 single, $28 under 10's
No smoking

BRUTHEN VIC. 3885

Bruthen Bed & Breakfast, Cnr. Main Street & Omeo Highway
Tel: (051) 57 5616
Owner/contact: Nick Margetts
Rooms: 3
Cost: $40 single, $65-$85 double; Dinner $10

BULN BULN EAST VIC. 3821

Bunurong Bed & Breakfast, Stolls Road
Tel: (056) 26 6289
Owner/contact: Wendy McKeown & Rob Devling
Rooms: 2 ensuite
Cost: $55 single, $90 double Ⓥ
Private lounge/dining area
MacAlister Lodge, 44 Ryans Road

COONGULLA VIC. 3860

Tel: (051) 48 0408
Owner/contact: David & Michelle Sanders
Rooms: 3
Home View, Heyfield Road

COWWARR VIC. 3857

Tel: (051) 48 9316 Fax: (051) 74 0858
Owner/contact: Barbara & Kevin Morgan
Rooms: 2
All meals available
Billabong Homestead, Paynesville Road (P.O. Box 42,

EAGLE POINT VIC. 3878

Bairnsdale, 3875)
Tel: (051) 56 7661
Owner/contact: Mrs. Maureen Newcomen
Rooms: 2
Swimming pool • Pets allowed • No children under 15
Gipsy Point Resort Hotel

GIPSY POINT VIC. 3891

Tel: (03) 846 1775
Owner/contact: Tom Payne
Rooms: 13 ensuite
Cost: Room only $40-$50; Breakfast $6.50-$9.50

Gipsy Point Lodge
Tel/Fax: (051) 58 8205
Owner/contact: Alan Robertson & Susan Webb (V)
Rooms: 8 ensuite
Cost: Per person - $85 dinner bed & breakfast, $95 full board
Boats for hire • No smoking indoors

The South East, Gippsland

INVERLOCH VIC. 3996

Fryers, 18 Ramsey Boulevard
Tel: (056) 74 1929
Rooms: 1 self contained unit

JOHNSONVILLE VIC. 3902

Meningie Homestead, Johnsons Road
Tel: (051) 56 4362
Owner/contact: Judy & David Moresi
Rooms: 3 double/twin ensuite
Cost: Bed & Breakfast - $60 double
Children half adult tariff ◆ *No smoking indoors*

KOONWARRA VIC. 3954

Koonwarra House, Kookaburra Drive
Tel: (056) 64 2250
Owner/contact: Gael Knepfer

LABERTOUCHE VIC. 3816

Tarween, Labertouche Road
Tel: (056) 28 7533

LAKES ENTRANCE VIC. 3809

Dostines, 37 Esplanade
Tel: (051) 55 2732
Owner/contact: Lance & Joan Dostine
Rooms: 2 s/c units
Cost: $65-$105 single, $80-$120 double
No children ◆ *No smoking* ◆ *Dinner by prior arrangement*

The South East, Gippsland

LOCH VIC. 3945

Tallwood Lodge, Henry's Road
Tel: (056) 59 6336 Fax: (056) 62 4337
Owner/contact: David & Kate Taylor
Rooms: 4 ensuite
Cost: $75 single, $100 double/twin
No smoking ◆ Dinner available by prior arrangement

MAFFRA VIC. 3860

Powerscourt Country House, R.M.B. 6095 Stratford Road
Tel: (051) 47 1897 Fax: (051) 47 1431
Owner/contact: Martin Van Ouyen (V)
Rooms: 5
Disabled access

MALLACOOTA VIC. 3892

Mareeba Lodge, 59 Mirrabooka Road
Tel: (051) 58 0378
Owner/contact: Anne Studd
Rooms: 2
Cost: $55-$65; Dinner $15-$18
Private guest lounge ◆ All meals by arrangement ◆ Children by arrangement

METUNG VIC. 3904

McMillans of Metung, 155 Main Road (P.O. Box 66)
Tel: (051) 56 2283
Owner/contact: John & Kaye McMillan (V)
Rooms: 12 s/c cottages
Cost: $75-$95 double, $15 extra adult, $10 child

Metung Hotel, Kurnai Avenue
Tel: (051) 56 2206
Rooms: 6

Terrazas Del Lago, P.O. Box 106
Tel: (051) 56 2666 Fax: (051) 56 2677

The Slipway Holiday Village, P.O. Box 82
Tel: (051) 56 2469 Ⓥ

ORBOST VIC. 3888

Gleann Eilg, P.O. Box 109
Tel/Fax: (051) 54 1542
Owner/contact: Brenda & Keith Murray
Rooms: 1
Cost: $35 single, $60 double; Dinner $20
No Children • No Smoking

Killarney, Duggans Road
Tel: (051) 54 1804
Owner/contact: Wendy & Max Nixon
Rooms: 2 suites
Cost: $75 single, $130 double
Working farm • No children • Dinner available by arrangement

Kuna Kuna, Buchan Road (P.O. Box 179)
Tel: (051) 54 1825
Owner/contact: Helen Johnstone
Rooms: 2 Ⓥ
Cost: Single - $35; Dinner bed & breakfast $60
No smoking • Host farm

PAYNESVILLE VIC. 3880

Mariners Cove Resort, The Esplanade
Tel: (051) 56 7444 Fax: (051) 56 7069
Owner/contact: Tony Spiekman
Rooms: 15 Ⓥ
Cost: Suite - $60-$108, $10 extra person

The South East, Gippsland

POOWONG VIC. 3988

Red House, McDonalds Track, Mountain View
Tel: (056) 59 7323
Owner/contact: Brian & Susan Coleman
Rooms: 2

SALE VIC. 3850

Bon Accord, 153-155 Dawson Street
Tel: (051) 44 5555 Fax: (051) 44 5555 Ⓥ
Owner/contact: Michelle Pugsley
Rooms: 2

TONIMBUK VIC. 3815

Tonimbuk Farm, Tonimbuk-Gembrook Road
Tel: (056) 29 8525
Owner/contact: Eleanor Viney
Rooms: 7 (doubles/singles/1 twin)
Horse riding available on property

WATTLE POINT VIC. 3875

Wattle Point Holiday Retreat, 11 Wattle Point Road (R.M.B. 7524 via Bairnsdale)
Tel/Fax: (051) 57 7517
Owner/contact: Wayne Miller
Rooms: 15 double and 93 s/c lodges Ⓥ
Cost: From $59 double, from $89 four people

MATERIAL ASSETS

Exquisite! Truly a masterpiece! Words used to describe the hand embroidered linen we offer. Personalised linen is an enchanting way to say someone is special. Our hand embroidered linen is second to none - original masterpieces in miniature, made to match your decor. A love of colour has always held our interest and this is extended to embroidered garden pictures to grace your home. These may be inspired by a favourite photograph, or be dreams of the garden you would like to enjoy.

To complement the beauty of antique furniture, we offer tapestries using modern and traditional themes. These are designed and worked by a master artisan using the vibrancy of colours found in fruit, flowers and the natural world. As single items, they stun the eye - as collections, they become MATERIAL ASSETS. Chairseats, footstools and cushions grace the sitting room, whilst romantic teacosies add charm to the kitchen.

We are always developing new products and are now able to offer patchwork quilts using the wealth of contemporary fabrics. Hand quilting is a feature of these luxurious items and they will become heirlooms for you to treasure.

MATERIAL ASSETS is a proudly Australian family business providing unique, exquisite pieces of work to grace your home.

Material Assets
Box 51, RUSHWORTH, VIC. 3612

The Dandenongs

For me the Dandenongs offer a beautiful natural environment strewn with interesting houses and stunning gardens, both public and private. There is, however, much more for the tourist. An abundance of craft and gift shops, tearooms, antiques and nurseries. The area is filled with scenic drives with destinations as diverse as Puffing Billy and the William Ricketts Sanctuary.

Romance is the staple of this area, either as a quiet and close getaway for Melbourne lovers or a beautiful environment for weddings, receptions and those all important photographs.

From Melbourne take the Burwood Highway to Ferntree Gully, and in just 50 kms. you are in the Dandenongs, a lush forested range popular for one hundred years as a cool scenic escape from the city. Mt. Dandenong is 633 m. and bestows on this small area its high rainfall. Nature is the great attraction, the forests and national parks with a plethora of walks in scenic temperate rain forest with beautiful mountain ash, tree ferns and bird life.

Woven through these forests are winding roads connecting the many small settlements. There are many charming houses along these country lanes with large and beautiful European gardens. Autumn is therefore colourful, but early Spring is of special note when the area blazes with the colours of azaleas and rhododendrons. The area is also famous for its nurseries. The bulb displays, daffodils and tulips, are spectacular, again in the Spring.

A drive around the Mt. Dandenong tourist road will take you past dozens of craft, antique and gift shops and dozens more tea rooms and restaurants with architecture varying from Tudor through Tyrolean to log cabin. Be warned, this drive can be exceedingly slow on fine Spring and Summer weekends, this being the most popular day trip destination close to Melbourne.

ATTRACTIONS

- Sherbrooke Forest - walking tracks, Lyre birds, Mountain Ash, The Sherbrooke Falls
- Doongalla Forest - walking tracks, magnificent Mountain Ash along the creek, the rare Long Leaved Box, and Red Stringybark
- Public Gardens:
    - Rhododendra Gardens, Olinda
    - Alfred Nicholas Memorial Garden
    - George Tindale Garden
    - Piranda Garden
    - William Ricketts Sanctuary - sculptures in a bush setting
- Nurseries, especially Tessalars
- Antiques, especially Laszlo Grdos
- Children - Puffing Billy and the adjacent large miniature railway

ACCOMMODATION

Arcadia

188-190 Falls Road, Olinda, 3788
Tel: (03) 751 1017
Contact: Geoff Simmons
Rooms: 2 & 1 Self contained cottage
Cost (B & B): From $75 - $125 double

Arcadia is a striking two storey cedar and glass home at Olinda in a quiet position away from the main road, opposite the National Rhododendron Gardens. The original cottage was built in 1932 and extensively renovated and extended in 1988. the cottage has a large country kitchen with bay windows and original colonial cottage furniture. The lounge features a floor to ceiling huon pine and cedar bookcase, a bay window seat and an open log fire with a spectacular 3 metre tall window overlooking the mature 2½ acre garden and trout ponds. Guests may elect to have their breakfast in front of the window and fire or in the new glass conservatory.

On entering the new section of the home from the low southside front entrance, one is struck by the height and light of the north facing two storey glass wall in the foyer with a staircase leading to the large first floor *Treetop Room.* Guests have exclusive use of the first floor, which includes an ensuite, external and internal balcony where breakfast is served overlooking the garden.

The ground floor *Garden Room* features a brass bed, picture windows, separate toilet and bathroom which has an original claw foot bath. Breakfast is served on a dropside trolley in the room.

Through the garden past beech and ash trees, rhododendrons, tennis court, in a private situation is the fully self-contained *Forest Cottage* with bedroom and ensuite, separate lounge kitchen, large sundeck and undercover parking. The cottage has a bright sunny outlook.

The house successfully integrates the old and new both in the architectural design, and the extensive use of early Australian antiques, art, pottery and artefacts collected when travelling overseas and has a comfortable and relaxing atmosphere. A substantial gourmet breakfast with local treats is provided.

Monreale

The Crescent, Sassafras
Tel: 03 755 1773 Fax: 03 755 2729
Contact: Peta and Laurie Rolls
Rooms: 3 double ensuite
Cost (B & B): From $80 double

This quality accommodation now has three double ensuite rooms. The garden continues to flourish, housekeeping and hospitality standards are still 5-Star.

Monreale was designed on several levels in the 20's as a guest house; then for 25 people, now for just three couples. The rooms are beautifully appointed and thankfully not terminally infected by the craft/kitch disease endemic to the area.

Each room has private facilities and shares a lovely private outdoor sitting area surrounded by the pretty garden. The guest sitting room is of real country-house quality with mahogany and chintz around an open fire.

Breakfast is taken in this room at a round table in the window, and is shared with the wild forest birds, notably the Crimson Rosellas, invited to the window sill. Three things are essential for a quality B & B: the bedroom should be private, comfortable and special in some way; the hosts hospitable; and breakfast spectacular. Breakfast at Monreale was spectacular. Peta and Laurie have created one of the most pleasing B & B's in Victoria.

Last year's winner of the Best Newcomer's Award - they certainly earn their place in Victoria's Top Ten.

Mary Cards Cottage

1498 Mt. Dandenong Tourist Road, Olinda
Tel: 03 751 1301
Contact: Kevin and Margaret Smith
Rooms: 3 suites
Cost:From $125 - $195

Kevin and Margaret moved to the Dandenongs, leaving the fast lane of fashion retailing behind them, and now enjoy the clean air, growing their own vegetables and fulfilling a dream.

They have built a blue stone cottage - nearly identical to the original, lived in by Mary Card, world famous crochet designer in 1902. Upstairs are 2 totally different rooms, one with spa, the other with private bathroom overlooking the English style garden. The rooms are totally self contained.

A third suite is well under way and will be the most romantic yet.

Kevin and Margaret provide a mouth watering selection of goodies in your fridge, champagne and the provisions for a full cooked breakfast. All cooking utensils, olive oil and sauces are supplied.

This is a romantic couple's haven.

Serendipity

Lot 6 Horizon Road, Selby, 3159
Tel: 03 754 4820
Contact: Caroline Richards
Rooms: 2 and 1 s/c suite
Cost: $75 single, $85 double, $100 suite

Caroline Richards is one of the most vibrant caring hosts in the Dandenongs and has converted the upper level of her house into a self contained apartment with kitchen facilities, including microwave, and a spacious living room with T.V., video and open fireplace.

She is more than happy to make easily heated food and there is a wonderful light, airy sponge to greet you on arrival!

Situated in a totally natural setting and very close to some of the Dandenongs' best attractions, Serendipity will be a memorable experience.

Penrith Country Estate

1411-1413 Mt. Dandenong Tourist Road, Mt. Dandenong
Tel: 03 751 2139
Contact: Kaye and Graeme Bradtke-Stevenson
Rooms: 3
Cost: $95-$160 double

Penrith is set on 6½ acres of botanical delight. The rooms are very romantic with ensuite (2 with spas) and breakfast is a speciality, served late, if you wish, in the room overlooking the pool and gardens.

Other meals by arrangement.

The Garden Cottages at Como

1465 Mt. Dandenong Tourist Road, Olinda, 3788
Tel: 03 751 2264 Mobile: 018 569 138 Fax: 03 751 1301
Contact: Michelle Wilson and Brett Billon
Rooms: 2 cottages
Cost: $75

The Garden Cottage: Raised above the lush garden, the verandah opens onto a charming cosy sitting room. The cottage atmosphere is enhanced by "found" materials, an open fire and antique furnishings. The kitchen is in keeping with its old stove and pots and pans hanging from meathooks. This is a romantic and secluded retreat, the bedroom charming with a four poster bed and pretty fabrics. Its bathroom is quaint, with a claw foot bath and polished brass fittings. Modern amenities ensure your comfort and self sufficiency. There is ducted heating, television and stereo. Provisions are supplied, including champagne, ground coffee and fresh flowers. A sought after hideaway for lovers. I visited as twenty dozen red roses were leaving!!

Forget Me Not Cottage: This has the same ambience but is architecturally different, being open-plan with a steeply sloping roof, and boasts a huge bath with views towards the city.

Alkira Cottages

Launching Place Road, Gembrook
Tel: (059) 68 1484
Contact: Andy or Mary Walker
Rooms: 2 s/c cottages
Cost: From $100 double, $15 extra person

There is a certain quality about Alkira that is hard to define. Perhaps it is the crisp, clean air or the sweeping views across the State Forest to the hills beyond. Nearly everyone comments on it, even the locals who have lived in the area all their lives. They stand at the top of the hill where the cottages are, look around and say "My word, this is a top spot here". Add to this a beautifully appointed cottage and you have all the makings of a remarkable weekend.

Each cottage is quite separate and unique with its own individual style and charm. Sleeping accommodation is for 6 - 8 people and one cottage is designed to allow easy wheelchair access. All linen and towels are provided.

Mary will cater to meet your requirements! A breakfast basket, or a casserole in the oven upon your arrival.

Crofter's Cottage

Chaundy Road, Belgrave Heights
Tel: (03) 754 6715 Fax: (03) 754 8705
Contact: Col & Rita Hickman
Rooms: s/c cottage
Cost (person/night): $50 Mon - Thurs, $75 Fri or Sun, $100 Sat

Set amidst 160 acres of green, rolling hills on the edge of the beautiful Blue Dandenongs, just 45 minutes from Melbourne, is the "Crofter's Cottage", a self contained cottage offering early settler style accommodation.

Once inside, the wonderful cornucopia of 19th Century Australiana is certain to cause a sharp intake of breath, and there is an immediate sense that the cottage has been magically preserved in time, and that its occupants have just popped out for a moment! Adding to this lived-in feel is the cosy glow from an impressive stone fireplace, the heart of the cottage.

The sturdy colonial brass beds are complemented by comfy handmade mattresses in the style of the old fashioned shake-up feather beds; and in the kitchen and bathroom the uneven stone floors add an exquisitely authentic touch which is enhanced by an antique meat safe, butter churns and a baker's oven built into the wall.

For breakfast the kitchen has been amply supplied with all the requirements for a hearty country breakfast, including fresh eggs from the farm and locally baked breads.

Guests are also warmly invited to experience life on a farm - with a difference. Col and Rita are devoted to raising the Falabella miniature horses - one of only two farms in Australia doing so. They also breed Alpacas, Ostriches and the long, shaggy haired Highland Cattle!

All this, together with the cottage's spectacular views, the delights of the Dandenongs and Col and Rita's warm and friendly hospitality, combine to provide an enchanting escape from all the hassles of modern life.

R.A.

Earlwood Manor and Ross Gallery

Mt. Dandenong Tourist Road, Sassafras
Tel: (03) 755 2321
Contact: Val Ross
Rooms: 3
Cost: From $90 double, $180 double suite

One stop shopping for marriage gifts, jewellery and especially rings of outstanding quality are available at the gallery. The Ross's also offer light luncheon, teas and facilities for small receptions.

The house, Earlwood, will come as a surprise. There is no need to go to Beverly Hills - here it is on your doorstep. The house is lush and theatrical, gold, gilt and glitz. My only concern is that a walk through the house in a wedding dress would result in a trail of devastation containing thousands of dollars worth of ornaments and object d'art.

The deluxe suite has a bay window with open views over the large ornamental garden and beyond. The garden is a fairyland of lights at night and melts into the surrounding forest. The large windows in the bathroom bring ferns and mountain ash inside, and the spa becomes an exotic rock pool amongst the trees.

The other double room has its own private bathroom.

Breakfast is a most professional and lavish affair with a sunny aspect overlooking a terrace - an attractive venue, weather permitting.

Val Ross is professional about any undertaking and has extraordinary energy. She loves the theatre, which her 41 visits to Phantom would indicate. This love of theatre has created plans for murder mystery weekends in combination with the Dandenongs' answer to Dynasty - Glenmoor.

Glenmoor

Tel: (03) 755 2204 or 018 33 6665 Fax: (03) 755 1361

Contact: Francine and Allan Millar

A stone manor flood-lit and fairy-lit behind electric gates, with a Ferrari and a Porsche squatting in the garage.

All three rooms have private facilities with huge baths, gold fittings and gilt mirrors everywhere. The list of facilities is endless - billiard room, spa, sauna, solarium, indoor heated pool, formal dining room, terrace and gallery.

A good place for a murder, a mystery or both.

The Dandenongs

BELGRAVE VIC. 3160

Foxes Hollow
Tel: (03) 751 1700
Owner/contact: Ross Gasking
Rooms: 3 s/c cottages
Cost: $75 - $200 per person per night
Various packages available

BELGRAVE HEIGHTS VIC. 3160

Crofter's Cottage, Chaundy Road
Tel: (03) 754 6715 Fax: (03) 754 8705
Owner/contact: Col & Rita Hickman (V)
Rooms: s/c cottage
Cost: $50-$100 single

Pinetree Cottage, 11 Marama Road
Tel: (03) 754 2745
Owner/contact: Bert & Sylvia Andrews
Rooms: s/c cottage
Cost: Double - $65 night, $260 week

CARRUM VIC. 3197

B & B at Mac's - Carrum, 49 Valetta Street
Tel: (03) 772 1435
Owner/contact: Brian McKenzie
Rooms: 2
Cost: $60 twin, $30 single
No smoking

EMERALD VIC. 3782

"Inglewood", 10 Sycamore Avenue
Tel: (059) 68 3796
Owner/contact: Pat & Brian MacRitchie

The Nook, 50 Lakeside Drive
Tel: (059) 68 4080
Owner/contact: Don & Val Jackson
Rooms: 1 ensuite
Cost: $85-$90 double, $20 child
No smoking

Pumpkin House, Lot 14 Stewart Road (P.O. Box 124, Kallista, 3791)
Tel: (059) 68 4104
Owner/contact: Mark Klaveren
Rooms: 2 s/c cottages
Cost: From $100 double

FERNY CREEK VIC. 3786

Menabilly, 57 One Tree Hill Road
Tel: (03) 755 2192
Owner/contact: Helen & Peter Rashleigh
Rooms: 2
Cost: $89-$90 double/twin

GEMBROOK VIC. 3783

Alkira Cottages, Launching Place Road
Tel: (059) 68 1484
Owner/contact: Andy & Mary Walker
Rooms: 2 s/c cottages (V)
Cost: From $100 double, $15 extra person, breakfast $5 each extra

KALORAMA VIC. 3766

Kalorama Chalet, 9 Falls Road
Tel: (03) 728 1185
Owner/contact: Hugo Wilhelm
Rooms: 13
Cost: $38 single, $48-50 double; Dinner (3 course) $13.50

The Dandenongs

MENZIES CREEK VIC. 3159

Kharwa, 174 Belgrave-Gembrook Road
Tel: (059) 68 3926
Owner/contact: Jill & Graham Berger
Rooms: 2
Cost: $65 double

MONBULK VIC. 3793

Bluegum Heights, Red Hill Road
Tel: (03) 756 7434
Owner/contact: Marjorie & Charles Adams
Rooms: 3
Cost: From $60 single, $80 double
No smoking ◆ *No children*

MOUNT DANDENONG VIC. 3767

Penrith Country Retreat, 1411-1413 Mt. Dandenong Tourist Road
Tel: (03) 751 2391
Owner/contact: Kaye & Graeme Bradke-Stevenson (V)
Rooms: 3
Cost: $95-$160 double/twin

Wyndham House, Observatory Road
Tel: (03) 751 1041
Owner/contact: Ken Chapman & Suzanne McLean
Rooms: 1
Cost: $90 double

OLINDA VIC. 3788

Arcadia, 188-190 Falls Road
Tel: (03) 751 1017
Owner/contact: Geoff Simmons & Lynne McDowell (V)
Rooms: 3
Cost: From $75-$125 double

The Dandenongs

Kenloch Manor, Mt. Dandenong Tourist Road
Tel: (03) 751 1680 or (03) 751 1008 Fax: (03) 751 1789
Owner/contact: Goff & Kath Martin
Rooms: 3
Cost: $95-$115 double

Mary Card's Cottage, 1498 Mt. Dandenong Tourist Road
Tel: (03) 751 1301
Owner/contact: Kevin & Margaret Smith
Rooms: 3 suites
Cost: From $125 double Ⓥ

The Garden Cottages at Como, 1465 Mt. Dandenong Tourist Road
Tel: (03) 751 2264 or (018) 569 138 Fax: (03) 751 1301
Owner/contact: Michelle Wilson & Brett Billon
Rooms: 2 s/c cottages
Cost: $75 Ⓥ

The Loft in the Mill, 1-3 Harold Street
Tel: (03) 751 1700 Fax: (03) 751 2030
Owner/contact: Janice Gasking
Rooms: 4 s/c units
Cost: $80 double

Winstanley's Country House, 13 Warwick Farm Road
Tel: (03) 755 1783 Fax: (03) 755 1323
Owner/contact: Anne & Alan Winstanley
Rooms: s/c suite
Cost: $90-$120 double/twin, weekend package $210 double/twin

MENZIES CREEK VIC. 3159

Charma, 75 The Crescent
Tel: (03) 755 1491 or (03) 755 2266
Owner/contact: Christine St. Aubyn & Paul Orange
Rooms: 1 and 1 suite
Cost: $65 single, 490 double, $25 extra adult, $10 child
Dinner by arrangement

Earlwood Manor, Mt. Dandenong Tourist Road
Tel: (03) 755 2321
Contact: Val Ross Ⓥ
Rooms: 3
Cost: From $90 double, $180 double/suite

Fleurbaix, 286 Mt. Dandenong Tourist Road
Tel: (03) 755 1185
Owner/contact: Maggie & Neil Adam
Rooms: 1 ensuite
Cost: $90 double
No children • No smoking

Glenmoor
Tel: (03) 755 2204 or 018 33 6665 Fax: (03) 755 1361 Ⓥ
Contact: Francine & Allan Millar

Le Manoir, 434 Mt. Dandenong Tourist Road
Tel: (03) 755 2254
Owner/contact: Jenny Hyland
Rooms: 1 suite
Cost: $65 single, $90 double, $25 per extra person
No smoking • Midweek discounts

Monreale Country House, The Crescent
Tel: (03) 755 1773 Fax: (03) 755 2729
Owner/contact: Laurie & Peta Rolls Ⓥ
Rooms: 3 ensuite
Cost: From $80 double
No smoking

Puckoon, 24 Mernda Road
Tel: (03) 751 1687
Owner/contact: Nancy Gooderham

SELBY VIC. 3159

Serendipity, Lot 6 Horizon Road
Tel: (03) 754 4820
Owner/contact: Caroline Richards
Rooms: 2 and s/c suite Ⓥ
Cost: $75 single, $85 double, $100 suite
No smoking

SEVILLE EAST VIC. 3139

Merrigum Cottage, 'Merrigum Herefords', Douthie Road
Tel: (059) 64 8462 Fax: (059) 64 8462
Owner/contact: Averell & Jane McCandless
Rooms: s/c cottage
Cost: $95 double

SHERBROOKE VIC. 3789

Cottages of Sherbrooke, Sherbrooke Lodge Road
Tel: (03) 755 1912
Owner/contact: Graeme & Dawne McPherson
Rooms: 3 s/c cottages
Cost: $95-$120 double
No children

Sherbrooke House, Sherbrooke Road at Poets Lane
Tel; (03) 755 2044 Fax: (03) 755 2089
Owner/contact: Ray Hall & Rob Hansen
Rooms: 16
Cost: All inclusive gourmet getaway - $140-$180 double

UPPER BEACONSFIELD VIC. 3808

Fern Hill. Lot 118A Salisbury Road
Tel/Fax: (059) 44 3116
Owner/contact: Faye and Keith Farthing
Rooms: 2

Maroondah Highway

An alternative route to the North East and the Victorian high country follows the Maroondah Highway to Lilydale. This is the gateway to the Yarra Valley wine producing area, an area regaining the importance it had one hundred years ago, with at least 32 vineyards now in operation. Those to visit include:

- De Bortolli Yarringa Estate - excellent restaurant. Recommended Pinot Noir, Shiraz and the Sauterne styles.
- Domaine Chandon - high quality sparkling wines. Restaurant style tasting room.
- Coldstream Hills James Halliday - the name of this wine writer and judge has lent cachet to the area. Top quality product.
- Fergussons
- Yarra Burn
- Kelly Brook

  } These are attractive family venues providing restaurants with spit-roasts.
- Long Gully Estate - consistently well made wines
- Oakridge Estate - a top quality cabernet
- St. Huberts - recently purchased by a multinational company
- Shantell -

The Yarra River flows from the upper Yarra Reservoir to Warburton and then follows the Warburton Highway to Yarra Junction and Woori Yallock, where it turns north to Healesville. These are small logging towns made attractive by the surrounding hills and the river. The largest, Warburton, has many walking tracks along the river and amongst the Mountain Ash of the rainforest. You will recognise the distinctive sound of the bell birds even if you have never heard them before.

HEALESVILLE

Healesville is at the head of the Yarra Valley on the Maroondah Highway. This is a beautiful area on the edge of the dividing range which, from here, is crossed via the Black Spur. The Maroondah Dam provides a scenic spot for relaxing at the edge of town.

Healesville Sanctuary is a prime Victorian Tourist Attraction, enabling visitors to easily view most native species of fauna. The enclosures are mostly open and present the animals in a natural environment. Other displays include a reptile house, also a nocturnal house for the many species that are only active at night, and a glass-sided platypus tank. The Sanctuary is well worth a visit or a day trip from Melbourne.

From Healesville the Maroondah Highway attacks the dividing range via the Black Spur. This is an attraction in itself, a marvellous rainforest lines the twisting road with astonishingly tall and regular columns of Mountain Ash. There is a dense fern under storey, with the umbrella-like tree ferns a forest in themselves.

Just before you leave the Spur at Narbethong, nestled into the forest is The Hermitage.

A detour north of the Yarra Valley makes a loop via Yarra Glen to Yea. On the way you drive through the forests of the Kinglake National Park. Accommodation is available at Lamon Farm, Kinglake.

If you pass through Yea, take the opportunity to visit the old cheese factory to sample and buy their traditional fetta and straccino (a good substitute for Parmesan) and farmhouse cheeses.

MARYSVILLE

A detour to Marysville is rewarding. This is a compact, pretty town cradled in the mountains. Tall native trees crowd the boundaries, the forest spilling over into the gardens and vacant blocks. The early settlers filled the town with exotic trees and these, now mature, provide a dazzling display in the autumn. There are many walks in the surrounding forest, the most popular being to the spectacular Steavenson Falls, which are floodlit at night. There is skiing close by at Lake Mountain.

Between the small settlements of Buxton and Taggerty, the Cathedral Range State Park is majestically obvious on your right. This is a good park for energetic walks and views. Accommodation is available close to the base of the Cathedral at Kingbilli. These stone cottages are owned by the 'Beaches', pioneers in self-contained accommodation. Meals are available at the Cathedral restaurant, Taggerty.

Shortly before reaching Alexandra there is a steep hill providing stunning views from the lookouts of the lush river flats around the town.

On the Alexandra side of the hill on the left is Stonlea, a convention centre with restaurant and bar.

ALEXANDRA

This small rural centre is the junction of the Maroondah and Goulburn Valley Highways. The Goulburn Valley Highway, straight ahead, follows the river to Eildon. Turning left these highways merge for a few miles and then separate, the Goulburn Valley Highway veering left to Seymour, and the Maroondah turning north around Lake Eildon, which it crosses at Bonnie Doon, to Mansfield and Mount Buller.

ATTRACTIONS

- Timber Tramway Museum
- McKenzie Native Reserve (orchids in winter and spring)
- Picnic Races (4 a year)

The Goulburn Valley Highway to Eildon offers fishing in trout ponds and scenic flights at Thornton. Further on a deer farm and the usually deserted Eildon Golf Club, a pretty undulating course with many resident kangaroos, then Snobs Creek Trout Hatchery with an excellent aquarium of native freshwater fish.

EILDON

The pondage below the wall is a pretty picnic spot. Excellent views from the wall and an interesting bustle at the Boat Harbour or Jerusalem Creek, a large houseboat anchorage. Eildon Weir is a huge and beautiful expanse of water winding between the forested hills. There are hundreds of inlets and bays where on a houseboat you can really get away from it all. Picnic craft are also available from the Boat Harbour.

ATTRACTIONS

For a really spectacular view, take the sky-line road which looks down on the lake and the seemingly endless blue hills around. This road takes you to Frazer National Park where you may hand-feed kangaroos, wombats and king parrots on the lake shore.
Sharing this view is the exclusive retreat, Eucalypt Ridge.

MANSFIELD

This is the service centre for the mountains and wilderness around Mt. Buller and Mt. Stirling and nearby Lake Eildon. The town connects via the Midland Highway with the Hume Highway at Benalla and with the flats around Wangaratta via the fabulously beautiful 'back road' to Whitfield in the King Valley. the Obelisk in the centre of town is to the memory of 3 police officers shot by Ned Kelly at Stringybark Creek near Tolmie in 1878. Mansfield is also notable as a saw-mill town and as the location for the films 'The Man from Snowy River I and II'

EILDON WEIR

This is a marvellous leisure resource, the largest and most under-utilized stretch of fresh water in Victoria. Except on Boxing Day and the Easter weekend, you may have a hundred inlets and bays in rugged mountain scenery all to yourself. To exploit this facility requires forward planning to secure a houseboat.

I suggest contact: Eildon Houseboats, Eildon Boat Harbour, Tel: (057) 74 2107

MT. BULLER

At 1800 metres, this mountain is arguably the prettiest in Australia, and certainly offers the most spectacular views since it is on the very edge of the dividing range. You may look one way and see purple mountains and deep valleys rolling on to the horizon, or the other over the flatter farming land to the west. there is a great variety of runs of decent length and degree of difficulty, some taking you from the bare mountain summit down below the snow gums into the mountain ash forests. Huge quantities of money have been spent supplying chair lifts on every quarter of the mountain so although, with its proximity to Melbourne, it is the most used and popular of Victorian resorts, the waiting time after a run is usually brief.

ACCOMMODATION

Atunga Cottage

512 Henley Road, Kangaroo Ground, 3097
Tel: (03) 712 0338 Fax: (03) 712 0633
Contact: Carolynn O'Brien
Rooms: s/c mudbrick cottage
Cost: $75 double, $10 extra person

Atunga, or Squirrel Nutkin Cottage as one delighted author called it, is a haven, 0.5 km. from the Yarra River and surrounded by natural bush. This idyllic mudbrick home run by Australis, a natural history travel company, has already found the niche market - artists, photographers, authors. Honeymooners, too, have reported upon it most favourably.

Lamon Farm

3555 Mount Slide Road, Kinglake, 3763
Tel: 057 86 1684
Contact: Marianne and Tony Monks
Rooms: 2 double ensuite, 1 twin ensuite
Cost (B & B) $100 double

This friendly B & B nestles on a hilltop overlooking Melbourne on the edge of the Kinglake National Park. This modern brick house has 3 guest rooms, all with ensuite, and a cosy upstairs guest lounge with a large open fire, books, magazines and a C.D. player.

Lamon Farm also produces wonderful chestnuts and strawberries, so don't be surprised to find a jar of strawberry jam awaiting you on departure.

Woodlands of Narbethong

Manby Road, Narbethong, 3778
Tel: (059) 63 7150 or (03) 529 2219
Contact: Gary & Vicky King

This extremely special spot is really just for 2. If you long to own a house in the country, surrounded by mountain ash and tree ferns, and creeks, with even a resident dog - this property is for you.

It is extremely comfortably furnished, open fire and a huge array of provisions for breakfast. Dinner can be provided if you make arrangements at the time of booking. Don't take your children - find kind friends to look after them. Go with your partner and have an experience to remember.

The Hermitage

Maroondah Highway, Narbethong, 3778
Tel: 059 63 7120
Contact: John and Val Stafford
Rooms: 6
Cost (B & B): From $40 single

This marvellous rambling building, originally owned by J.W. Lindt, is now in the cherished possession of John and Val Stafford, and is quite unashamedly one of my favourite places in Victoria.

I recently attended a wedding held there - never was there a more romantic setting or a happier looking couple married under the vast oak tree.

It doesn't matter at what time of year you visit The Hermitage, the gardens, originally laid out by Baron Ferdinard Von Mueller, are a constant ever-changing delight. The gentle, nurturing talents of John and Val are everywhere - even your butter at breakfast time will have a wildflower to decorate it.

St. Fillan

723 Maroondah Highway, Narbethong, 3778
Tel: (059) 63 7126
Contact: Rex & Helen Goulding
Rooms: s/c suite
Cost (B & B): $90 double

A pair of iron gates opposite the Marysville turn is the entrance to St. Fillian's. First built by Sir James Munro in 1886 as his country property, with a garden designed by Von Mueller, St. Fillian's is a glorious spot.

The present house, a two storey weatherboard, was built in the early 1930's and has been occupied by Ron and Helen Goulding for the last 25 years. They have recently converted the maid's quarters into an attractive, comfortable self-contained cottage. Beautifully polished jarrah floor boards gleam at you as you walk in through the front door.

Helen provides a continental breakfast and will bring eggs and bacon in to you. No cooking facilities are provided, but St. Fillian's is close to the recently refurbished Narbethong pub and Marysville - dinner would not be a problem.

The garden is stunning - ,a vast array of shrubs and flowers. Great in any season. This place is a nature lover's delight.

Dalrymples Guest Cottages

18 Falls Road, Marysville, 3779
Tel: (059) 63 3416
Contact: Bob & Di McNamara
Rooms: 3 s/c cottages, 1 s/c house

These delightful one bedroomed cottages nestle amongst tall trees in Marysville. They are most comfortably furnished, and whilst there are no cooking facilities, Di's breakfast basket is of ample quantities for the hungriest of appetites.

The newly acquired double storey house sleeps six easily. Two bathrooms, one with spa, and a large living area with open fire. All this accommodation gets booked heavily, so reservations are a must.

Mathilde's of Marysville

19 Red Hill Road, Marysville, 3779
Tel: (059) 63 3697
Contact: Joseph Baraké
Rooms: 3 ensuite
Cost (B & B): $100, Dinner $30 per person

This is a new B & B which I didn't have time to visit, but the response from guests that have stayed have all been very encouraging.

The Oaks Homestead

Goulburn Valley Highway, Alexandra, 3174
Tel: (057) 72 1572
Contact: Brigitte Vernon
Rooms: 3 ensuite
Cost (B & B): $125 - $145, Dinner $40 per person

Since taking over The Oaks Homestead in March 1993 Bridgitte has made some delightful changes. The Blue Room now has its own charmingly Provençal style bathroom - terracotta flooring and rough white plaster. It is lovely. All the rooms are now 'ensuite'.

The homestead is gracious and exceedingly comfortable - and the food good.

Bill Bourke is available for those wanting to learn the art of fly fishing, either by the day or in three-day residential schools.

This is the type of place where you can be really energetic, or just relax in a comfy chair and do nothing.

A qualified masseur is available by appointment.

Mittagong Homestead

462 Spring Creek Road, Alexandra, 3714
Tel: (057) 72 1586 Fax: (057) 72 2425
Contact: Robyn Palmer-Price
Rooms: 2 self contained cabins
Cost (B & B): $60 per person twin share

Mittagong Homestead is expanding. Up until now guests have had their own private wing of the homestead - 2 double rooms with ensuite, lounge, dining room, sitting room with T.V. and stereo. Outside; solar heated salt water swimming pool, sauna, tennis court and bicycles.

But, Robyn is into caring for her guests, and she has noticed a demand for spas and self contained, so from December 1993 there will be 2 fully self contained 'Woolshed' cabins.

Each cabin will have 2 bedrooms with king size beds, electric blankets, linen provided, an open fire, a spa, laundry, T.V. and stereo. With full cooked breakfast provisions provided, and evening meals by arrangement, what more can one ask for?

Pendaven Country House

159 Halls Flat Road, Alexandra, 3714 (P.O. Box 167)
Tel: 057 72 2452
Contact: Penny and David Paxman
Rooms: 6 double ensuite with T.V. and fridge, 1 with wheelchair access
Cost (double/night): $125 - $195 B&B, $195 - $280 DB&B

Perched high on a hilltop with astounding views of the Goulburn Valley, Pendaven is a modern, stylish guest house. The large lounge/dining areas have 7 metre high cathedral ceilings and polished timber floors. The dining room is set with individual tables and Penny's food is good, healthy country cooking.

Downstairs there is a sauna and a large heated circular spa, with that amazing view.

Eucalypt Ridge

564 Skyline road, Eildon, 3713
Tel: (057) 74 2033 or (03) 807 1170
Fax: (057) 74 2610 or (03) 888 2206
Contact: Corinne & Brian Dixon
Rooms: 4 double suites
Cost (all inclusive) $1,600 per couple per weekend

After 3 years of exacting construction, "Eucalypt Ridge" commenced operations in July 1991. In the past, the barrier to the best of Victoria's bush was finding a country retreat where nature could be experienced in hedonistic comfort.

"Eucalypt Ridge", 144 km. north-east of Melbourne, has been designed in every way to welcome guests and provide them with the rare opportunity to feel the beauty of Victoria and enjoy the hospitality and luxurious appointments - Italian furnishings, commissioned works of art, crockery by Villeroy and Boch and cutlery by Christofle and Alessi.

Your hostess, Corinne, is a chef trained in Australia, Thailand and Italy and her cuisine is exemplary. Pasta, bread and ice-creams are all made in the kitchen. The finest Yarra Valley wines are selected to compliment the evening degustation menus. The open bar includes French champagne, your choice of cocktail, and spirits for the most discerning connoisseur.

"Eucalypt Ridge" accommodates just eight guests in four suites, all with luxurious marble ensuites and private balconies facing towards the northern sun, Lake Eildon, Fraser National Park and the surrounding mountains.

Play tennis, water ski, fish the giant lake or tiny streams, take a drive in the lodge's limousine, or a cruise on its luxury launch - it's all included.

For the not-so-active, risk a large armchair and enjoy the ultimate sound experience with the compliments of Bang and Olufsen whilst browsing through a book from the comprehensive library.

"Eucalypt Ridge", with its special capacity to lavish personal care on eight people, is an ideal setting for hosting special guests, business associates or celebrating a special occasion.

Sample Breakfast Menu

Fruit Juices

Freshly squeezed Orange Juice
Freshly squeezed Grapefruit Juice
Apple Juice
Fresh Fruit Platter of Seasonal Fruits

Cereals

Muesli, Special K
Corn Flakes, Weet Bix
Yoghurt

Breads for Toasting

Four varieties of bread baked on the premises:
Sourdough Rye, Wholemeal,
Fruit Loaf, Triticale Sourdough
Assortment of homemade seasonal jams
Honey, Vegemite

Beverages

Coffees: filtered, cappuccino, espresso, macciato
Teas: Earl Grey, English Breakfast,
Prince of Wales, herbal

Brilliant Estate

R.M.B. 2050, Yarck, 3719
Tel: (057) 73 4212 Fax: (057) 73 4340
Contact: Dinah & Lorraine Jones

Brilliant Estate is just two hours north of Melbourne off the Maroondah Highway. Here Dinah Jones organises a variety of 'art' weekend workshops.

The cost includes accommodation in the renovated shearers' quarters in twin bedded rooms. You need to take your own doona or sleeping bag and towels.

All meals are provided - with lunch in the garden (weather permitting) and dinner in the homestead.

The next course is on 'gilding' - for further information on forthcoming courses, I suggest you contact Dinah Jones.

Howqua-Dale Gourmet Retreat

Howqua River Road, via Mansfield, 3722 (P.O. Box 379)
Tel: (057) 77 3503 Fax: (057) 77 3896
Contact: Marieke Brugman & Sarah Stegley
Rooms: 6 ensuite
Cost (person/night): $250 all inclusive

The prestigious U.S. 'Andrew Harper's Hideaway Report' votes Howqua-Dale Gourmet Retreat as 'Gourmet Sanctuary of the Year'. This is the 13th year for this connoisseur's guide to peaceful and unspoilt places and its annual citations of the best of the best internationally. This makes Howqua-Dale the extremely rare two-time recipient of the Award.

Howqua-Dale this year includes Spa Week programmes with health, fitness and beauty treatments, as well as enticing and delicious light food. There is a weekend cooking school for men only and they have also enlarged the programme of residential classes.

The Celebrity Chefs programme continues.

The best only get better.

Sample Menu - Howqua-Dale

Sushi & Champagne

Grilled Scampi with poached leeks, crispy seaweed and a shallot fondue sauce

Mallee Guinea Fowl roasted, served with a lentil pilau and wild mushrooms

Chocolate hazelnut praline meringue torte with coffee cream and strawberry guava sauce

Stoneys High Country Adventure Pty. Ltd.

P.O. Box 287, Mansfield, 3722
Tel: (057) 75 2212 Fax: (057) 75 2598

A review of Mansfield would not be complete without reference to Graeme Stoney. His adventures are certainly an attraction and he has to supply food and accommodation.

The Stoney family offer you an overnight escape with a difference.

Throughout the Spring, Summer and Autumn, trail rides depart from the family's cattle out station, Stockyard Creek. The rides cover a large area of the Great Dividing Range. You will experience some of the most breathtaking scenery in Australia and discover why both 'Man from Snowy River' films were made here.

The weekend trips are based at Stockyard Creek with its Pioneer homestead and bunkhouse. From here they go on dam rides along the Howqua River and follow bridle tracks blazed through the bush over a century ago by early cattlemen and gold rush.

In the winter the horses are turned out and cross country ski trips are held instead. This offers you a great opportunity to visit and enjoy the back country of the Victorian Alps. The skiing and views are spectacular and the Stoneys are warm, wonderful people. Enjoy an experience of a lifetime, Winter or Summer.

ALEXANDRA VIC. 3714

Australian Bush Pioneer Farm
Tel: (057) 74 7378
Owner/contact: Bronwyn Rayner
Rooms: 2 and s/c cottage

Cairn-Brae, 191 Conolly's Creek Road (R.M.B. 4168)
Tel: (057) 72 2187
Owner/contact: Roe Cumming
Rooms: 2
Lunch/picnic basket by arrangement • No smoking

Mittagong Homestead, Spring Creek Road
Tel: (057) 72 1586 Fax: (057) 72 2425
Owner/contact: Robyn Price
Rooms: 2 ensuite
Cost: $60 per person twin share (V)
Dinner by arrangement

The Oaks Homestead, R.M.B. 5295 Goulburn Valley Highway
Tel/Fax: (057) 72 1572
Owner/contact: Brigitte Vernon (V)
Rooms: 3 ensuite
Cost: $125-$145 double; Dinner $50 per person

Pendaven Country House, 159 Halls Flat Road (P.O. Box 167)
Tel: (057) 72 2452
Owner/contact: Penny & David Paxman (V)
Rooms: 6 ensuite
Cost: Double - $125-$195, Dinner bed & breakfast $195-$280

Sherntarl Lodge, Maintongoon Road (P.O. Box 128)
Tel: (057) 72 1637
Owner/contact: Jennie & Mark Quittner
Rooms: s/c cabin
Cost: $60 night, $120 weekend
Children under 10 years free

EILDON VIC.

Eucalypt Ridge, 564 Skyline Road
Tel: (057) 74 2033 or (03) 807 1170 Fax: (057) 74 2610 or (03) 888 2206
Owner/contact: Corinne & Brian Dixon (V)
Rooms: 4 ensuite
Cost: All inclusive, Weekend Package $720 per person (double occ.), $870 per person (single occ.)
No children ◆ *No smoking*

GRUYERE VIC. 3770

Woodlands Sanctuary, Woodland Way
Tel: (059) 64 9432
Owner/contact: Garth & Audrey Willey
Cost: From $100 double

HEALESVILLE VIC. 3777

"Brentwood", Myers Creek Road
Tel: (059) 62 5028
Owner/contact: Pat & Gustaaf Van Driel
Rooms: 2, ensuite
Cost: From $80 double, $60 single

Catnip Cottage Herb Farm, 79 Don Road
Tel: (059) 62 3208
Owner/contact: Barbara Flynn
Cost: $80 double

Naini Tal Lodge, Nyora Road
Tel: (059) 62 3415
Owner/contact: Brenda & Campbell Newman
Cost: From $100 double, $60 single

Peacehaven Mountain Retreat, 3 Nyora Road
Tel: (059) 62 2831
Owner/contact: Celia & John Elliott
Rooms: s/c unit
Cost: $60 twin, $40 single

"**Priya Darshana**", Heath Road
Tel: (059) 62 5114
Owner/contact: June & Maurice Van Cuylenburg
Rooms: 1 ensuite and s/c cottage
Cost: From $65 double

Strathvea Guest House, Myers Creek Road
Tel: (059) 62 4109
Owner/contact: Dianne Clarke
Rooms: 8
Cost: Dinner, bed & breakfast - $90-$120 single; Weekend $380 double
No smoking

"**Wide Horizons**", Juliet Crescent
Tel: (059) 62 4119
Owner/contact: Corry & Peter Skilbeck
Cost: From $90 double
Opening Easter 1994

Maroondah Highway

HOWQUADALE VIC. 3722

Howqua-Dale, Howqua River Road (P.O. Box 379, Mansfield)
Tel: (057) 77 3503
Owner/contact: Sarah Stegley & Marieke Brugman
Rooms: 6 ensuite (V)
Cost: Fully inclusive - $250 single
Gourmet cooking schools ◆ No smoking ◆ No children

KANGAROO GROUND VIC. 3097

Atunga Cottage, 512 Henley Road
Tel: (03) 712 0338 Fax: (03) 712 0633
Owner/contact: Mrs. Carolynn O'Brien (V)
Rooms: s/c cottage
Cost: $75 double, $10 extra person

KINGLAKE VIC. 3763

Lamon Farm, 3555 Mt. Slide Road
Tel: (057) 86 1684
Owner/contact: Marianne & Tony Monks
Rooms: 3, ensuite (V)
Cost: $100 double
Dinner by arrangement ◆ No children

LAUNCHING PLACE VIC. 3139

Hill N Dale Homestead & Ferny Glade Cottage, Don Road
Tel: (059) 67 3361
Owner/contact: Tony & Susan Stanley
Rooms: 2 and two s/c cottages
Cost: $90 double, DB&B from $65 single; Cottages from $105 daily

MANSFIELD VIC. 3722

Merrilea, 22 Kidstone Parade
Tel: (057) 75 1148
Owner/contact: Dianne Dunstan
Rooms: 5
Cost: $75 double
No smoking

Sawpit Gully Lodge, Lot 4 Sawpit Gully Rd (P.O. Box 421)
Tel: (057) 76 9562
Owner/contact: Pam Bryant
Rooms: 7
Cost: Single - $40, Dinner bed & breakfast $60

Stoneys High Country Adventure Pty. Ltd., P.O. Box 287
Tel: (057) 75 2212 Fax: (057) 75 2598 (V)
Owner/contact: Chris Stoney

129 Highton Lane
Tel: (057) 75 1259
Owner/contact: Joy Whyte
Rooms: 3
Cost: $30 single, $10 child

MARYSVILLE VIC. 3779

Barree Cottages, McLean Street
Tel/Fax: (059) 63 3287

Dalrymples Guest Cottages, 18 Falls Road
Tel: (059) 63 3416 (V)
Owner/contact: Bob & Di McNamara
Rooms: 3 s/c cottages, 1 s/c house

ElKanah, Buxton Road
Tel: (059) 63 3229
Owner/contact: Enid Maea
Rooms: 38
Cost: Fully inclusive - $72 single, $124 married couple
No smoking • No alcohol

Kerami House, Kerami Crescent
Tel: (059) 63 3260
Owner/Contact: Janet or Denis
Rooms: $4, ensuite
Cost: $290 W/E package, dinner $40 double, B & B $100 double midweek only

Marylands Country House, 22 Falls Road
Tel: (059) 63 3204
Rooms: 42

Mathilde's of Marysville, 19 Red Hill Road
Tel: (059) 63 3697
Owner/contact: Joseph Baraké Ⓥ
Rooms: 3 ensuite
Cost: $100; Dinner $30 per person

Nanda Binya Lodge, Woods Point Road
Tel: (059) 63 3433
Contact: Manager
Rooms: 5

MERRIJIG VIC. 3722

Brumbys Run, Buttercup Road (Merrijig Free Bag, Mansfield)
Tel: (057) 77 5768
Owner/contact: Jenny & Barry Ross
Rooms: 5
Cost: $45 single, $75 double
Meals by arrangement • Children over 12 • No smoking in house

Merrijig Lodge, Mt. Buller Road
Tel: (057) 77 5590
Owner/contact: Chris Dunlop
Rooms: 14
Cost: $25 Bed & Breakfast, $18 self catering

MILLGROVE VIC. 3799

"Inglebe", 77A Prices Road
Tel: (059) 66 9375
Owner/contact: Barb & Spud Murphy
Cost: From $90 double
Dinner by arrangement

MIRIMBAH VIC. 3722

Highlander Lodge, 4 Summit View Court (R.M.B. 4547 Mansfield)
Tel: (057) 77 5511
Owner/contact: Elva & Jack Smith
Rooms: 4
Cost: $35-$48 single, $10-$20 child

Mürren, Mt. Buller Road (R.M.B. 4540)
Tel: (057) 77 5663
Owner/contact: Gaye Adamson
Rooms: 3
Cost: $90-$105 double, $35 extra person
Dinner available on request

NARBETHONG VIC. 3778

Henry VIII Manor House, Maroondah Highway
Tel: (059) 63 7167
Owner/contact: Dennis Cosh
Cost: From $75 double

St. Fillan, 723 Maroondah Highway
Tel: (059) 63 7126
Owner/contact: Helen & Rex Goulding
Rooms: 1 s/c suite (V)
Cost: $90 double
No children ◆ No smoking

The Hermitage, Maroondah Highway
Tel: (059) 63 7120
Owner/contact: Val & John Stafford (V)
Rooms: 6
Cost: From $40 single, $80 double/twin
Dinner by arrangement

Woodlands of Narbethong, Manby Road
Tel: (059) 63 7150 or (03) 529 2219
Contact: Gary & Vicky King (V)
Rooms: s/c cottage

TAGGERTY VIC. 3714

Australian Bush Settlement, R.M.B. 2618 Maroondah Highway
Tel: (057) 74 7378
Rooms: 2

TOOLANGI VIC. 3777

Tallawalla Lodge, Spraggs Road
Tel/Fax: (059) 62 9219
Owner/contact: Jenny & Peter Sexton
Cost: From $70 double

WARBURTON VIC. 3799

Magnolia Cottage, 33 Blackwood Avenue
Tel: (059) 66 9469 or (059) 66 9127
Owner/contact: Marie Hormann
Rooms: 3
Cost: $50 single, $85 double
No children ◆ No smoking inside ◆ Dinner available

Warburton Waters, Warburton Highway (P.O. Box 310)
Tel: (059) 66 9166
Owner/contact: Pam & Jim Conway
Rooms: 17
Children by arrangement

WHITTLESEA VIC. 3757

Hiltonvale Homestead, 485 Wallan Road
Tel: (03) 716 2744
Owner/contact: Diana Lawrence
Rooms: 3
Cost: $30-$40 single
Dinner available by arrangement

WOORI YALLOCK VIC. 3139

Cherry Tree House, Lot 12 Warburton Highway, Cnr. Allsops Road
Tel: (059) 64 7577
Owner/contact: Margaret & John Baker
Rooms: 2
Cost: From $75 double

YARCK VIC. 3719

Brilliant Estate, R.M.B. 2050
Tel: (057) 73 4212 Fax: (057) 73 4340
Owner/contact: Dinah & Lorraine Jones (V)
Art weekend workshops ◆ All meals provided

YARRA JUNCTION VIC. 3797

Tarrango Farm, 273 Tarrango Road
Tel: (059) 67 2123
Owner/contact: Yvonne Nardella
Rooms: 2 and s/c house
Cost: From $85 double
Dinner by arrangement

North East
Hume Highway

If you tire of the changeable climate of Melbourne and need some sun on your back go to the north east of Victoria. It is amazing, as soon as you drive over the Dividing Range which encircles Melbourne and then follows the coast around to Sydney and beyond, the rainfall drops dramatically. The North East enjoys a continental climate unaffected by the sea and protected by the range. When the skies are clear in winter, severe frosts at night melt into pleasant short sleeve days. In the summer, though the days may be 100°F the nights are still cool and from December until the autumn break, which is prayed for in March, but often does not arrive until May, cloudless days are guaranteed.

Though hot in the summer, when the grass is brittle and bleached, the humidity is so low that outdoor activity is still enjoyable. Many outdoor activities are available with the scenic proximity of the mountainous Dividing Range offering winter sports and summer forest wilderness together with many permanent rivers and lakes. This is the place to bring your boat and skis, and boots.

The quick way out of the clouds is the Hume Freeway to Seymour, the gateway to the North East. At Seymour you cross the Goulburn River, the south-western boundary of the North East. The other major river of Victoria, the Murray, forms the northern boundary.

As you follow the Hume to Albury/Wodonga the foothills of the range are always present on your right hand side and the view to the left a broad flat landscape.

SEYMOUR

Noteable for the Goulburn River and the army base at Puckapunyal. The Freeway by-passes the town and so shall we, unless you need food or drink.

VINEYARDS

- Mitchelton Vineyard (The excellent Preece range is particularly good value!). The Valmorbida family are creating a tourist centre here with a viewing tower, new cellar door area and the Major Mitchell restaurant on the banks of the Goulburn. Daytime and twilight cruises are available in the summer.
- Chateau Tahbilk. Established in 1860 there is a fine historic feel to the old winery. The marsanne is noteworthy (it is said that half the world's marsanne is produced by Mitchelton & Tahbilk).
- Paul Osicka. Grayton, halfway between Nagambie and Heathcote. Historic ambience and excellent quality.
- Walkershire Wines (At Bailieston). Produce a huge Shiraz Cabernet blend.

EUROA

The town is a pleasant place to break a journey, having a pretty park on the river, some simple eating places and pubs. The Seven Creeks Run Woolshed is a tourist attraction, as are the scenic drives into the hills, especially to Gooram Falls and Polly McQuinns.

VIOLET TOWN

A small settlement with a single short street of pretty weatherboard shops, most of them empty. The railway station probably has the neatest garden on VicRail and there is a monthly craft and produce market.

BENALLA

The centre of the town has been beautified by the creation of a lake on the Broken River and a new streetscape with replanted trees created to repair the damage of the 1960's modernization. It is now by-passed by the freeway.

ATTRACTIONS

- Benalla Art Gallery (Ledger collection)
- Rose Gardens on the Broken River
- Lake Mokoan - good fishing and bird life
- Aerodrome:
  - Premiere gliding centre
  - Hot-air balloons
- Access to Mt. Buller, Midland Highway South; Shepparton and the irrigation areas by the Midland Highway North.

Note that Benalla is an excellent centre from which to explore this area, with easy access to the extensive irrigation areas to the north with its orchards and green summer crops. To the south there are many pleasant scenic roads into the hills and the Midland Highway passes Lake Nillahcoutie on its way to Mansfield.

WANGARATTA

With 16,500 people, this is the largest town on the Hume between Melbourne and the border with N.S.W. It has a substantial feeling with two storey buildings and more than one commercial street. Of historical interest is the connection with Ned Kelly.

The ovens and King Rivers meet here and along their banks are pleasant parks and picnic areas.

Note the Wangaratta Air World display of antique civil aircraft.

The surrounding area is rich farmland, with many important vineyards. Other interesting crops include tobacco and hops in the river valleys, and the cherries from the Warby Ranges.

North East, Hume Highway

Here the Ovens River flows north to join the Murray at Lake Mulwala. This is a popular boating area, especially from the towns of Yarrawonga and Mulwala.

RUTHERGLEN

Rutherglen is on the northern side of the Highway and is the centre of the most important wine growing area in Victoria.

VINEYARDS

- Rosewood, Bill Chambers - good value, excellent fortified wines.
- Campbells - up-market operation.
- Bullers Calliope - large range. Bird park.
- All Saints Vineyard & Cellars, Andrew Sutherland Smith - large range and impressive historic winery.
- Morris Mia Mia Vineyard, Mick Morris - a generous and talented 6th generation wine maker. Produces some of the best fortified wines in the world at very reasonable prices. Also try the durif, and superb cabernet
- Stanton & Killeen - another of the oldest established families of the area. Mostly fortifieds and an excellent durif.
- Jones Winery - excellent vintage port.
- St. Leonards Vineyard - owned by Brown Bros. of Rutherglen. Beautiful location overlooking the Murray River.
- Fairfield - the original home of the Morris family, this used to be the largest vineyard in the Southern Hemisphere with 350 hectares of vines. The mansion has been recently restored.
- Mt. Prior Vineyard

The other areas making up this important North East wine growing area are:

GLENROWAN

- Baileys (attractive 'cellar' tasting area)
- Taminick Cellar
- H.J.T. - Harry J. Timson has a small vineyard on the shore of Lake Mokoan. High quality wines.

MARKWOOD

- Markwood Estate Vineyard

OXLEY

- John Gehrig Wines - on the King River. Makes a good chardonnay.

BARNAWARTHA

- Gehrig Bros. Vineyard

CHILTERN

- Gayfers Vineyard

MILAWA

- Brown Brothers - large, innovative winemakers producing a large range of high quality varietal wines. Excellent marketers and always developing new styles and experimenting with new areas.

Milawa is on the Snow Road and is a favourite tourist stop. Other attractions include the cheese factory (washed rind cheeses) and the mustard farm.

FOOD

- The Old Emu

Many small country roads lead into the hills. The Ovens and King Valleys are particularly attractive.
Lake William Hovell and Paradise Falls are at the head of the King Valley.
The Ovens Valley is green even in summer, with crops of tobacco, hops, pines and walnuts. The road leads to the mountain and ski resorts of Falls Creek, Hotham and Mt.

Buffalo. Myrtleford and Bright are famous for their autumn colours.
Mount Buffalo National Park has fabulous walks and views with Lake Catani and the Eurobin Falls at the top and Lake Buffalo at the foot of the mountain.
The historic townships of Beechworth and Yackandandah are major attractions north of the Ovens Highway.

YACKANDANDAH

The town has been classified by the National Trust and is exceptionally beautiful. Tree lined streets of original verandahed buildings in a pretty hilly rural landscape.

ATTRACTIONS

- Art and craft shops
- Old gold diggings

BEECHWORTH

A larger town, this was the centre of the gold fields and has also been classified as historically important by the National Trust.
Many of the public buildings are of interest, especially the Post Office and the Powder Magazine. Tanswells Hotel is a restored lacework building offering accommodation and a restaurant. Note the Woolshed Falls historic walk and the Gorge scenic drive.

ACCOMMODATION

Bellbourie Estate

Hume & Hovell Road, Seymour, 3660
Tel: (057) 92 3505 Fax: (057) 92 3908
Contact: Geof & Judy Horton
Rooms: 2 ensuite
Cost (B & B): $120 double, Dinner for two $90

An ex-Aspro House, this is a panelled Kew hunting lodge popped into the country. A stunning garden and wonderful park on the banks of the Goulburn River, heated swimming pool, tennis court, golf driving range and putting green. Geoff Horton at the time of writing was still offering Clydesdale wagon rides.

Two double ensuite rooms, open fires and excellent food and hospitality. Very elegant.

Taffy's

Lyns Lane Road, Longwood, 3665
Tel: (057) 98 5325
Contact: Jill & Bernard Hayes
Rooms: 3 Self contained cottages

Take the Ruffy road up into the Strathbogie Range and follow the signs to Taffys. Created a few years ago by a Welsh Stonemason (and his wife Ann who now owns the Sages Cottage at Baxter), this charming collection of rustic buildings is very isolated.

Jill and Bernard Hayes, latterly of Hayguns in Euroa, now operate the restaurant and the three cottages. The restaurant seats 45 and is reminiscent of eighteenth century Europe with deep sills to the small windows, a loose-laid floor of hardwood offcuts and an impressive open fire with huge bellows. The buildings are on a high ridge which gives a splendid view north across 100 km. of flat farmland over Shepparton to the Murray River beyond.

The cottages are authentically quaint with kerosene lamps and warmed by pot belly stoves. They are very cosy and a God-send after a good night in the restaurant, since here you are one heck of a long, winding way from anything else.
Breakfast basket is supplied.

Blind Creek

R.M.B. 4110, Tatong Road, Benalla, 3672
Tel: (057) 62 2792 Fax: (057) 62 4078
Contact: Jane & Norton Grimwade
Rooms: 2
Cost (B & B): $105 double, $70 single
(D, B & B): $265 double, $100 single

This modern architect designed country house is decorated with great attention to detail by Jane Grimwade. Two double rooms share a bathroom, but only one couple is accommodated unless two are travelling together.
The garden is beautiful - a real country garden, and the hours of work and their green fingers are now showing real dividends.
The food is excellent and they typically serve north eastern wines.

Yaridni Bed & Breakfast Host Farm

R.M.B. 1090, Goorambat, 3725 (Yarrawonga Road, Benalla)
Tel: (057) 65 1273 Fax: (057) 64 1352
Contact: Rhyllis Siggers
Rooms: 3
Cost: $95 double B & B, $$85 single D, B & B
$95 full accommodation

At Yaridni you will experience genuine country hospitality, good food and wine. Just 13 kms. off the Hume Freeway between Benalla and Winton, this is a great spot for a night's

stopover between Sydney and Melbourne - or Sydney and Adelaide.
Rhyllis' innovative four course dinners are superb and served in the formal dining room.
There is one double room with ensuite and one double with shared facilities. A large family room with billiard and table tennis tables and T.V. make a break from the farm activities.

Koendidda Country House

R.M.B. 2137, Barnawatha, 3688
Tel: 060 26 7340 Fax: 060 26 7300
Contact: John and Jan Ingram
Rooms: 4 large ensuite
Cost (B & B): $65 single, (D, B & B) $105 single

Just 5 minutes from the Hume Freeway and central to the wineries of the North East is one of the region's finest examples of a spacious and colonial homestead (1856-58). Sited right on the backs of the meandering Indigo Creek, amidst hectares of landscaped bushland gardens, Jan and John Ingram are proud of the 2 storey fully restored Georgian style period house.
Complementary champagne or sherry is served pre-dinner in the elegant sitting room - log fire adding a glow to the many fine pieces of Georgian furniture. After dinner complementary port or Muscat is served in either the informal sitting room in winter, or in the warmer months in the gazebo.
The house features wide halls and high ceilings, central heating and air conditioning. All guest bedrooms have private bathrooms.
John is an ardent conservationist and the grounds of Koendidda are home to 500 species of flora and over 100 species of birds. Restoration of the Indigo Creek and the incorporation of wetland pondage with its growing population of amphibians, including platypus, beaver rats and native fish is a recently completed project.

Mountain bikes are available for riding the great country lanes or exploring the Chiltern Regional Park.
Koendidda is an ideal location to break the interstate journey or simply to take in Yackandandah, Beechworth or Rutherglen.

Finches of Beechworth

3 Finch Street, Beechworth, 3747
Tel: (057) 28 2655 Fax: (057) 28 2656
Contact: Jennifer Wilkinson
Rooms: 6
Cost: Double - $140, $210 dinner bed & breakfast

An historic home dating back to the 1880's, Finches is set in a half acre of beautiful English-style cottage garden perfumed with a profusion of flowers, including a Wisteria charmingly entwined around the house's large shady verandah.
Finches offers luxurious Victorian-style accommodation. There are six double bedrooms featuring mahogany beds and amoires, complemented by sumptuous chintz drapes. Five bedrooms have ensuites and one has a private bathroom. The lounge is a delightful combination of open fire, comfortable soft furnishings and elegant antiques, amking it a lavish, yet homely, retreat.

Kinross

34 Loch Street, Beechworth, 3747
Tel: (057) 28 2351
Contact: Steve & Anne Fanning
Rooms: 5 ensuite
Cost (B & B): From $120 double, $95 single
Dinner $39 per person

Steve and Anne Fanning have done a wonderful renovation on the old Manse. The five double (or twin) bedrooms are all ensuite, with open fireplaces and fine antique furniture.
Anne's cooking has gained Kinross a fine reputation. Hearty breakfasts and beautifully presented 4 course dinners are served by Steve in the dining room.

Sample Breakfast Menu - Kinross

Beechworth apple juice
Freshly squeezed orange juice
Tomato juice

Cornflakes, Just Right,
Nutrigrain, Muesli
Balance Oat Bran Flakes
Sultana Bran

Eggs - poached, scrambled, fried
Bacon, Sausages, Black Pudding
Scrambled egg with smoked trout
Eggs Benedict, Eggs Washington

Toast
Marmalades, Jams

Plunger coffee
Twinnings teas -
Darjeeling, English breakfast
Irish breakfast, Earl Grey

Lakeside

P.O. Box 17, Rutherglen, 3685
Tel: (060) 32 8650 Fax: (060) 32 8118
Contact: Helen & Peter Chambers
Rooms: 3
Cost (per person): $40 B&B, $90 DB&B $100 All inc.

Lakeside homestead is situated on the banks of Lake Moodemere, a grand old homestead built in the 1850's. The property is a mixed farm with grapes, cereal crops and sheep, situated in the centre of the wine district adjacent to state forests. There is easy access to canoes, swimming, golf, tennis and historic townships.

Enjoy the serenity of country life, dinner and a local Muscat by a cosy fire.

Mount Buffalo Chalet

Mt. Buffalo National Park (P.O. Box 76, Porepunkah, 3740)
Tel: (057) 55 1500
Contact: Alan Carruthers
Rooms: 100

Fresh, mountain air, great accommodation and that ability to relax well away from the city sprawl. The Mount Buffalo Chalet, recently renovated, has it all, and a lot more.

Bushwalkers, anglers, skiers and horseriders are all catered for at the Chalet, at various times of the year. That's the beauty of the Chalet; it's an all year proposition – one that's difficult to refuse.

High season tariffs range from $155 a day for the tower suites to $132 for the front rooms. The facility and non facility rooms are even cheaper!

Cobram Homestead

Murray Valley Highway, Cobram East, 3644
Tel: (058) 73 5393 Fax: (058) 73 5395
Contact: Sally & John Cummins
Rooms: 4
Cost (B & B): $70 single, $125 double,
Dinner $30 per person

The magnificent driveway of well over a kilometre of lush willow trees and century old peppercorns never quite prepares the "first time" visitor for the majestic greeting the homestead and its grounds offer.

Set on a gentle rise amongst English gardens and rolling lawns extending down to the banks of the Murray River, the views and surrounds are breathtaking.

Classified by the National Trust (settled in 1845) the property and homestead have great historical significance, as well as offering guests luxury and charm and tranquil, lazy weekend and overnight stays.

Decorated and furnished in all its original splendour, the Federation Homestead has three double bedrooms and one twin (share bathroom) available and wonderful country breakfasts begin the days overlooking the river.

Sally and John Cummins delight in sharing their home, and in spoiling their guests, and will arrange dinner if required, as well as picnic hampers and barbeques.

North East, Hume Highway

ARCADIA VIC 3613

Dorilla Park, R.M.B. Arcadia
Tel: (058) 27 1383
Owner/contact: L.M. & P. Willis
Rooms: 2 single/twin
Cost: $60 single, $90 twin
Working farm ◆ Dinner available by prior arrangement

AVENEL VIC. 3664

Harvest Home Hotel, 1 Bank Street
Tel: (057) 96 2339 Fax: (057) 96 2580
Owner/contact: Suzie McKay & Ian Bevan-Davies
Rooms: 7
Cost: Dinner Bed & Breakfast - $90 single

BARNAWARTHA VIC. 3688

Koendidda, R.M.B. 2137 Pooleys Road, Indigo Valley
Tel: (060) 26 7340 Fax: (060) 26 7300
Owner/contact: Jan and John Ingram
Rooms: 4 ensuite (V)
Cost: Single - $65, $105 dinner bed & breakfast
No children ◆ No smoking

BEECHWORTH VIC. 3747

Burnbrae, Gorge Road
Tel: (057) 28 1091
Owner/contact: Judi Borschman and Alec Armitage
Rooms: 4 double
Dinner by arrangement ◆ No children

Finches of Beechworth, 3 Finch Street
Tel: (057) 28 2655 Fax: (057) 28 2656
Owner/contact: Jennifer Wilkinson
Rooms: 6
Cost: Double - $140, $210 dinner bed & breakfast (V)
No smoking

Foxgloves, 21 Loch Street
Tel: (057) 28 1322
Owner/contact: Patricia & Simon Meade
Rooms: 3 ensuite
Cost: $90 double

Kinross, 34 Loch Street
Tel: (057) 28 2351
Owner/contact: Steve and Anne Fanning
Rooms: 5 ensuite (V)
Cost: From $120 double, $95 single; Dinner $39 single

Rose Cottage, 42 Camp Street
Tel: (057) 28 1069
Owner/contact: Tony & Lynn McCure
Rooms: 4
Cost: $55 single, $80 double/twin

BENALLA VIC. 3672

Belmont Bed & Breakfast, 80 Arundel Street
Tel: (057) 62 6575
Owner/Contact: Carolyn Leonard
Rooms: 3
Cost: $90 double, $55 single

Blind Creek, R.M.B. 4110 Tatong Road
Tel: (057) 62 2792 Fax: (057) 62 4078
Owner/contact: Jane & Norton Grimwade
Rooms: 2
Cost: $70 single, $105 double/twin; Dinner bed & Breakfast (V)
$100 single, $165 double

Yaridni B & B, Yarrawonga Road (R.M.B. 1090, Goorambat, 3725)
Tel: (057) 64 1273 Fax: (057) 64 1352
Owner/contact: Rhyllis Siggers
Rooms: 3 Ⓥ
Cost: From $95 double; $85 single dinner bed & breakfast, $95 single full board
Children welcome • Smoking outside only

BRIGHT VIC. 3741

Bright Alps Guest House & Ski Lodge, 83-85 Delany Avenue
Tel: (057) 55 1197
Owner/contact: Andrew & Carole Wilson
Rooms: 19
Cost: $63 double

Rosedale Guest House, 117 Gavan Street
Tel: (057) 55 1059
Owner/contact: Keith Morrison
Rooms: 16
Cost: $29 single, $15 under 14's, $7 under 5's; Dinner $18
Children/Family orientated

Thorley Manor, Bright-Wandiligong Road (Box 75)
Tel/Fax: (057) 55 1538
Owner/contact: Jim & Alison Anton
Rooms: s/c suite
Cost: Fully inclusive ski package - $280-300 double/weekend

Yarrara, 3 Walkers Lane
Tel: (057) 55 1850
Owner/contact: D.F. Whitecross
Rooms: 2
Cost: $25 single
No children

North East, Hume Highway

BUNDALONG VIC. 3730

Leigh Park
Tel: (057) 26 8488 Fax: (057) 26 8480
Owner/contact: Gwen & Len Stone
Rooms: 2 and 6 s/c cottages
Host farm

BUNGIL VIC. 3690

The Herb and Horse Colonial, Murray Valley Highway
(R.M.B. 4023, Wodonga)
Tel: (060) 72 9553

COBRAM EAST VIC. 3644

Cobram Homestead, Murray Valley Highway
Tel: (058) 73 5393 Fax: (058) 73 5395
Owner/contact: Sally & John Cummins (V)
Rooms: 4
Cost: $70 single, $125 double; Dinner $30 single

CORRYONG VIC. 3707

Alpine Gateway Lodge, 96 Hanson Street (P.O. Box 61
Tel: (060) 76 1269
Owner/contact: Mary S. Shaw
Rooms: 4
Cost: Bed only - $28 single, $38 double; B & B - $33.50-$35 single, $49-$53 double

Snowy Mountain, Sullivan Street, Towong
Tel: (060) 76 8252
Rooms: 4
Dinner available

FALLS CREEK VIC. 3699

Astra, Sitzmark Street
Tel: (057) 58 3496
Owner/contact: Roy & Pam Morris
Rooms: 24 ensuite
Cost: Summer - $55 Single B & B, $85 Single Full Board; Winter - $108-$155 Single
No children under 5

Cedarwood Alpine Lodge, 5 Schuss Street (P.O. Box 124)
Tel: (057) 58 3393
Booking contact: Wanderer Ski Holidays. Tel: (03) 525 577
Manager/contact: Geoff Van Wachem
Rooms: 27
Packages available • *Booking essential*

Cooroona Lodge, 8 Slalom Street
Tel: (057) 58 3244
Owner/contact: Mrs. Mary-Lou Irwin
Rooms: 13 ensuite
Cost: $35 single, $17.50 under 14's

Diana Lodge, Falls Creek Road (P.O. Box 483, Swan Hill, 3585)
Tel: (057) 58 3214 or (050) 37 6227
Rooms: 15

Halleys Lodge, P.O. Box 56
Tel: (057) 58 3363
Owner/contact: J.B. & L.M. Lawther
Rooms: 19 ensuite
Cost: Breakfast dinner & light lunch - from $400 for 5 nights
Winter only

Julians, Slalom Street
Tel: (057) 58 3211 or (03) 428 5324
Owner/contact: Julian Newton-Brown
Rooms: 21 ensuite

Karelia Alpine Lodge, 70 Parallel Street
Tel: (03) 439 7736 or (057) 58 3273
Owner/contact: Jerry Brazda
Rooms: 18 ensuite
Cost: Single - From $35 Summer & Autumn, from $50 Winter

Lakeside Lodge, Schuss Street, (P.O. Box 192, Collingwood, 3066)
Tel: (03) 888 5477 or (057) 58 3302
Manager/contact: Peter & Susan Broadhurst
Rooms: 16
Ski season only

Pretty Valley Alpine Lodge, Slalom Street (P.O. Box 52)
Tel: (057) 58 3210
Owner/contact: Barry & Maureen Jones
Rooms: 26

Silver Ski Lodge, Slalom Street
Tel: (057) 58 3303 or (03) 598 4542
Owner/contact: Mike & Jan or John Potucek
Rooms: 30

Snowdrift Lodge, Falls Creek Road (11 Arkaringa Crescent, Black Rock, 3193)
Tel: (057) 58 3303 or (03) 598 4542
Owner/contact: Deanne & Tony Beckwith
Rooms: 19

Trackers Mountain Lodge, 88 Schuss Street
Tel: (057) 58 3346
Owner/contact: Baldy Blackwell
Rooms: 19 ensuite
Cost: $40 single, $20 child
Dinner available ◆ 1991 Victorian Tourist winner

Viking Alpine Lodge, 72 Parallel Street (P.O. Box 121)
Tel: (057) 58 3247
Owner/contact: Michael & Carol Bartholomew
Rooms: 18 ensuite
Cost: $45 Per Double Room, $15 Each Extra Adult, $7.50 Child

LONGWOOD VIC. 3665

Taffy's, Lyns Lane Road
Tel: (057) 98 5325
Owner/contact: Jill & Bernard Hayes (V)
Rooms: 3 s/c cottages

MILAWA VIC. 3678

Ercildoon, Oxley Road (Snow Road)
Tel: (057) 27 3222
Owner/contact: Malcolm & Dorothy Gardner
Rooms: 4
Cost: $50 single, $65 twin, $65-$70 double
No children ◆ No smoking

MITTA MITTA VIC. 3701

Callaghans Creek Lodge, Callaghans Creek Road
Tel: (060) 72 3676
Owner/contact: Melissa Nichol
Rooms: 4
No children

MOUNT BAW BAW VIC. 3833

Watzmann Haus, Alpine Village
Tel: (051) 65 1124
Owner/contact: Max Otter
Rooms: 6
Closed in summer◆ No children

MOUNT BUFFALO VIC. 3745

Conservation & Environment, Mt. Buffalo Park
Tel: (057) 55 1988
Manager/contact: Paul Heisler
Rooms: 8 bunk style, 12 motel suite

Mt. Buffalo Chalet, Mt. Buffalo National Park (P.O. Box 76, Porepunkah, 3740)
Tel: (057) 55 1500 Reservations: (008) 037 038
Manager/contact: Mr. Alan Carruthers Ⓥ
Rooms: 100

MOUNT BULLER VIC. 3723

Alpine Retreat Ski Lodge, 48 Stirling Road
Tel: (057) 77 2678
Owner/contact: Karl & Danny Matern
Rooms: 25 ensuite
Cost: Dinner, Bed & Breakfast - $70-$100

Avalanche, 10 Delatite Lane (25 Quarry Road, Mitcham, 3132)
Tel: (03) 874 7990
Owner: Bill Short
Contact: The Manager
Rooms: 18
Family orientated lodge

Lantern Lodge, 18 Goal Post Road (P.O. Box 21)
Tel: (057) 77 6326 or (03) 723 3586 Fax: (057) 77 6385
Owner/contact: Lillian Aldinger
Rooms: 16
Cost: Winter dinner bed & breakfast $70-$105 single, Summer bed & breakfast $45 single
No smoking

MOUNT HOTHAM VIC. 3741

Zirkys Lodge, Alpine Highway (P.O. Box 46, Bright)
Tel: (057) 59 3518 Fax: (057) 59 3652
Owner/contact: Heather Zirknitzer
Rooms: 6 ensuite
Cost: $90 single
Dinner available

MUDGEGONGA VIC. 3737

Orange Grove, R.M.B. 2430 Blacks Flat Road
Tel: (057) 53 4513
Owner/contact: Mary Brewer
Rooms: 3
Cost: $40 single, $20 child; Dinner $25 (3 course)

NAGAMBIE VIC. 3608

Laundon Guest House, Murchison Road
Tel: (057) 94 2897
Owner/contact: Jacquie Anton
Rooms: 7

OMEO VIC. 3898

The Manse, Cnr. Omeo Highway & Day Avenue (P.O. Box 125)
Tel: (051) 59 1441 or (03) 589 6029
Owner/contact: Norma Anderson
Rooms: 5
Facilities for disabled

The Willows Guest Cottage, Anglers Rest
Tel/Fax: (051) 59 7241
Owner/contact: Geoff & Jenny Vardy
Rooms: 2 s/c
Cost: Full board - $80 single, $50 child

RUTHERGLEN VIC. 3685

Lakeside, P.O. Box 17
Tel: (060) 32 8650 Fax: (060) 32 8118
Owner/contact: Helen & Peter Chambers
Rooms: 3 Ⓥ
Cost: Single - $40, dinner bed & breakfast $90
No smoking

Mount Ophir Country Homestead, R.M.B. 1180 Stillards Lane
Tel: (060) 32 9920 or (060) 32 9079
Owner/contact: Ruth Penhall
Rooms: 4
Cost: Single - from $45, from $85 dinner bed & breakfast
No smoking

SEYMOUR VIC. 3660

Bellbourie Estate, Hume & Hovell Road
Tel: (057) 92 3505 Fax: (057) 92 3908
Owner/contact: Judy Horton
Rooms: 2 ensuite Ⓥ
Cost: $120 double, Dinner for two $90
No children

STANLEY VIC. 3743

Pioneer Cottage, P.O. Stanley
Tel: (057) 28 6603
Owner/contact: J. Indian & S.J. Routledge
Rooms: 1 cottage
Cost: $35 single, $15 under 15's
No smoking

TAWONGA SOUTH VIC. 3698

The Valley View Lodge, 9 Allamar Court
Tel: (057) 57 1033
Owner/contact: Richard & Judy Ellis
Rooms: 11 ensuite
Cost: $55 double, $15 extra person
Dinner available

WAHGUNYAH VIC. 3687

The House at Mt. Prior, P.O. Box
Tel: (060) 26 5256 Fax: (060) 26 5601
Owner/contact: Trish Hennessy
Rooms: 5
Cost: P.O.A.

WANGARATTA VIC. 3678

Old Boorhaman, R.M.B. 4721 Yarrawonga Road, Peechelba East
Tel: (057) 26 9265
Owner/contact: Val & Michael Boothby
Rooms: 2
working farm

WODONGA VIC. 3691

The Willows, R.M.B. 1139
Tel: (060) 28 9231
Owner/contact: Gwen & Fred Keat
Rooms: 2
Cost: $60 Single, $30 Children

Quamby B & B, R.M.B. 4223 Yarrawonga Road
Tel: (057) 26 9291 Fax: (057) 26 9402
Owner/contact: Chiffra & Bernard Clarke
Rooms: 3
Cost: $65 single, $95-$105 double/twin
Smoking outdoors only

Calder Highway to the North; The Central Goldfields

The main centres of population in this area are Kyneton, Daylesford, Hepburn Springs, Maldon and Castlemaine, but there are many small settlements of interest. In the north Harcourt, Chewton, Guildford and Fryers Town and further south Malmsbury, Woodend, Trentham and Lancefield.

Leave Melbourne on the Tullamarine Freeway and then take the Calder Highway (Routh 79). This small area is filled with history with its many charming little gold towns.

Major Mitchell first surveyed the area climbing to the summit of Mt. Macedon in 1836. Here, at a height of 1,000 metres, the whole Port Phillip basin can be viewed.

The towns date from 1850, when the gold boom brought thousands of people to the area. Gold created these towns and, with their consequent wealth, a burgeoning of grand public buildings.

Mount Macedon

Only 40 kilometres from Melbourne, Mt. Macedon has long been established as a cool summer haven for the wealthy of Melbourne. Many of these fine residences were decimated by the fires of 1983. Much of the old has been replaced by new architecture, but the gardens with their fine deciduous trees have survived.

There are many aspects to Mt. Macedon for the tourist. The Mount itself offers the most spectacular views. There are many walks in the state park. Hanging Rock is close by and the locals recommend the walk to Sanatorium Lake at the top of the hill.

When ever the weather report says snow down to 800 metres, families rush to the mountain, the closest place to Melbourne for the kids to build a snowman.

Wineries are a feature of the area. Many private gardens are open at the weekends to the public. there is an excellent craft shop at Macedon called Finches, and many quality nurseries.

Mt. Macedon General Store is a great venue for information and local gossip, and a snack inside or out.

ATTRACTIONS

- Mt. Macedon Golf Club - 9 greens, 18 holes
- Macedon Ranges Regional Park
- Wombat State Forest
- Hanging Rock Reserve - Hanging Rock Picnic Races New Year's Day & Australia Day
- Vineyards

KYNETON

A promising entry to the town with the Campaspe River following the highway, and most attractive public gardens. The uneven verandahs on the old shops present a charming streetscape. Enjoy the many delights of this town.

Piper Street, the Calder Highway on the way north out of town, is a concentrated delight. A clutch of antique shops, an 'antique' sweet shop and the museum.

The Kyneton Museum

67 Piper Street

Housed in a blue stone bank building C.1865. On entry it appears tiny, but on further exploration it has an extensive and fascinating collection of exhibits: Squatters homestead, cellar, farmyard, outbuildings, stone coach house and farm machinery, dairy, hedging and fencing, old market building, and on - 2 hours is not enough. Hopefully, Patricia Williams will be in charge; a delight in herself.

Leave time to look at the shops across the road - put the kids into the excellent old lolly shop, look next door at Mljo for good recycled clothing, buy an antique and then hopefully it's time for a beer at the Red Ox, a few doors further back towards town.

The Red Ox:

Great to find such an enjoyable watering hole in the country. The interior is not particularly charming, but the owners are. Imported English and Australian beers and Guinness on tap. A sensational local cider from Harcourt. This is an excellent steak house with pop music and a beer garden and the friendliest staff. They are very obliging and knowledgeable about the area and the food is good, with a touch of city sophistication.

ATTRACTIONS

- Racecourse (especially the day after the Melbourne Cup)
- Ten wineries (especially Virgin Hills).
- Gardens
    - Botanic
    - Malmsbury
    - Alister Clark Rose Garden
    - Kyneton Gardens on the Campaspe River
- Kyneton Museum

A few km. out of Kyneton on the right look out for:

- Bleak House - rose nursery. Wonderful garden walk in the summer, bleak in the winter. The Garden Shop tea room sells books and Chris Canning cards.

MALMSBURY

Eleven km. from Kyneton, a small settlement with pleasant public gardens, famous for Mrs. Robbs Bake House on the left near the pub.

HARCOURT

A spot for a picnic in the Oak Forest - a cider and a look at Mt. Alexander, where there is a Koala Reserve.

Harcourt is the apple centre of Victoria. Roadside sales are available, and 4 km. out of Harcourt on the Bendigo Road is Mt. Alexander Wines. Taste and buy:

- Harcourt Cider
- Champagne Cider
- Pear Cider
- Pear Champagne

Harcourt Cider is brilliant - even for the most jaded palate.

CHEWTON

A scattered settlement - old gold workings and a modern mine on the creek front, but the valley remains scenic.

Look for Badgers Keep Nursery and Garden, and hope it is open. It seems this wonderful place with its unique plants is open less and less as the meticulous owners tire of keeping visitors' children off the plants and beds.

CASTLEMAINE

Only a few minutes away from Chewton. Clustered around the town centre, bounded by Mostyn Street, Barker Street and Hargraves Street, are many original buildings of the 1850's and 60's; walk this precinct and visit the Botanical Gardens.

ATTRACTIONS

- The Market Museum (in the restored market building)
- Buda - a grand historic house and garden. Roses are named and displayed for sale. The cypress hedge dating from 1865 is a notable feature.
- Botanic Gardens

MALDON

Only fifteen minutes from Castlemaine, it is a tiny authentic Victorian jewel. The whole town was classified by the National Trust in 1966 because it 'possesses a most unique and well preserved variety of historic architecture'. An Historic Tour walk brochure is available at the excellent Visitors' Centre, and describes Maldon as 'having few spectacular buildings', but that its appeal is in its intactness and the concentration of the elements which make up a 19th century mining town.
There is a plethora of self-contained accommodation in Maldon; some genuinely old, like Lavender & Lace, Tressiders, and School Cottage, others newly-constructed but in old-style. Maldon Tourist Information will supply you with details of these.

ATTRACTIONS

- Shops. The proprietors have provided an interesting range of merchandise.
- Calders Cottage and Garden - something for everyone, plus the ultimate in Australian Kitch.
- Spotted Dingo Studio - original contemporary jewellery and metalwork.
- The Maldon Gallery, Book Shop and Print Shop.
- The Old Grain Store - a large and excellent range of antiques.
- Lavender & Lace. Dianne and Spencer Tunks sell lavender and lace near to the Kangaroo Pub. They also have accommodation.

Kangaroo Pub

With beer garden. Between Castlemaine & Bendigo - close to Lake Cairn Curran. Cobb & Co. stables out the back, verandah posts and lace over slate paved footpath with bench seats, this pub and so many other of Maldon's buildings make this hamlet famous for its low scale character.

Authentic as an 1857 colonial pub can be, it has the fortune of never having been ravaged by a succession of alterations to obliterate its historic beginnings.

Dining in the Tapestry Room Restaurant, where lace tablecloths, tapestries and period bits and pieces reflect the era when Maldon was awash with Welsh miners, seeking gold from the ground and passing on their renowned skills as stonemasons, slate roofers and paviours.

Graeme and Coral Gibb preside over this only so named "Kangaroo Hotel" in Australia. The leafy courtyard is just the place to be when Maldon turns on its famous hot days. The coldest ales, finest wines and best fare in town.

No accommodation available

ATTRACTIONS

SURROUNDING AREA

- Nuggetty Ranges and Mt. Moorul. Behind the cemetery, 1,496 ft. above sea level. Consisting of huge granite boulders, it offers a good walk and spectacular views.
- Mt. Tarrengower and Lookout Tower. Higher, at 1,872 ft., giving 360° views.
- Carmans Tunnel and the North British Mine.
- Lake Cairn Curran near Newstead. Good bathing, picnic and barbecue facilities. Boat launching ramp and children's amusements. (By the way, the pub in Newstead was offering a counter meal for $3 - amazing.)

Head south again to Hepburn Springs and Daylesford via Yandoit and Franklinford.

HEPBURN SPRINGS

The spa complex is a major Victorian attraction, as are the mineral springs scattered along the steep valley. The facility is well organised, with a plethora of therapeutic and relaxing offerings. This fine building, established in 1895, has been thoroughly modernised and is spacious and attractive. Unfortunately, everyone complains about the add-ons: $5 for a bath robe, $1 for a towel, $1 for a locker, plus various deposits - do try it, but take a calculator to work out the bill.

Outside, the walk along the floor of the valley to the various springs is interesting and pleasant amongst the old trees.

DAYLESFORD

Known for the Lake House.

ATTRACTIONS

- Convent Gallery - good breakfast and lunch here - a quality gallery
- Antique shops.

LANCEFIELD

Things are happening in Lancefield! The majestic old building on the corssroads has become the Antique Centre of Victoria. This 55 roomed, 3 storey building called 'Macedonia House' was built in 1889 as a hotel for the then industrious farming community of Lancefield. In February this year Bill and Heather Coleby bought the property and they have almost finished the conversion of the wonderful edifice - each room is filled to capacity with antiques and Edwardiana. A must visit.

At the other end of town 'The Gallery and Nursery' are also worth a visit. The Gallery has new exhibitions every 8 weeks and the nursery is a delight.

A little out of town is the Cleveland Vineyard. Keith and Lynette Brien are restoring this 1860 house into a glorious family home with bed and breakfast accommodation - due to open 1994, but visit now to taste the Pinot and Chardonnay.

Heading back towards Melbourne - down a dirt track to the right is a real surprise. The Copes-Williams Vineyard. Here is the 8th Lord Taverner's Pitch in Australia - the only ground on private land. This is social cricket in a village green setting, complete with pavillion.

Then there is the wine - Cope-Williams Romsey Brut - and Rosé, table wines and a cricketers Portwine. Lunch is good in the tasting room - try a Romsey Roll. Accommodation is planned for 1994.

ACCOMMODATION

The Stables

Huntley Burn, Main Road, Mt. Macedon, 3441
Tel: (054) 26 1411
Contact: Penny Tate
Rooms: s/c accommodation
Cost: $250 double, weekend

If you have the facility to plan, here you may experience the magic of Mt. Macedon and other things.

The reality of Huntley Burn would impoverish any attempt at description. Just drive through their gateway to a country estate and enter a wild garden where a mansion once stood. Lost in the fires of '83, now a riot of growth covers the bones of a magnificent property.

Preferably arrive at night driving an old sports car, and bear left to the stables, where you will stay. You now are characters in your own romantic story, entering the film set for an Evelyn Waugh novel, or have stumbled into someone else's dream. It feels as though your host, perhaps an aristocratic lady still waiting for her lover killed in the war, has suddenly left, leaving you a courteous note saying 'enjoy your stay' and apologising for being called away. There is a feeling of being players in a carefully constructed game, a mystery. What has happened here, who is the owner, what is the significance of the oak cupboard containing nothing but an old teddy bear and a black bra?

I felt a bit like Goldilocks, as I compulsively rummaged through all the drawers to find more clues before the bears came home.

I promise you will at the least enjoy it, but probably you will become totally, romantically gooey over the experience. Just see what is written in the guest book by people who were presumably normal before they stayed here.

If, whilst you are here, you never leave the garden and stables, you will have experienced Mt. Macedon.

I should mention that there is a loft for kids, but you would no more bring children here than your speed-boat and golf clubs. Also you have some unusual companions who are gentle, quiet and charming and totally in keeping with the atmosphere.
Penny Tate is the creator, director, the lady - I have no idea who he was.

Mountain Inn

351 Main Road, Mt. Macedon, 3441
Tel: (054) 26 1755
Contact: David, Rosemary & Sarah Kennon
Rooms: 9
Cost: $70 double, $85 double ensuite
$10 reduction Monday - Thursday

This warm hued brick building grows out of the hill and is as close to an English pub as you will find in Australia.
The bar food is innovative and of excellent value. Fine dining in the Green Room is no longer available; they now serve a bistro menu. If you require more elaborate food, Mistys over the road is still going strong.
Breakfast is served in the sunroom, or on the deck just outside in the summer. Croquet is no longer available, the lawn is now well used with tables and seating in the shade of the grand oak. There is a hard tennis court and, by local request, a hitching rail for horses.
There are three ensuite rooms, one with a window to the road; the other two have direct access to the garden at the back. Two more double rooms with handbasins share a large bathroom on this level. Upstairs, four small double rooms complete the accommodation.
Throughout the pub is a comfortable homely feeling with a pleasant rural atmosphere.

Ballantrae Mews

385 Mt. Macedon Road, Mt. Macedon, 3441
Tel: (054) 26 2078
Contact: Peter & Bunty Jackson
Rooms: s/c unit
Cost (B & B): $85 double

On a large steep block of over six acres, 2½ of which is garden and the rest a gully hideaway for much wildlife, including a tame Koala.

The accommodation is a modern weatherboard structure built above a garage workshop area. This elevation gives splended ivews over the gully to open countryside. One very large room has a double bed at one end, sitting area around a wood heater centrally and spacious kitchen with all modern appliances, including a microwave at the other end.

I found the hosts to be extremely obliging - they freely make available laundry facilities in the main house and you are invited up there for breakfast if you so desire. (Nice dog too!)

Pond Cottage and Viewly Hill

Chasers Lane, Pipers Creek
Tel: (054) 22 1447
Contact: Dougal & Nellie Ramsay
Rooms: s/c cottages
Cost: $75-$90 each first two, then $40-$48

Just an easy hour's drive from Melbourne, Pond Cottage and Viewly Hill are two secluded self-contained cottages located on 520 glorious rolling acres, not far from historic Woodend and Kyneton.

Set amidst a magnificent 7 acre Garden of Eden, picturesque Pond Cottage nestles on the bank of a tranquil lake, where trout lie sleeping and swans serenely glide. Inside, the cottage is a perfect blend of Murray pine flooring and comfy, casual modern sofas. The two upstairs bedrooms have been

designed so that you wake up to spectacular views of the lake and garden! Have a hit of tennis or a dip in the pool.
Dating back to the 1850's, Viewly Hill is a farm homestead which has been completely rebuilt as luxurious accommodation for up to 8 people - each room has its own ensuite and there are cosy open fires in addition to central heating. Here you can explore the farm, or play croquet.
The cottages' two kitchens are generously supplied with delightful country fare - including farm eggs, fresh herbs and fruit juices specially brought in from Batlow in N.S.W.

The Gallery Cottage

R.M.B. 1890, Lancefield Road, Carlsruhe, 3442
Tel: (054) 22 2636 Fax: (054) 22 3504
Contact: Bill & Pat Ross
Rooms: Self contained cottage
Cost (B & B): $130 - $150 double

The plainness of the outside of this cedar cottage belies the comfort within, where we find Pat's flair for arrrangements in the mixture of old and new to provide for our every need.
The breakfast provisions left in the cottage include fresh fruit, fruit juice, all sorts of cereals, mueslies, porridge, farm eggs and bacon with wholemeal bread for toast and an assortment of jams, marmalade, honey and Vegemite.
Should guests require an evening meal, it is served in the Chooks & Choos (restored Guards Van) restaurant.

The Bentinck Country House

2 - 8 Carlisle Street, Woodend, 3442 (P.O. Box 498)
Tel: (054) 27 2944 Fax: (054) 27 2232
Contact: Ross Plowman
Rooms: 30
Cost (D, B & B): From $110 - $150 single

The gravel drive is crunchy, the facade imposing and the delightful gardens extensive and include a lake with a bridge to an island summer house, a swimming pool and two en tout cas tennis courts.

A cantelevered Georgian circular staircase dominates the large hall reception area. Through glass doors to the right, a huge sitting room with large comfortable furniture and a roaring fire welcomes the guest. The feeling is of quality and solid luxury. Twenty four of the twenty nine rooms are ensuite; all are beautifully furnished.

Three double bedrooms share two bathrooms upstairs, whilst the other two double rooms without private facilities share two bathrooms on the ground floor. The sitting area on the landing at the head of the stairs opens onto a balcony above the front door.

The Bentinck has a reputation as a high quality convention centre with a sophisticated dining room, but the independent traveller may be assured of a warm welcome, comfort and quality.

Kyneton Country House

66 Jennings Street, Kyneton, 3444
Tel: (054) 22 3556
Contact: Mary & Paul Reid
Rooms: 4
Cost - Double (full): $230 one day, $330 two days (1 dinner)
Ensuite $25 per night
(Midweek B & B): From $75 single, From $100 double

This is a grand Victorian detached villa in a famously neatly maintained cottage garden.
The house has been beautifully restored and offers four double rooms. The ensuite room attracts a $40 supplement.
Booking is suggested two weeks ahead.

Dunbar

Metcalfe-Redesdale Road, Metcalfe, 3448
Tel: (054) 23 2388 Fax: (054) 23 2600
Contact: Doreen & Bruce Orchard
Rooms: 4
Cost: From $75 single, $35 children

Dunbar at Metcalfe, 10 km. N.E. of Malmsbury is a working farm which offers visitors genuine country hospitality. Bruce and Doreen Orchard have restored their century-old homestead to provide accommodation for up to ten guests. The property runs 1,400 fine wool Merinos and has lots of farmyard animals. Be warned that there are also 2 self-contained cottages which sleep up to 8 people - so school holidays can be busy - but if you are looking for genuine warmth and country hospitality, enjoy Dunbar, an excellent host farm.

Thompson's Tranquil Valley Farm

Hoopers Road, Chewton, 3451
Tel: (054) 72 2118
Contact: Mary Thompson
Rooms: 1 double suite in farmhouse, 1 s/c unit
Cost:$65 - $75

Friendly budget farm accommodation. Take Fryers Road, Dunn Road and then Hoopers Road.

A simple house in a lovely quiet valley. Guarded by two very lazy, fat red healers; they may be a danger to your tyres, but not to your heels, don't worry. The unit is private, situated at the end of the house, overlooking the little valley.

Mary Thompson advertises her environment as allergy-free, and uses organically grown fruit and vegetables and free range eggs. Kids are welcome, there is plenty of room, and at $65 on a weekday night and $75 at weekends, it is excellent value.

Holcombe Homestead

R.M.B. 3683, Glenlyon, 3461
Tel: (053) 48 7514 Fax: (053) 48 7742
Contact: Annette & John Marshall
Rooms: s/c house
Cost (person/day): $75 first 2 guests, $45 each extra guest

This is a warm hued brick building, imposing, with most ornate chimneys and neat presentation. A country mansion, a retreat.
This is no ordinary self-contained period house, but a Victorian homestead, furnished with appropriate, ornate pieces. Pine trees shelter the large lawn and a floodlit Flexipave tennis court.
The accommodation includes three double bedrooms, which share the single bathroom. The kitchen has all modern appliances, including a dishwasher. For that special occasion there is an imposing dining room, furnished in Regency style, a proper venue for a lavish dinner party.
The verandah affords shade from which to contemplate the immense surrounding countryside.
Although this is a self catering proposition, provisions may be supplied by prior arrangement.

Whispering Oaks

Simpson Street, Campbells Creek, Castlemaine, 3450
Tel: (054) 72 3930
Contact: Chris & Brian Sartori
Rooms: Self contained cottage

This tiny double-fronted brick cottage is set at right angles to the unmade Simpson Street and looks over an extensive garden to open countryside. It consists of one room with polished floorboards. At one end is a couch and fireplace; at the other a double brass bed. It is compact and cute.

For breakfast you may either help yourself to the dried fruits, cereals and break provided, or you may order a cooked breakfast from the interesting menu offering porridge; bacon and eggs; filled savoury muffins; croissant; or a fluffy omelette. The garden is fairly open, but there is a pleasant sitting area beneath the oaks, after which the property is named.

Coach & Rose

68 Mostyn Street, Castlemaine, 3450
Tel: (054) 72 4850
Contact: Stephen & Jannina Biggs
Rooms: 4 ensuite
Cost (B & B): From $85 double

This establishment exemplifies our criteria of genuine Australian hospitality. There are four double motel-type ensuite units, comfortable and pleasantly furnished.

Jannina Biggs is a delight and her breakfast offerings, innovative and unusual, are taken in the conservatory. The accommodation is new, built onto the back of an old coach house. In the cellar is a sitting room with T.V. and a games room with a snooker table. For sunny days, a rose garden has been created as a sitting area.

Ellimatta

233 Barker Street, Castlemaine, 3450
Tel: (054) 72 4454
Contact: Lloyd & Margaret Everett
Rooms: 5
Cost (B & B): $85 - $100 double

This is a mini version of the Bendigo Shamrock Hotel and is located in the centre of Castlemaine. The broad upstairs verandah is a great place to gain a different perspective on the world going by.

This historic building has been beautifully restored and provides accommodation of 4 double bedrooms and one family room. Only one room is ensuite, but the others give a choice between open fires or French doors onto the balcony. A private sitting room offers tea and coffee facilities.

Margaret Everett is the ideal hostess, most generous in her promotion of the area. She is willing to share her time and knowledge with the visitor.

Continental breakfast may be served on the verandah. Cooked breakfast is included in the tariff and the a-la-carte restaurant is of continuing good reputation, with local produce such as Bacchus Marsh venison medallions. The owners also offer a picnic 'gourmet lunch' for house guests.

The wine list features local wines at reasonable prices and a range of local and interstate beers.

The Stables

The Diggers Rest, 61 Main Road, Campbell's Creek, Castlemaine, 3450
Tel: (054) 72 2480
Contact:Lyn & Graeme Bennett
Rooms: Self contained accommodation

If you like antiques and are driving through Campbell's Creek, you would have to stop at Diggers Rest. Behind this shop, the stables have been converted faithfully and, dare I say,

fanatically, in 1850's style to provide self-catering accommodation.
The ground floor is surfaced with huge blocks of slate, some 4 inches thick, which came out from Europe as ballast at that time. The refrigerator, stove and plumbing are obviously not from the period. The sitting area is comfortable, and warmed by an open fire.
The loft of the stables is one large bedroom which may have anything from one to three iron four-poster beds, according to requirement. These are dressed romantically with net and lace.

Halfway House Cottage

R.M.B. Muckleford, via Castlemaine, 3451
Tel: (054) 75 1113
Contact: Pamela & Graeme Christmas
Rooms: s/c cottage

Halfway House Cottage is situated on a rural property of 5 hectares on the Castlemaine to Maldon Road, midway between these two historic towns.
The cottage is designed to accommodate couples who desire to experience the charm of a quiet romantic retreat, and is fully self-contained.
They can also enjoy the comfort of a cosy wood fire.

Sussex Field

Sandy Creek Road, Maldon, 3463
Tel: (054) 72 4720 or (054) 75 2320
Contact: Carole Gleen

This collection of buildings, sheds and barns is nothing short of remarkable. A sunshine gate, pole fences, adze timber yards and sheds with slab walls surround the farm house with its stone walls. Behind these structures is a barn with the roof timbers supported by crude tree trunks and all covered by thatch and green sprouting turf. All is in perfect working order, apparently frozen in time but in fact has been painstakingly restored with found timber from derelict buildings in the area.

Accommodation is available either in the original mud-brick cottage set apart from the homestead, or you can take the farm house, itself true to the period.
Contact Carol, a comfortable stay in unique surroundings is assured.

The Barn

64 Main Street, Maldon, 3463
Tel: (054) 75 2015
Contact: John
Rooms: 2 ensuite s/c units
Cost (B & B): $90 double

On the main street, opposite Calder's Cottage and Garden, tucked away in a cottage garden behind the shop fronts. The Barn has been cleverly converted into 2 units. Upstairs, you look out onto peppercorn trees and downstairs onto the garden. Each unit has a double bedroom, living area and bathroom. One has an open fire, the other a pot belly stove, and both are quiet and secluded yet centrally located in Maldon.

"Lavender Lace & Living"

High Street, Maldon, 3463
Tel: (054) 75 2357 or (054) 75 1075
Contact: Spenser & Dianne Tunks
Rooms: s/c accommodation for one couple
Cost (B & B): $75 double

This offers historic plush in an original stone cottage with the obligatory, but so welcoming, log fire. Also lots of lavender and lace, of course. Romantic.

Tressiders Cottage

High Street, Maldon, 3463
Tel: (054) 75 2357 or (054) 75 1075
Contact: Spenser & Dianne Tunks
Rooms: s/c cottage, sleeps 8
Cost (B & B): $85 double, $50 single

More grand, with the same attention to detail and comfort. Four double rooms, minimum booking 2 couples at $85 per couple at weekends.

Railway Cottage

Maldon, 3463
Tel: (054) 75 2114 Fax: (054) 75 2114
Contact: Karl Liffman
Rooms: Self contained cottage

Karl is another fanatic for authenticity in restoration. A genuine wood stove dominates the tiny kitchen of this cottage, although a hotplate and microwave cooker, together with a large refrigerator are sensible concessions to the twentieth century. The bathroom has a large enamel claw-foot bath with shower and also a basin, all with original plumbing. A double

wooden wash trough duplicates the washing machine and dryer.
One double bedroom and a twin bedroom occupy the front of the house; the sitting room, kitchen and bathroom are at the back.
The cottage is surrounded by a pretty, old fashioned garden which appears mature after only one season of Karl's horticultural magic.

Spring Cottage

Maldon, 3463
Tel: (054) 75 2114 Fax: (054) 75 2114
Contact: Karl Liffman
Rooms: Self contained cottage
Cost: $85 - $100 double

My favourite in Maldon. Turn into Spring Street at the gnome factory and it is situated at the end of this tiny valley; on the left, with peppercorn trees, and a wormwood hedge in front, the cottage is set back a little way up the hill.
It is partially obscured by the most charming cottage garden full of period plants 'of sustenance' - for the miner - all labelled. Karl, the owner, is a remarkable industrious man with an encyclopaedic knowledge of plants and an obsession for the genuine and original. This is a perfect little haven, faithfully restored with 2 bedrooms.
The unique garden of Spring Cottage is currently under siege by rabbits.

Eaglehawk Restaurant and Accommodation

Contact: Sally & Peter Bishop
Rooms: Self contained units

The Eaglehawk Pub, now a restaurant with accommodation, occupies a large Federation-style building, three kilometres north of Maldon. It has a pleasant, well-stocked bar and two connecting dining rooms with open fires.

The accommodation units are newly built and architecturally in harmony with the original building. They are set around a pleasant garden with a swimming pool. Parking is provided behind the units, so the garden provides a pleasant oasis for contemplation from your porch.
Although basically a motel, it has atmosphere, quality and style which transcends that appellation. If you do not want self-catering accommodation, this provides the best quality in Maldon.
The menu changes with the seasons; Chef Lee Aldridge.

Villa Parma

Hepburn Springs, 3461
Tel: (053) 48 3512
Contact: Franchiek Kasek
Rooms: 3

James of Linton House is totally besotted by the Villa. I was stunned. A Tuscan building has been dropped, and I do mean dropped, into Hepburn Springs. It has a totally genuine, ancient feeling. Inside packed with antiques, it is necessary in some rooms to turn sideways as you thread your way past the furniture to the fireplace. Two double bedrooms and a single bedroom share the bathroom, so queues may form.
There is a drawing room upstairs, and a small sitting room downstairs, each with open fires. Normally just bed and breakfast, but your obliging host will prepare an interesting dinner by prior arrangement.
A definite, different experience, probably for the under 40's. I would not send my mother or my accountant.
The garden is extensive and currently in design stage, or are they excavating the ruins of a Roman temple?

Dudley House

101 Main Road, Hepburn Springs, 3461
Tel: (053) 48 3033 Fax: (053) 48 3033
Contact: Kay & Peter Lipman
Rooms: 4
Cost (B & B): From $110

Dudley House has softened and offers comfort, quality and hospitality.

It has a great position overlooking the Hepburn Springs and offers four beautifully appointed double rooms, 2 with ensuite and 2 with private facilities, and commodious common areas.

Peter and Kay have recently purchased the cottage next door. Mrs. O'Grady's sleeps 6, with 2 renovated bathrooms, and is different from Dudley House.

Mooltan Guest House

129 Main Road, Hepburn Springs, 3461
Tel: (053) 48 3555
Contact: Eddie Beacham
Rooms: 11
Cost (B & B): $75-$100 double, midweek
(D,B & B) $220-$280 double, weekend package

Most conveniently located, overlooking the spa and Wombat Forest across the creek.

This is a rambling, warm and friendly Edwardian building. Eleven bedrooms, all with wide verandahs. Eight upstairs (6, 7 & 8 are the best) sharing 2 bathrooms; 3 ensuite rooms below. This is a proud family enterprise, a son supplying stained glass for the windows and a daughter helping father with the carpentry. The proprietor, Eddie Beacham, will make you very welcome. Dinner is available (and a tennis court soon will be).

Cliston

R.M.B. 3999, Daylesford-Malmsbury Road, Drummond, 3461
Tel: (054) 23 9155
Contact: Max & Kath Pilbeam
Rooms: 2 & Self contained cottage

The proprietors entertain you royally at this 4-Star host farm. The house provides for guests one double bedroom and one twin room, each ensuite, also a sunroom and sitting room. Max is a beef farmer with an additional interest in rare farm animals which are being lost to the gene pool, since they are no longer deemed to be efficient enough for modern production targets. On a stroll around the farm you may bump into a black pig or startle a gorgeously dotted rooster.

The tariff includes all meals and your entertainment. Kath is a most hospitable hostess and good cook.

The Pilbeams also offer a large, self-contained cottage for those wishing to cater for themselves, or who require more privacy. Three bedrooms, one queen, one twin and one double, are serviced by a bathroom and separate lavatory. there is wood and electric heating and comfortable sitting areas which open onto a large verandah, which has superb views over the renowned Virgin Hills Vineyard.

Linton House

68 Central Springs Road, Daylesford, 3460
Tel: (053) 48 2331
Contact: James Booth

This large weatherboard house overlooks the lake at Daylesford. James Booth is a charming, talented, wonderfully hospitable person. He has created 2 apartments of immense style.

One is pale greys, sisal carpet with antique furnishings - including a superb reading stand over the large claw bath. The other has an open fire in the bathroom, and the apartment is in the old ballroom/library - warm hued timber panelling.

He provides good breakfast provisions in the compact kitchen area, and we suggest you dine out in one of Daylesford's many restaurants

The Balconies

Daylesford, 3450
Tel: (053) 48 1322
Contact: Geoff & Theo
Rooms: 4

This is a huge, modern U-shaped, brick veneer house with wide verandahs and the best view in Daylesford. It looks over its own dams, stepped down to the lake shore and the Boathouse Restaurant on the far side.

Inside, the generous proportions of the hallway and sitting areas lend a feeling of luxury augmented by the quality fabrics and furnishings. There are 4 double bedrooms, two of which are ensuite; the two others share a bathroom. Again, these rooms are of generous size and beautifully finished.

Downstairs there is a sheltered courtyard with a spa. On one side of this courtyard is an indoor heated swimming pool, whilst on the other side is a large games room. Dinner is served by prior arrangement.

Wombat Hill Cottage

Daylesford, 3460
Tel:
Contact: Joan Brodie
Rooms: Self contained cottage

Owned by Joan Brodie, co-proprietor of the gift shop, Benjamin Bandicoot, located on the main street.

The cottage, on a hill above the town centre, provides self catering accommodation. There are two comfortable double bedrooms and one bathroom. Communal areas are quaint, warm and charming, but the outstanding features of this cottage are firstly the extensive gardens, and secondly the splendid view over Daylesford to the Korweingburra Forest.

The back of the house is open-plan, a combined kitchen, dining room and sitting room with a slate floor. There is also a laundry and, at the front of the house, another sitting room.

Jajarawong Cottages

R.M.B. 2543, Yandoit Creek Road, Yandoit via Daylesford, 3460
Tel: (054) 76 4362
Contact: Ron & Sandra Rumbelow
Rooms: 4 s/c cottages
Cost (B & B): From $80 double

2 bedroom fully self contained mudbrick stone and timber cottages with gas lights, wood heaters and sauna. Dinner available.

Lavandula

Carol White's lavender farm. Housed in a stone farmhouse and barn built in 1856, with cobbled floors and exposed beams is an emporium where you may buy a range of lavender products. Also local honey, hand crafted furniture, pottery and wrought iron. A few antiques are also available. Beautiful surroundings.

CARLSRUHE VIC. 3442

The Gallery Cottage, The Gallery Carlsruhe, R.M.B. 1890 Lancefield Road
Tel: (054) 22 2636 Fax: (054) 22 3504
Owner/contact: Bill & Pat Ross
Rooms: s/c cottage, sleeps 6
Cost: $150 couple/night

Ⓥ

CASTLEMAINE VIC. 3450

Coach & Rose, 68 Mostyn Street
Tel: (054) 72 4850
Owner/contact: Stephen & Jannina Biggs
Rooms: 4 double ensuite
Cost: From $85 double
No children

Ⓥ

Ellimatta Restaurant & Guest House, 233 Barker Street
Tel: (054) 72 4454
Owner/contact: Lloyd & Margaret Everett
Rooms: 5
Cost: $85-$100 double

Ⓥ

Inverness Park
Tel: (054) 70 5078
Rooms: s/c cottage

The Diggers Rest, 61 Main Road, Campbells Creek
Tel: (054) 72 2480
Owner/contact: Lyn & Graeme Bennett
Rooms: s/c accommodation

Ⓥ

Whispering Oaks, Simpson Street, Campbells Creek
Owner/contact: Chris & Brian Sertori
Tel: (054) 72 3930
Rooms: s/c cottage

Ⓥ

CHEWTON VIC. 3451

Golden Point, R.S.D. 181 Golden Point Road
Tel: (054) 72 3714
Owner/contact: James Evans
Rooms: Self-contained cottage

Thompsons Tranquil Valley Farm, Hoopers Road
Tel: (054) 72 2118
Owner/contact: Mary Thompson (V)
Rooms: 2 units (1 in farmhouse, 1 s/c)
Cost: $65-$75 single
No smoking

DAYLESFORD VIC. 3460

Ambleside, 15 Leggatt Street
Tel: (053) 48 2691
Contact: Eric & Joan Firth
Rooms: 2 ensuite
No children ♦ *No smoking*

Central Springs, Will's Square
Tel: (053) 48 3134
Rooms: 26 (double/twin/family)
Dinner available

Lake House, King Street
Tel: (053) 48 3329
Owner/contact: Alla & Allan Wolf-Tasker
Rooms: 11 ensuite
Cost: Dinner, bed & breakfast - from $105 single
No children at weekends

Linton House, 68 Central Springs Road
Tel: (053) 48 2331
Owner/contact: James Booth
Rooms: 2 s/c apartments (V)
Cost: $110 double
No children

The Balconies
Tel: (053) 48 1322
Owner/contact: Geoff & Theo (V)
Rooms: 4

Wombat Hill Cottage (V)
Owner/contact: Joan Brodie
Rooms: s/c cottage

DRUMMOND VIC. 3461

Cliston, R.M.B. 3999 Daylesford-Malmsbury Road
Tel: (054) 23 9155
Owner/Contact: Kathryn & Max Pilbeam (V)
Rooms: 2 double/twin, ensuite and 3 bedroom cottage
Host farm

FARADAY VIC. 3450

Rainbow Ridge
Tel: (054) 73 3278
Owner/contact: Heather & Alan Elliot
Rooms: s/c house (2 guests)
Wood fire and B.B.Q. ◆ *Pets by arrangement*

FRANKLINFORD VIC. 3461

Truro Homestead, R.M.B. 2390
Tel: (054) 76 4207
Owner/contact: Joy & Eric Sartori
Rooms: 2
Cost: $85 double
No smoking

GISBORNE VIC. 3437

Sun Valley Lodge, R.M.B. 220 Melton Road
Tel: (054) 28 3415
Owner/contact: Marie & Bob Park
Cost: $65 single, $80 double; Dinner $22.50 per person

GLENLYON VIC. 3461

Holcombe Homestead Country Retreat, R.M.B. 3683
Tel: (053) 48 7514 Fax: (053) 48 7742
Owner/contact: Annette & John Marshall
Rooms: Self-contained house (6 guests) Ⓥ
Cost: $120-$150 double

Oldeborg
Tel/Fax: (053) 48 7538
Owner/contact: Julie Thomson
Rooms: 2 (double/twin) and 2 s/c cottages
Working farm

GUILDFORD VIC. 3451

Country Garden, Cnr. Turner & Franklin Streets
Tel: (054) 73 4462

Loddon, Fryers Street
Tel: (054) 73 4232
Owner/contact: Neil & Christine Patterson
Rooms: 1 double
No children

HEPBURN SPRINGS VIC. 3461

Dudley House, 101 Main Road
Tel/Fax: (053) 48 3033
Owner/contact: Kay & Peter Lipman
Rooms: 4 Ⓥ
Cost: From $110 double
No smoking • No children

Liberty House, 20 Mineral Springs Crescent (Box 54)
Tel: (053) 48 2809
Owner/contact: Susan Brewer
Rooms: 10 double/twin

Mooltan, 129 Main Road
Tel: (053) 48 3555 Ⓥ
Owner/contact: Eddie Beacham
Rooms: 11
Cost: $75-$100 double midweek; Weekend package D, B & B $220-$280 double
Dinner available

The Hepburn Chalet, 78 Main Road
Tel: (053) 48 2344
Manager/contact: Kaye Scott
Rooms: 24
Cost: $50 single, $60-$78
Meals by arrangement

Villa Parma
Tel: (053) 48 3512 Ⓥ
Owner/contact: Franchiek Kasek
Rooms: 3

Calder Highway, The Goldfields

KYNETON VIC. 3444

Kyneton Country House, 66 Jennings Street
Tel: (054) 22 3556
Owner/contact: Paul & Mary Reid
Rooms: 4 (V)
Cost: Midweek - From $75 single, $100 double
No smoking

Woodbine, Cnr. Foster Lane & Fiddlers Green Road (P.O. Box 568)
Tel: (054) 22 2837 or (054) 22 3428
Owner/contact: Michael & Rosemary Pithie
Rooms: s/c cottage
Cost: $115 double
Dinner available

LAANECOORIE VIC. 3463

Laanwaan
Tel: (054) 35 7250
Rooms: 2 double
Dinner available ◆ *Working farm*

LANCEFIELD VIC. 3435

Cleveland, Shannons Road
Tel: (054) 29 1449
Owner/contact: Keith & Lynette Brien

'Fairways', 19 Golf House Lane
Tel: (054) 29 1903
Owner/contact: Maggie & Philip Brackley
Rooms: 4 ensuite
Cost: All inclusive - $89 single

Homestay, Main Road
Tel: (056) 59 6336
Rooms: 2
Dinner available

MALDON VIC. 3463

Adair House, 36 Adair Street
Tel: (054) 75 1031
Owner/contact: Margaret Sleeham
Rooms: 2 double
All meals by arrangement ◆ Children over 12 ◆ No smoking

Benyon Cottages, Anzac Hill
Tel: (03) 435 4271 or (054) 75 2779
Owner/contact: Beverley Watters
Rooms: s/c cottages
Cost: Weekend - double $130, four $190

Calder House, 44 High Street
Tel: (054) 75 2912
Contact: Richard & Trish Vincent
Rooms: 6
Cost: Double - $99, Dinner bed & breakfast $165
Fully licenced restaurant

Eaglehawk Restaurant & Accommodation
Contact: Sally & Peter Bishop (V)
Rooms: s/c units

Lavender Lace & Living, High Street
Tel: (054) 75 2357 or (054) 75 1075 (V)
Owner/contact: Dianne & Spenser Tunks
Rooms: s/c cottage
Cost: $75 double
No children

Lemonwood Cottage, *Bells Reef Road*
Tel: (054) 75 2120 or (03) 735 5273 or (018) 992 602
Owner/contact: Pat & Fred Cox
Rooms: s/c cottage
Dinner by arrangement ◆ *No children*

Maldara Cashmere Farm, Popeks Road (P.O. Box 140)
Tel: (054) 75 2091
Owner/contact: Merv & Jean Smith
Rooms: 3
Cost: $65 double, $14 children over 4
Children under 4 free

Palm House, 2 High Street
Tel: (054) 75 2532 or (054) 75 2209

Railway Cottage, Reef Street
Tel/Fax: (054) 75 2114 Ⓥ
Owner/contact: Karl Liffman
Rooms: Self-contained cottage
Cost: $85-$100

School Cottage, 115 High Street
Tel: (054) 75 2658
Owner/contact: Robert McGuirk & Bev Gray
Rooms: Self-contained cottage
Cost: $35 single, $60 double

Scotch Pie House, 63 Main Street
Tel: (054) 75 2654
Owner/contact: Ray & Ellen Stanyer
Cost: $40 single, $70 double, $15 children

Spring Cottage, 13 Spring Street
Tel/Fax: (054) 75 2114
Owner/contact: Karl Liffman
Rooms: Self-contained cottage (V)
Cost: $85-$100 double
No children

Sussex Fields, Sandy Creek Road
Tel: (054) 72 4720 or (054) 75 2320
Owner/contact: Carole Gleen (V)
Rooms: Self-contained
Cost: From $70 double

The Barn, 64 Main Street
Tel: (054) 75 2015 (V)
Contact: John
Rooms: 2 s/c units
Cost: $90 double

Tobin Cottage, 6 Church Street
Tel: (054) 75 1163
Owner/contact: Ashley Petersen
Rooms: s/c cottage
Cost: Bed & breakfast provisions - $95 double

Tressiders Cottage, High Street (V)
Tel: (054) 75 2357 or (054) 75 1075
Owner/contact: Dianne & Spenser Tunks
Rooms: s/c cottage
Cost: $50 single, $85 double per day

MALMSBURY VIC. 3446

Malmsbury Cottage, Mollison Street, Calder Highway
Tel: (054) 23 2432
Owner/contact: Dawn Warner
Rooms: 3 double/twin
Cost: $40 single, $80 double
Dinner by arrangement

Hopewell Cottage, Ross Street (P.O. Box 196)
Tel: (054) 23 2470
Owner/contact: Barry & Maria Simpson
Rooms: s/c cottage
Cost: $29.50-$60 single
Dinner by arrangement

MELTON VIC. 3337

Kimberley, 16 Canopus Circuit (R.M.B. 8572 RSD Melton)
Tel: (053) 67 3429
Owner/contact: Shirley Davis
Rooms: 3 single/double ensuite
Cost: $40 single, $70 double
No smoking ◆ No children

METCALFE VIC. 3448

Dunbar Homestead, Metcalfe-Redesdale Road
Tel: (054) 23 2388 Fax: (054) 23 2600
Owner/contact: Doreen & Bruce Orchard
Rooms: 4 rooms in homestead and 2 s/c cottages (V)
Cost: Homestead - from $75 single, $35 children
Host farm

MOUNT MACEDON VIC. 3441

Ballantrae Mews, 385 Mt. Macedon Road
Tel: (054) 26 2078
Owner/contact: Peter & Bunty Jackson
Rooms: s/c cottage
Cost: $85 double
No smoking

Ⓥ

Evesham Cottage, 4 Turntable Road
Tel: (054) 26 2111
Owner/contact: Margaret Barber
Rooms: s/c cottage
Cost: $85 double

Huntley Burn
Tel: (054) 26 1411
Owner/contact: Penny Tate
Rooms: 2 Self-contained cottages (The Stables/The Cottage)
Cost: The Cottage - $60 double; The Stables - $200-$250 double/weekend

Ⓥ

Mountain Inn, 351 Mt. Macedon Road
Tel: (054) 26 1755
Owner/contact: Mrs. David Kennon
Rooms: 9 doubles
Cost: $70-$85 double

Ⓥ

MUCKLEFORD VIC. 3450

Halfway House Cottage, Castlemaine-Maldon Road (R.M.B. Muckleford via Castlemaine)
Tel: (054) 75 1113
Owner/contact: Pamela & Graeme Christmas
Rooms: s/c cottage
Cost: $85 double
No smoking

Ⓥ

MOUNT MACEDON VIC. 3441

Willowbank Farm Cottage, Muckleford School Road (R.M.B. Muckleford via Castlemaine)
Tel: (03) 489 5865 Fax: (054) 72 2483
Rooms: s/c cottage

PIPERS CREEK VIC.

Pond Cottage & Viewly Hill, Chasers Lane
Tel: (054) 22 1447
Owner/contact: Dougal & Nellie Ramsey
Rooms: 2 s/c cottages
Cost: Bed & breakfast provisions - $75-$90 single first 2, $40-$48 extra person (V)

TRENTHAM VIC. 3458

Blue Mount Bed & Breakfast, R.M.B. 276
Tel: (054) 24 1296
Owner/contact: Kerry Proctor
Rooms: s/c unit
Cost: Bed & breakfast provisions - $55 single

Serendipity, R.M.B. 620 Kyneton Road
Tel: (054) 24 8251

WOODEND VIC. 3442

Ard Choille, Turner Avenue
Tel: (054) 27 2482
Owner/contact: Mrs. H. Cotten
Rooms: 2 ensuite
Cost: $85 - $125
No smoking • No children

The Bentinck Country House, 2 - 8 Carlisle Street (P.O. Box 498)
Tel: (054) 27 2944 Fax: (054) 27 2232
Owner/contact: Ross Plowman (V)
Rooms: 30 (24 with ensuites)
Cost: Dinner, Bed & Breakfast - $110-$150 single

YANDOIT VIC. 3461

Jajarawong Country Cottages, R.M.B. 2543 Yandoit Creek Road (via Daylesford 3460)
Tel: (054) 76 4362
Owner/contact: Sandra & Ron Rumbelow
Rooms: 4 s/c cottages for 6 guests (V)
Cost: From $80 double

Dinner by arrangement ◆ No pets

Midland Highway Bendigo & Echuca

From Harcourt you may travel to Echuca via Bendigo.

BENDIGO

A little smaller than Ballarat and further north, Bendigo is probably Victoria's most famous gold mining town. There is not the concentration of large Victorian buildings found in Ballarat, but those in the city centre are of grander proportions. The Shamrock Hotel and the newly renovated Court House and Post Office vie with each other from opposite sides of the street for ;your attention and perhaps patronage.

The Sacred Heart Cathedral is the largest outside Melbourne.

ATTRACTIONS

- Bendigo Art Gallery and Alfa Art Gallery in View Street
- Antique Market, High Street
- Central Deborah Mine (in working order)
- The Chinese Joss house at Erin Point
- Dudley House and Gardens
- Sandhurst Town, a recreation of a colonial town with gold diggings and eucalyptus distillery
- Bendigo Pottery, display and sale
- Wineries, especially:
    - Chateau Dore
    - Chateau Le Amon
    - Balgownie

ROCHESTER

This is a dairy centre on the Campaspe river. Noteworthy is the Campaspe Syphon, an engineering feat which enables the Waranga-Mallee irrigation channel to pass under the Campaspe river. Fishing is popular in these channels, but the only real reason to visit Rochester is Random House.

ECHUCA-MOAMA

Echuca-Moama is at the junction of the Murray, Campaspe and Goulburn rivers. The Murray and its riverboats were important features of Australian pioneering history. Wentworth, Swan Hill and Echuca were all commercial ports in the heyday of river traffic. Echuca, the most important of these, has preserved many original buildings and restored the Port, a massive red gum wharf which now is home to the Pevensey and the Emmylou, a paddle steamer used for overnight trips. Alternatively the diesel powered paddle-wheelers Canberra and Pride of the Murray have one hour excursions. There are pleasant walks around town and along the river banks.

VINEYARDS

- Tisdall - commercial varietal wines from local warm climate fruit.
- (Tisdalls) Mt. Helen - more complex, cooler climate wines.

ACCOMMODATION

Ravenswood Homestead

Calder Highway, Ravenswood, 3453
Tel: (054) 35 3284
Contact: Erika & Edmund Beilharz
Rooms: 7

South of Bendigo, halfway between Harcourt and Bendigo, on the Calder Highway.

An imposing entrance in park-like surroundings. The drive, lined with poplars, leads to a pleasant garden in front of a large red brick house built in 1857.

Accommodation is supplied in the converted adjacent buildings which house three family suites and four double rooms, all with their own bathrooms. They are pleasantly familiar, in cottage style with iron beds and wicker furniture. Tea, coffee, heaters and electric blankets are supplied.

Meals are served in the servants' congregation room unless there is a large group, who may request to eat in the dining room of the homestead. Food is straightforward country fare of soup, roasts and sweets.

An additional facility is the garden room with an open fire, television and table tennis.

Villa Heidi

35 MacKenzie Street, Bendigo, 3550
Tel: (054) 41 4265
Contact: Heidi Teague
Rooms: 2
Cost (B & B): $40 single, $70 double

Heidi Teague has your welfare at heart, and probably the welfare of the rest of the world it is such a big heart.

She lives downstairs in this compact Victorian Terrace. There are two comfortable guest rooms upstairs which share a bathroom. The back room is best, having its own little verandah, looking down over Bendigo.

The house is packed with nicknacks through which you thread your way downstairs for breakfast in the kitchen. Healthy can be tasty and generous. Organic muesli, organic porridge, freshly vitamised carrot apple and celery, grilled grapefruit, wholemeal bread and perhaps a boiled egg (no bacon; it may harm you).
Heidi is such good value.

The Shamrock Hotel

Pall Mall, Bendigo, 3550
Tel: (054) 43 0333 Fax: (054) 42 4494
Contact: Bob Vagg
Rooms: 14 ensuite, Others available

At the heart of Bendigo, the history of Bendigo and from its magnificent first floor verandah the feeling of Bendigo now, and then, in the gold rush.
Marshall Waters has moved on so the food has yet to prove itself, yet I recommend a visit.
This superb building - an Australian equivalent to an Indian Summer Palace - is an icon of Victorian history to be appreciated and experienced.
The traveller, here, will taste a true rural Victorian city from a hospitable pile of ornate antiquity.
There is a large busy corner Bistro downstairs and an a la carte restaurant upstairs open at weekends only.

The Cottages

Cnr. Niemann & Anderson Streets, Bendigo, 3550
Tel: (054) 41 5613
Owner/Contact: Chris & Mavis Willson
Rooms: 3 s/c cottages
Cost: From $110 double

The Cottages, Bendigo, are located within a kilometre of the city centre, a few hundred metres from all sporting facilities, close to the famous View Street with its art galleries, theatre and antique shops. Take an easy stroll to many of Bendigo's

most historic buildings, including many wonderful 19th Century mansions build by Australia's early Gold Tzars.
There are three cottages set in a renowned cottage garden. The resident owners have created an environment where couples or friends can escape to their own private world of beauty and tranquility – hosts who have travelled the world and really appreciate what makes a "great escape".
Full English breakfast, in your own private courtyard, cottage or with your hosts in their home.

Random House

22 Bridge Road, Rochester, 3561
Contact: Len Keeper & Doug Hall
Tel: (054) 84 1792 Fax: (054) 84 2014
Rooms: 4

Random House is one of our favourite places in Victoria. This majestic Victorian Homestead, situated on the beautiful Campaspe River, is at Rochester.
Len Keeper and Doug Hall are delightfully entertaining hosts - and it is their attention to every detail that makes Random House so special.
Magnificent antique furniture, original paintings and a host of treasures adorn the rooms. Three double and one twin

bedroom are all lavishly appointed and each offers its own ensuite facility.
Len's culinary flair is obvious at dinner. A word of warning - after his dinners you need a run before tackling his enormous breakfasts.

Sample Menu - Random House

Pre-dinner Savouries

Cheese Vol-au-Vents
Smoked Salmon

Soup

Smoked ham and tomato soup

Dinner

Seafood Terrine with Herb Mayonnaise
Pork fillet with Rosemary Sauce and seasonal vegetables

Dessert

Pear en croute with Hazelnute Creme Patissiere
Coffee and Petits Fours

Murray House Bed & Breakfast

55 Francis Street, Echuca, 3564
Tel: (054) 82 4944
Contact: Cliff & Jeanette Moore
Rooms: 5 & s/c cottage
Cost (B & B): $70 single, $98 double
Cottage $60 per day double, $75 for four

Murray House is nestled in a quiet treelined street of Echuca, and has retained the atmosphere of the 1930's.
Murray House accommodates families, double or twin rooms, all featuring their own ensuite. An additional feature is the self contained flat with 2 bedrooms, bathroom and lounge/dining room, plus roomy kitchen.
Breakfast is of mammoth proportions - Jeanette certainly makes sure no-one leaves the table hungry - fruit juices, scrambled eggs with smoked trout, omelette, vegetable fritata.

The River Gallery

578 High Street, Echuca, 3564
Tel: (054) 80 6902
Contact: Robin
Rooms: 6 ensuite

The River Gallery is centrally located in the heart of Echuca's historical Murray River Port. Situated within an 1870's building, the charm of last century has been captured whilst still providing guests with the comforts and convenience of today.

There are six elegant rooms decorated in different themes - Early Australian, Victorian, French Provincial, Italian, French and Scottish. All rooms have ensuites, T.V.'s, fridges, tea and coffee facilities, and open fires. Three open onto balconies and two have spas.

There is also a colonial style breakfast room looking out onto a charming courtyard.

BENDIGO VIC. 3550

Nanga Gnulle Country Home, 40 Harley Street
Tel: (054) 43 7891 Fax: (054) 43 3397
Owner/contact: Peg and Rob Green
Rooms: 2
No children ◆ No smoking

Shamrock Hotel, Pall Mall
Tel: (054) 43 0333 Fax: (054) 42 4494 Ⓥ
Owner/contact: Bob Vagg
Rooms: 14 ensuite, others available

The Cottages, Cnr. Niemann & Anderson Streets
Tel: (054) 41 5631 Ⓥ
Owner/contact: Chris & Mavis Willson
Rooms: 3 s/c cottages
Cost: From $110

Villa Heidi, 35 MacKenzie Street, Central Bendigo
Tel: (054) 41 4265 Ⓥ
Rooms: 2 twin
Owner/contact: Heidi Teague
Cost: $40 single, $70 double
No smoking

CLOVERLEA VIC. 3822

Dingley Dell, Darnum-Allambee Road
Tel: (056) 27 8473
Owner/contact: Chris Onslow
Rooms: 2 (1 double/1 twin)
Host farm

COBRAM EAST VIC. 3644

Cobram Homestead, Murray Valley Highway
Tel: (058) 73 5393 Fax: (058) 73 5395
Owner/contact: Sally & John Cummins
Rooms: 4
Cost: $70 single, $125 double; Dinner $30 single

(V)

EAGLEHAWK VIC. 3556

Neangar House, View Point
Tel: (054) 46 8204
Contact: Patricia & Hugh Sayle
Cost: $50 single, $70 double
Tea rooms and restaurant facilities available

ECHUCA VIC. 3564

Murray House Bed & Breakfast, 55 Francis Street
Tel: (054) 82 4944
Owner/contact: Cliff & Jeanette Moore
Rooms: 5 and s/c cottage
Cost: $70 single, $98 double; Cottage $60 day/double
Dinner available by prior arrangement

(V)

Steam Packet Inn, Murray Esplanade
Tel: (054) 82 3411
Owner/contact: James Hawkins
Rooms: 10
Cost: Double/Twin - $82, Dinner bed & breakfast $105

The River Gallery, 578 High Street
Tel: (054) 80 6902
Owner/contact: Robin
Rooms: 6 ensuite

(V)

KANGAROO FLAT VIC. 3555

Warrawee, Lot 81 Sheltons Road
Tel: (054) 47 7194
Owner/contact: Jennie Williams
Rooms: 2 twin ensuite
Cost: $45 single, $80 double
No smoking inside • No toddlers

NEWSTEAD VIC. 3462

Valley View Farm, Mia Mia Road
Tel: (054) 76 2565
Owner/contact: Patricia Parsons
Rooms: 3
Cost: $70 double; Dinner $15

RAVENSWOOD VIC. 3453

Ravenswood Historic Homestead, Calder Highway
Tel: (054) 35 3284
Owner/contact: Erika & Edmund Beilharz (V)
Rooms: 7 units

ROCHESTER VIC. 3561

Random House Country Retreat, 22 Bridge Road (P.O. Box 111)
Tel: (054) 84 1792 Fax: ((054) 84 2014
Owner/contact: Len Keeper & Doug Hall (V)
Rooms: 4
No children • Dinner by arrangement

YARRAWONGA VIC. 3730

Riverside Lodge, 4 Linthorpe Drive
Tel: (057) 43 1011
Owner/contact: Vivien & Barry Shepherd
Rooms: 4 ensuite
Cost: $45 - $65 double/twin
No children

Melbourne to Ballarat The Grampians

A four lane freeway takes you from Melbourne to Ballarat in just over an hour.

Noted for its weather, Ballarat has been an important country commercial centre since before the 1850's gold rush. The large ornate Victorian buildings are signs of past wealth and now, in response to the potential for new wealth from the tourist industry, the buildings are being restored and used to good effect.

The National Trust publishes an interesting guide book to this architectural heritage titled 'Walking Ballarat'.

ATTRACTIONS

- Buildings of the town centre:
    - Lydiard Street - the most consistent streetscape
    - Sturt Street - the main street
    - Camp Street
- Her Majesty's Theatre - Opera Week at Easter
- Ballarat Fine Art Gallery
- Railway Station and Gates
- Lake Wendouree and the adjacent Botanical Gardens (with its statuary)
- Begonia Festival in March

- The Mining Exchange. Fifty dealers selling antiques and collectables
- Sovereign Hill - a major Victorian tourist attraction. A tasteful and interesting 'Theme Park' depicting a gold mining settlement with working displays, shops and mine tours, as well as the opportunity to 'pan' for gold. It has just been nominated as the premiere tourist attraction of its type in Australia.

BUNINYONG

Near Ballarat, to the south. Pretty little historic township with antique shops, and an excellent bakery.

CLUNES

To the north of Ballarat is the original gold mining town of Clunes on the way to Avoca.

AVOCA - MOONAMBEL

The main street in Avoca is of grand proportions, being almost as wide as it is long. Two storey shops are scattered along each side, interspersed with small cottages and vacant blocks.
If you are looking for the wineries of the Pyrenees, they are scattered around in the Avoca district.

PYRENEES REGION

There are 3 major functions held in this area every year.

- The Taltarni Cup (Caulfield Cup Day) held at the Avoca track. The Talterni Winery presents its wines for sale by the glass or the bottle.
- Tour de Pyrenees - 16th to 17th April. A major push-bike race.
- The Pyrenees Picnic Races held each year on Anzac Day. This incorporates a Food and Wine Harvest Picnic and, of course, 2-up.

VINEYARDS

- Chateau Remy - true hand-made mellow Champenoise and producer of Blue Pyrenees (with a nose of eucalypt).
-

- Summerfield - Blue stone tasting room.
- Mountain Creek - Scenic.
- Taltarni - Very attractive winery.
- Warrenmang - Open 7 days Pyrenees Vintage Village. A-la-carte restaurant. Overnight cottages amongst the vines. Pool, spa, tennis courts.
- Dalwhinnie - Highland vineyard; spectacular views.
- Redbank - Sally's Paddock
- Mount Avoca - Some of my favourite wines. Highly recommended for quality and reasonable prices

Pyrenees Mountain Village

Warrenmang Vineyard, Mountain Creek Road,
Moonambel, 3478
Tel: (054) 67 2233 Fax: (054) 67 2309
Contact: Athalie Bazzani
Rooms: 18
Cost (B & B): From $49.50 single

'Mountain village' captures the feeling, the architectural style of this complex.

Commodious common areas, a quality large restaurant and bar, offering interesting food, especially game, accompanied by local wines. A huge log blazes in the slate fireplace; a good spot for the pre-dinner drinks. Tennis courts, pool and tasting room offering produce from Warrenmang and other local producers.

Accommodation is in neat timber cottages in two rows - obviously try to book one at the front, which gives romantic views down over the sloping vineyard and the neat rows of vines filling a gentle valley.

The vineyard is an island in the surrounding bush landscape and fulfils much of its promise.

Sample Menu - Warrenmang

Entrée

Oven roasted Quail, boned and served with a variety of lettuces tossed with mango & avocado slices, quail eggs, cherry tomatoes and croutons all dressed in a raspberry vinaigrette.

Ravioli filled with a mousse of local yabbies, cucumber, capsicum, asparagus and seasonings gently poached in a rich lobster sauce flavoured with basil.

Main Course

Saddle of Pyrenees Hare, oven baked and served sliced on a bed of creamed spinach with wild rice and a dry sherry sauce.

Ocean Trout Steaks, steamed and presented on a bed of mushroom ducelle and accompanied by a puff pastry case filled with crisp asparagus spears and a smoked salmon cream sauce.

Dessert

Hot Souffle flavoured with a purée of local berries and accompanied by a crème chantilly infused with mint.

Mille-Feuille filled with fresh strawberries and a rich caramel pastry cream then served accompanied by an almond anglaise.

A fine selection of local Cheeses and Fruit served with oatmeal biscuits and walnut bread, also available as a 4th course

Coffee and Chocolates

GREAT WESTERN

A small settlement of a dozen houses on the Western Highway between Ararat and Stawell. This is an important wine making district, the cellars at Bests and Great Western are worth a visit.

VINEYARDS

- Seppelts - the tour of Victoria's largest and oldest sparkling wine producer is worthwhile
- Best - excellent; visit the old cellars
- Boroka
- Montara

HALLS GAP

What a surprise, after miles of hardly undulating, hungry country sparsely scattered with small trees, the wall of the Grampians looms above you. Suddenly you enter the green valleys, rushing streams and high crags of Halls Gap.

Scenically this is a major tourist destination. Unfortunately it primarily attracts very earnest bushwalkers whose preference is for cheap or family accommodation. Facilities are pretty basic.

ATTRACTIONS

- Brambuk. The Aboriginal centre is interesting architecturally
- Grampian View Motel is classic 1950's accommodation, but does have kangaroos hopping around and koalas in the trees

Halls Gap is the gateway to the Grampians and the road through this gateway to Zumstein passing McKenzie Falls is a five star experience. I must congratulate the National Parks Organisation for their unobtrusive work in the organisation and maintenance of the park and its walking tracks.

Just a few minutes from Halls Gap is an area named Wonderland. Walks here include:

- Grand Canyon
- Splitters Falls

- Elephant Hide
- Halls Gap
- Venus Baths

Try Grand Canyon. With the odd iron rail and white arrows signing the way, you are led to the canyon over boulders along creeks off into the wilderness. This is more than a stroll - it is a safe adventure which is well worth the effort.

The drive on to Zumstein is through spectacular scenery of dramatic rock formations, stark yet colourful, and all the lookouts are worth the detour. Remember the Grampians are famous for their wildflowers in springtime.

Kangaroos abound, especially at Zumstein, where they are tame enough to be hand fed. There there is also a profusion of Black Boys, the rare and ancient grass trees.

One detour, to McKenzie Falls, is especially worthwhile. Again, National Parks have made this attraction accessible, without excessive intrusion (except for the kiosk).

Walking down to Broken Falls, the first viewing point may seem sufficient exercise, but I highly recommend the full trip to the bottom to view McKenzie Falls; you will not be disappointed.

As you travel south on the Henty Highway through low lying Red Gum forests, your continual companion is the Grampian Range on your left. At Cavendish cross the Wannon River and turn left at the pub on to the Monanger Road. This, via Victorian Point Road, is the scenic route back to Halls Gap.

HAMILTON

Hamilton is a large country town with important saleyards. If there is an auction of sheep or cattle in progress, this is worth a look and to mingle with the crowd. This is one of my favourite rural pastimes, admiring the stock and the repartee between auctioneer and buyers.

ACCOMMODATION

The Old Methodist Church

802 Warrenheip Street, Buninyong, 3357
Tel: 053 41 3786 or 03 886 405
Contact: Peter & Lainie Ivanoff
Rooms: Self contained accommodation
Cost (B & B) $65 single

Undoubtedly in the top half dozen self contained accommodation offered in this book. A converted church, it has historic and aesthetic appeal combined with the most lavish furnishing and finishes. This renovation would grace the pages of Architectural Digest. The surroundings are pleasant in a quiet area away from the centre of the village, the large garden has mature trees, a tennis court and vegetable garden which you may freely use.

The main living area utilizes half of the ground floor and the spacious feeling is enhanced by the high vaulted ceiling. There is an ultra-modern kitchen, and large laundry, equipped with every electrical gadget. The adjacent vestry is elegantly converted to a bathroom with a huge shower servicing the two double bedrooms downstairs. A spiral staircase leads to the mezzanine floor comprising a cosy sitting area with T.V. and stereo which leads to the master bedroom with its ensuite.

Interesting works of art and antiques collected on Asian travels give a unique connected ambience to the whole interior. Highly recommended.

Balfour

Scotts Lane, Scotsburn, via Buninyong, 3357 (P.O. Box 473)
Tel: (053) 41 8039
Contact: Merrin & Ed Davis
Rooms: 2 ensuite
Cost (B & B): $65 single, $90 double

Set on a picturesque 40 acre yabby farm, Balfour is 5 km. towards Geelong from Buninyong.
Accommodation is in two double ensuite rooms, off a large private sitting room, with wood space heater and small kitchen. Outstanding views over undulating pastures to Mt. Buninyong, and quiet walks along untravelled lanes, make this a wonderful, peaceful refuge for any guests fortunate enough to come this way.

"Brim Brim"

Lal Lal Street, Buninyong, 3357
Tel: (053) 41 8038
Contact: Marcia & Cromwell Beggs
Rooms: 3 & s/c accommodation

Buninyong is Victoria's first inland town, established in 1842, and is 10 minutes direct south-east of Ballarat on the Midland Highway, or 75 minutes from Melbourne.
"Brim Brim" (Aboriginal for natural spring) was built in 1857 for John Warrington Rogers, a well known Mining Court Judge at the time.
The property is of many acres and the homestead itself is a magnificently restored triple brick construction on blue stone foundations, set in five acres of beautiful gardens.
"Brim Brim" has a tennis court, croquet lawn, beautiful lily pond, billiards and reading rooms, plus a separate conference

centre, air-conditioned and centrally heated, seating 120, for those who want to have industry or commercial training in a relaxed country atmosphere.

There are three bedrooms, one with ensuite facilities, and two with adjacent private bathrooms.

There is also a separate self-contained three bedroom accommodation with all facilities, in the former manager's residence, with veranda on three sides, commanding some of the most outstanding views in the district.

Both residences are centrally heated and also have open fireplaces.

"Brim Brim" gardens are also available for weddings and afternoon teas.

Ballarat Terrace

229 Lydiard Street North, Ballarat, 3350
Tel: (053) 33 2216
Contact: Bernie & Evelyn Ebbs
Rooms: 3
Cost (B & B): $70 single, $95-$125 double

Bernie and Evelyn Ebbs were pioneers in the provision of top quality bed and breakfast accommodation in Victoria. All new operators should measure themselves against this establishment. A classified house with appropriate furniture, plus a knowledge of their target market.

There are three areas of accommodation. The Maids Quarters at the back of the house is warm and quiet, comprising a double and single room with bathroom. Next is the Brass Room, with the appropriate bed and ensuite.

The large front room has become one of Victoria's 'honeymoon suites' and is booked for weeks ahead. It has a beautiful half Tester bed and other well chosen furniture, and French doors to the upstairs verandah. The bathroom is cleverly and unobtrusively incorporated into the room without affecting its proportions.

Breakfast is taken downstairs at the window of the comfortable guest sitting room.

Ballarat Terrace is strictly B & B, but your hosts are happy to arrange restaurant bookings for you.

Craigs Royal Hotel

10 Lydiard Street South, Ballarat, 3350
Tel: (053) 31 1377
Contact: Robert Vagg
Rooms: 26
Cost (B & B): From $60 to $120 double/twin

On Lydiard Street, but on the other side of Sturt Street from Ballarat Terrace, is this imposing building with two towers.

The Prince Albert Room has an ensuite with spa and features the fabulous bed originally provided for the room on the occasion of Prince Albert's visit to Ballarat. The towers each incorporate a suite nicely furnished with a stairway to a sitting room at the top of the tower. We have not stayed here, but look forward to the opportunity. For residents, a Club Bar and private sitting room are also available.

I must report the imminent arrival of 30 poker machines for a tabaret downstairs, but am assured that this will be soberly conducted with a strict dress code. Hopefully the subsidy provided from the machines will assist the eventual completion of the restoration of this wonderful building.

Reports please!

Ravenswood Cottage

404 Havelock Street, Ballarat, 3350
Tel: (053) 32 8296 Fax: (053) 31 3358
Contact: Eleanor & Peter Veal
Rooms: s/c cottage
Cost: $180 double, weekend (2 nights)
From $65 per night mid-week, $15 per extra person

Ravenswood is a tastefully restored Victorian Cottage in a spacious old world garden setting just three blocks from historic Lydiard Street (one of Australia's best preserved streetscapes dating back to the gold mining era).
The cottage combines charm of the last century with modern amenities such as gas heating, electric blankets, hot bath/shower and colour television.
The cottage includes separate lounge with open fire, dining and kitchen areas, and three large bedrooms provide ample space for six adults.
Spacious private grounds provide an ideal setting for relaxed outdoor living.
Ravenswood Cottage is only 1.3 km. from Ballarat's C.B.D. and 3 km. from the world renowned Sovereign Hill.

Keebles of Clunes

114 Bailey Street, Clunes, 3370
Tel: (053) 45 3220 Fax: (053) 45 3200
Rooms: 6, ensuite
Cost (Double): $120 weekdays, $400 weekend package

Joy Keebles commitment to excellence in the kitchen has to be admired, justifying her visits to Paris to hone her skills.

Allan has not given up his day job, but his influence shows in the integration of many features to create an exquisite small hotel. Keebles of Clunes looks small outside, but they have created space enough inside to provide a sitting room, library, games room with a pool table, formal dining room and a conservatory for breakfast. Upstairs they provide six double rooms, two with an extra single bed, all rooms ensuite.

The environment is relaxed and comfortable, the garden pretty and the food in itself worth the trip from Melbourne. A true quality small hotel with two acres of gardens on the banks of the Creswick Creek.

Sample Menu - Keebles of Clunes

Soup

Soupe du Jour

Entrée

Pear & Leek Pie with a creamy cheese filling

or

Suppli di Riso - Mushroom Risotto Croquettes with Mozzarella & Chive Centres

Main Course

Boned Rack of Lamb with Horseradish & Caper Sauce

or

Fillet of Chicken with a moist Orange & Pistachio Stuffing - served with a creamy orange sauce

Dessert

Delicious Chocolate Roulade with Crème de Menthe Filling - served with Creme Anglais

Coffee/Tea and Chocolates

The Hermitage

Great Western, 3377
Tel: (053) 56 2361
Contact: Meryl Bowyers
Rooms: s/c cottage

The Hermitage is the best accommodation for miles. The cottage next to the shop is available for bed and breakfast and is set in a large secluded cottage garden. Meryl, the owner, is a lovely lady and makes this a special place.

Banool

R.S.D. Balmoral, 3407
Tel: (055) 74 3334 Fax: (055) 74 3334
Contact: Sue & Neil Lawrance
Rooms: s/c log cabin
Cost: $100 per person per day

Banool Log Cabin is situated in beautiful undulating Redgum country, with spectacular views to the Grampians.
The comfortable 2 bedroom self-contained cottage has a cosy living room, T.V. and slow combustion fire.
Sue provides breakfast provisions in the cottage, but a splendid dinner is taken in the homestead.
The bonus on staying here is Bridge - Neil and Sue may invite you to join them for a game after dinner. There is also a table in the cottage.
But, if Bridge isn't your idea of fun, there is swimming, croquet and tennis, plus access to some stunning local gardens.

The Hilton

'Cherrymount', Glenthompson, 3293
Tel: (055) 77 4396
Contact: David & Pru McCulloch
Rooms: s/c cottage
Cost (full board): $90 single

This simple cottage, which surprisingly sleeps 7 - 1 double, 2 twins and 1 single - is really best utilised by one couple. The large double room with ensuite boasts a fine, extremely comfortable bed with 180° views over the surrounding countryside. The sitting room has an open fire and the McCullochs leave you a generous supply of firewood.

The kitchen is adequate, with breakfast provisions aplenty. But, staying here you have an option - drinks and dinner in the homestead with David and Pru. David is an ex-Carlton player, so expect some footy chatter along with the day to day farming conversation. Cherrymount is a large property and there is lots of opportunity to have some hands-on experience.

Mountain View Motel

Ararat Road, Halls Gap, 3381
Tel: (053) 56 4364 Fax: (053) 56 4262
Contact: David Ginn & Ross Barker
Rooms: 14,
4 two bedroom lodges & 2 one bedroom lodges
Cost: $66 - $140

Spacious grounds, well off the road outside town. Tennis courts and swimming pool. Very reasonable motel rooms at low prices and four neat self contained cottages, each with a verandah, full facilities and two bedrooms. Very hospitable and efficiently run.

Glenisla

R.S.D. 250, Via Cavendish, 3314
Tel: (053) 80 1532 or (053) 80 1535 Fax: (053) 80 1532
Contact: Evie & Eric Barber
Rooms: 4
Cost (full): $92 single

Western District farming is real Australian farming, with Merino sheep, Hereford cattle and broad acres on properties settled for 150 years.

Eric and Evie Barber offer a unique insight into this lifestyle. Eric pioneered farm experience hospitality and in Glenisla had the perfect instrument. By any measure the homestead is historic, attractive and beautifully presented. You park behind the house, which is hidden by a tall, neatly clipped Cypress hedge, in which there is a pretty gateway. This area is framed by huge red gums and shaded by two old Yew trees.

Opposite the house is the original stable and smithy, with slab walls and stone paved floor. Inside it is hung with harness and saddles, and the forge is in perfect working order.

The Homestead is of warm pink sandstone, trimmed in cream painted timber with a classic dull red roof.

Through the gate is a neat old garden which leads to a stone paved courtyard, around which the buildings have been converted to provide four suites, all with bathrooms. There are the store-room, the kitchen and the staff rooms. Two further bedrooms are available inside the house.

There is a wonderful verandah at the front of the house, covered in wisteria, which looks out over the flat farmland to the nearby Grampians.

The food is plentiful and wholesome, and the experience is made complete by the kind, knowledgeable attention of your hosts.

Arrandoovong

R.M.B. 1285, Branxholme, 3302
Tel: (055) 78 6221 Fax: (055) 78 6249
Contact: Bill & Jeanie Sharp
Rooms: 3
Cost (B & B): $90 double, $65 single, Dinner $25

History, garden and tranquillity lovers will delight in 'Arrandoovong', one of the true remaining showpieces of Victorian country splendour.

Situated on 500 hectares of premium Merino grazing country, the grand two storey bluestone homestead was built in the 1850's, a replication of gracious living in Scotland. It is surrounded by a magnificent balcony onto which the main guest rooms open and splendid views can be enjoyed.

The historic gardens are dominated by giant English oaks and a permanent stream shaded by poplars, elms and old pines - the most idyllic setting for picturesque walks and relaxation.

Accommodation features spacious Victorian rooms and luxurious queen size beds.

The hearty breakfast includes seasonal fruits, cereals, homemade jams, fresh farm eggs, lashings of bacon, piping hot toast as well as a bottomless cup of coffee/tea. Upon arrangement, a delicious home cooked, three-course dinner will be served to guests.

Your hosts, Jeanie and Bill, are there to ensure you are thoroughly pampered during your memorable stay. Relax on the balcony or verandah, enjoy coffee and 'goodies' by the open fire, stroll around the picturesque gardens....

Stoneycroft

South Mokanger, Cavendish, 3314
Tel: (055) 74 2398 Fax: (055) 74 2307
Rooms: s/c cottage

This is a host farm, and our interest is in the self contained blue stone cottage 100m. beyond the shearing shed.

This shed is remarkable for its size, its architecture and for being wholly constructed in blue stone.

The surroundings to the cottage are bare, it sits alone in a paddock. The building is 130 years old and spacious, comprising a bunk room for kids, double bedroom and a large kitchen and sitting. There is a fireplace, plenty of firewood and that feeling you could be nowhere else but the Western District.

This is an isolated but excellent base from which to explore the area.

AVOCA VIC. 3467

Avoca Heritage School Bed & Breakfast, 124 Rutherford Street
Tel: (054) 65 3691

The Old Rectory Guest House, 102 Rutherford Street
Tel: (054) 65 3560
Contact: Helen Reid
Rooms: 4
Cost: Dinner, bed & breakfast - $170 double

BALLARAT VIC. 3350

Al Hayatt, 800 Mair Street
Tel: (053) 32 1396
Owner/contact: Rosalie & Malcolm White
Rooms: 3
Cost: $65 single, $80 double
Dinner by arrangement

Ballarat Terrace, 229 Lydiard Street North
Tel: (053) 33 2216
Owner/contact: Evelyn and Bernie Ebbs (V)
Rooms: 3
Cost: $70 single, $95 - $125 double/twin
No smoking

Craigs Royal Hotel, 10 Lydiard Street South
Tel: (053) 31 1377 (V)
Owner/contact: Robert Vagg
Rooms: 26
Cost: $60-$120 double

Dunvegan, 806 Mair Street
Tel: (053) 32 2505
Owner/contact: Alf and Judy Hancock
Rooms: 3 ensuite
Cost: $70 single, $85 double, $15 extra person
Dinner by arrangement

Lindenhoe, 315 Drummond Street South
Tel: (053) 32 6950

Ravenswood Cottage, 404 Havelock Street
Tel: (053) 32 8296 Fax: (053) 31 3358 (V)
Owner/contact: Eleanor & Peter Veal
Rooms: s/c 3 bedroom cottage
Cost: $180 double/weekend, from $65/night midweek, $15 extra person
No smoking

Roseneath, 702A Dana Street
Tel: (053) 32 1512
Owner/contact: John & Margaret Corbett
Rooms: s/c unit
Cost: From $75 double
No children

Woodside, 120 Fisken Road, Mt. Helen
Tel: (053) 41 3451
Owner/contact: Joan & David Goldsmith
Rooms: 2
Cost: $40 single, $70 double
No children ◆ No smoking

BALMORAL VIC. 3407

Banool, RSD Balmoral
Tel/Fax: (055) 74 3226
Owner/contact: Sue & Neil Lawrance
Rooms: s/c log cabin
Cost: $100

Ⓥ

BEAUFORT VIC. 3373

'Wirranee Park' Rural Retreat, R.M.B. 786 Balls Road
Tel: (053) 49 7267 Fax: (053) 49 7223
Owner/contact: Douglas & Pauline Ball
Rooms: 3
Cost: $100 single, $130 double
No smoking • Children by prior arrangement

BRANXHOLME VIC. 3302

Arrandoovong, R.M.B. 1285 Chrome Road
Tel: (055) 78 6221 Fax: (055) 78 6249
Owner/contact: Jeanie & Bill Sharp
Rooms: 3
Cost: From $90 double, $65 single
Dinner by arrangement • Smoking outside • Working farm

Ⓥ

Inverary Homestead, Caroona Lane, RSD 1450
Tel: (055) 78 6212
Owner/contact: Stuart and Margaret Dufty
Rooms: 3
Cost: $60 single, $85 double
Dinner by arrangement • Working farm

BUNINYONG VIC. 3357

The Old Methodist Church, 802 Warrenheip Street
Tel: (053) 41 3786 or (03) 886 405
Owner/contact: Peter & Lainie Ivanoff
Rooms: s/c accommodation
Cost: $65 single

Ⓥ

Balfour, Scotts Lane, Scotsburn
Tel: (053) 41 8039
Owner/contact: Merrin & Ed Davis (V)
Rooms: 2 ensuite
Cost: $65 single, $90 double

Brim Brim, Lal Lal Street
Tel: (053) 41 8038 (V)
Owner/contact: Marcia & Cromwell Beggs
Rooms: 3 and s/c house

"The Eyrie" in the Eagle Store, 505 Warrenheip Street
Tel: (053) 41 2259
Owner/contact: Elizabeth & Tim Gilfillan
Rooms: 2 ensuite
Cost: $80-$90 double, $120 four persons
Dinner available by arrangement

CAVENDISH VIC. 3314

Stoneycroft Homestead, 'South Mokanger'
Tel: (055) 74 2398 Fax: (055) 74 2307
Owner/contact: Jill & Rob Gardner
Rooms: s/c cottage (V)
Cost: Bed & Breakfast - $75 double
Dinner by arrangement

CLUNES VIC. 3370

Keebles of Clunes, 114 Bailey Street
Tel: (053) 45 3220 Fax: (053) 45 3200
Owner/contact: Joy & Alan Keeble
Rooms: 6 ensuite (V)
Cost: $120 double/weekday, $400 double/weekend package
No children

DUNKELD VIC. 3294

Woodhouse Homestead, Woodhouse Lane
Tel: (055) 77 8223
Contact: Ron & Ros Plowright
Rooms: 2
Cost: $68 single, $118 double
Dinner available

ELMHURST VIC. 3469

Old Strathconon, Sandy Lane
Tel: (053) 53 7273
Owner/contact: David & Margo Green
Rooms: 3 (1 double/2 twin)

GLENISLA VIC. 3408

Glenisla Homestead, R.S.D. 250 Henty Highway, via Cavendish
Tel: (053) 80 1532 or (053) 80 1535 Fax: (053) 80 1532
Owner/contact: Eric A. Barber (V)
Rooms: 4
Cost: Full accommodation - $92 double

GLENTHOMPSON VIC. 3293

Stirling
Tel: (055) 77 4223
Owner/contact: Bruce & Elisabeth Cuming

The Hilton, 'Cherrymount'
Tel: (055) 77 4396 (V)
Contact: David & Pru McCulloch
Rooms: s/c cottage
Cost: Full board - $90 single

GREAT WESTERN VIC. 3377

The Hermitage
Tel: (053) 56 2361
Owner/contact: Meryl Bowyers (V)
Rooms: s/c cottage
Cost: $95 per night, including breakfast

HALLS GAP VIC. 3381

Banksia Cottage, Tandara Road
Tel: (018) 181 498
Contact: Graeme & Ruth McGregor
Rooms: s/c cottage
Cost: $65 per night for cottage

Mountain Grand, Dunkeld Road
Tel: (053) 56 4254
Owner/contact: David & Gerrie MacFie
Manager: Andrew O'Bryen
Rooms:10 ensuite

Mountain View Resort, Ararat Road
Tel: (053) 56 4364 Fax: (053) 56 4262 (V)
Owner/contact: David Ginn & Ross Barker
Rooms: 14 ensuite and 6 s/c lodges
Cost: $66-$140

Rocklyn, R.M.B. 2084 Dunkeld Road
Tel: (053) 56 4250
Owner/contact: Eve Fairs
Rooms: 10

HAMILTON VIC. 3300

Acton Lodge
Tel: (055) 72 5818
Owner/Contact: Ern & Marie Rentsch

Hewlett House
Tel: (055) 72 2494
Owner/Contact: Graeme & Anthea Struck

Murrufield, Glenelg Highway (P.O. Box 98)
Tel: (055) 72 3687
Owner/contact: Wilma Preston
Rooms: 2
Meals by arrangement

HORSHAM VIC. 3400

Garretts, "Casa Del Sol", 25 Landy Street
Tel: (053) 82 3928
Owner/contact: Denise & James Garrett
Rooms: 2
Cost: $45 single, $65 double
Dinner by arrangement ◆ *No smoking* ◆ *No children*

KANIVA VIC. 3419

Parlawidgee, P.O. Box 10A
Tel: (053) 92 2613
Owner/contact: Bob & Dawn Meyer
Rooms: 2
Cost: Dinner bed & breakfast - $50 single
Host farm ◆ *No children* ◆ *No smoking*

KINGOWER VIC. 3517

Passing Clouds, R.M.B. Kurting Road
Tel: (054) 38 8287 (accommodation), (054) 38 8287 or 38 8257 (vineyard)
Fax: (054) 38 8246
Manageress: Fay Roberts
Owner: Graeme Leith & Sue MacKinnon
Rooms: 2 ensuite
Meals by arrangement ◆ *Vineyard*

Lakeview, Glenelg Highway (P.O. Box 69)

LAKE BOLAC VIC. 3351

Tel: (053) 50 2240 or (053) 50 2218
Owner/contact: Brian O'Rorke or Thomas Spittal
Rooms: 3
Cost: $70 double, $45 single

Baloo, Cnr. Glengleeson & Main Highway

MACARTHUR VIC. 3286

Tel: (055) 76 1171
Owner/contact: Ellen & Bob Hill
Rooms: 3
Cost: $40 single, $75 double; Dinner $15
Working farm ◆ Child concession

"**Menenia**"

MININERA VIC. 3351

Tel/Fax: (053) 50 6536
Owner/contact: Adele Coutts
Rooms: 1 ensuite
Cost: $60 single, $96 double
Dinner by arrangement

Warrenmang Vineyard, Mountain Creek Road

MOONAMBEL VIC. 3478

Tel: (054) 67 2233 Fax: (054) 67 2309
Owner/contact: Athalie Bazzani
Rooms: 18
Cost: From $49.50 single (V)
Restaurant ◆ Not suitable for children

Glenhoe

PENSHURST VIC. 3289

Tel: (055) 73 5280
Owner/Contact: Glenys Scholfield & Richard Canapini

QUANTONG VIC. 3405

Banksia Hill, Hutchinsons Road (R.M.B. 5349, Horsham, 3401)
Tel: (053) 84 0264
Owner/contact: Jan & Peter Grenfell
Rooms: 2 ensuite
Cost: $35 single, $65 double
Dinner by arrangement • Smoking outdoors only • Commercial native flower farm

ST. ARNAUD VIC. 3478

The St. Arnaud Old Post Office & Josephine Coppens Gallery, 2 Napier Street
Tel: (054) 95 2313
Owner/contact: Josephine Coppens
Rooms: 2 ensuite
Cost: $70 double, $80 twin, $35 children
Dinner by arrangement • No smoking

Vyalla, 43 Alma Street
Tel: (054) 95 2427
Owner/contact: Serge Barbes
Rooms: 3
Cost: $65 single, $95 double
No smoking • No children • Dinner by arrangement

STAWELL VIC. 3380

Bellellen Rise, R.M.B. 2032
Tel/Fax: (053) 58 2750
Owner/contact: Pat & Norman Reid
Rooms: 2
Cost: $70 single, $95 double/twin, $135 triple; Dinner $25, by arrangement
No smoking • Children over 12 by arrangement

Clovelly House, 7 Clifton Avenue
Owner/contact: Margot Chapman
Rooms: 3 ensuite
Cost: $95 double/twin
Children by arrangement • Smoking outdoors only • Dinner by arrangement

TALBOT VIC. 3371

Bull & Mouth Restaurant Miners Cottages, Cnr. Balaarat St. & Balaarat St. Nth.
Tel: (054) 63 2325
Owner/contact: Barry & Dorothea Levy
Rooms: 3 s/c cottages
Cost: Diners $60 double, non diners $85 double, $15 extra person
Linen provided • No children

TARNAGULLA VIC. 3551

Tarnagulla, Commercial Road
Tel: (054) 38 7366
Manager/contact: Helen & John Chapman
Rooms: 2

WALLINDUC VIC. 3352

Naringal Homestead, Naringal
Tel: (055) 96 5122
Owner/contact: Elizabeth & Michael Rowe
Rooms: 2 and 2 s/c cottages
Cost: Homestead $300 single/day all inclusive; Cottage $100 double/day B & B, $200 double/day all meals

Princes Highway Lakes & Crater Country to Warrnambool

From Geelong the quickest road to the west and Warnambool is the Princes Highway.

One hundred kilometres west of Geelong, between the Princes Highway and the Hamilton Highway, 40 kilometres to the north, lies the lakes and crater country. Many large and small lakes, some fresh and some salt, are scattered over this old volcanic plain. Some are just depressions in the lava field, collecting run-off, and others are ancestral lakes formed by lava flows cutting across water courses. Crater lakes form in the cone of extinct volcanoes, the largest and most spectacular of these being Tower Hill at Koroit. The main towns of interest in this area are:

CAMPERDOWN

A pleasant town with its avenues of Elm trees and over 50 buildings of historical interest. The surrounding area offers lake fishing at Bullen Merri and Purrumbeete. Mt. Leura Lookout has splendid views over the lake-studded plain and north to Lake Goranjamite, the largest salt lake in Victoria.

COBDEN

A small dairy town.

TIMBOON

To the south, on the northern fringe of the Otways. The town is set in hilly dairy country and has the famous Timboon Cheese Factory a few kilometres out of town. Service here is generous and friendly, and the large range of interesting cheeses makes a visit worthwhile.

DARLINGTON

This is a small settlement on the north western side of lakes and crater country.

BIRREGURRA (COLAC)

This quaint but tiny settlement, 15 minutes from Colac, has suddenly become a centre of new B & B premises. This is probably the result of the presence and active encouragement from George of Sunnybrae Country Restaurant (Tel: 052-36-2276).

The sophisticated restaurant is a pleasant surprise in this rural backwater. The menu is innovative and the execution extremely professional; all in a bucolic setting.

Highly recommended.

Sample Menu

Angelo Cardoso's Proscuitto with fennel & pear salad

Shin of Veal as an Italian style roast on Risotto
Crab Soufflé with a curry sauce made from the stock
Scallops with Roti & jicama

Fresh custard apples with lime & coconut sorbet
White chocolate mousse with strawberries and rhubarb & jasmine ice-cream
Valentina Harris light Tiramisu with coffee sorbet

Elliminook

Warncoort Road, Birregurra, 3242
Tel: (052) 36 2080 Fax: c/- (052) 31 3424
Contact: Jill & Peter Falkiner
Rooms: 2

The house, built in 1865, presents a pleasant prospect as you enter the well tended, mature gardens via the circular drive.

A huge hoop pine and a Cedar of Lebanon dominate the garden with its neat bluestone bordered flower beds. The broad front verandah, with its comfortable cane furniture, invites you to the front door.

The renovations of this old homestead have been carried out with sensitivity and style by use of plain wood finishes. On one side of the front door is a comfortable sitting room with open fire, and on the other the dining room. There are two wings extending from the back of the main house, joined by a glassed verandah.

The garden room, with its adjacent large bathroom, is the best of the two double bedrooms. The warmth of handmade bricks surrounding the open fire, two chintz covered chairs and a large comfortable bed make your country house haven a simple delight.

Breakfast is usually served in the gallery, the glass verandah. Your hosts are the charming and energetic (with this garden they have to be) Jill and Peter Falkiner.

I continually return to the theme that B & B accommodation must offer a special ambience, somewhere to be, and enjoy a total environment within which the guests may relax. This, Elliminook provides.

Kooraweera

R.M.B. 2235, Camperdown, 3260
Tel: (055) 93 8235
Contact: Jill and David Deane
Rooms: 2
Cost (B & B): $60 double, $35 single

The surreal volcanic plain, so flat, interspersed with lakes and odd humps of hill, is home to many large old established farms. It is a pleasant relief to drive from this flatness into a shady undulating garden of two manicured acres. The backdrop to a substantial old weatherboard house includes a lake glimpsed through the trees.
There are three lakes on the property and apparently the salt lake is heaven for swimming or wind surfing. Tennis is also available.
The period furniture has obviously come with the house, as has the silver. A double room is offered in the house with an open fire, basin and adjacent bathroom.
The garden room at the back of the house is large with a sitting area of its own. At the time of writing it was still necessary to wend one's way to the inside bathroom for a shower, so both rooms were let only if people were travelling together.
Food is a feature here, as well as service. Meals can be taken in the dining room, on the terrace, or in your room. The meals are well planned, generous and well executed. David is a genial sheep farmer and, together, your hosts will ensure a pleasant stay.

Bydowne House

33 Parrott Street, Cobden, 3266
Tel: (055) 95 1886
Contact: Jim & Marion Fairweather
Rooms: 2
Cost: $85 - $100 double, $50 - $60 single

This is quite the best house in Cobden. Formerly a nursing home, it is huge but since you can never take it all in at once it has a cottage feeling inside and out. It is surrounded by a thick, high hedge so, though in town, you could be anywhere. The pretty garden is shod with a croquet lawn and more tree ferns than in the Otways.

There are 3 double rooms and a single. The Camelia Room and Rose Room are double and have access to the verandah. The Iris Room is a single, and these three have the use of a sensational bathroom with stained glass, a shower and a double bath. You are guarantied private use of this facility since only one of these rooms is let at a time, unless a group is travelling together.

The Tulip Suite consists of a bedroom with an iron bed, bathroom and a connecting internal verandah which serves as a sitting area.

The home has a warm friendly feeling. Breakfast is served in the breakfast room, whilst dinner is by arrangement. A small T.V. room is available if you need to watch the news and football results.

Yellangip Country House

Pura Pura Road, Darlington, 3271
Tel: (055) 97 9203 Fax: (055) 97 9203
Contact: Carmel English and Peter Judson
Rooms: 5 ensuite
Cost (B & B): $140 - $180 double, Dinner $35 per person

This substantial Edwardian country house has elegance and charm. the high ceilinged rooms are huge, yet with good proportions. the extraordinary antique furnishings of the bedrooms are in keeping with the period and in their sheer sheer scale.

The five rooms offered each uses a different timber. The Walnut Room has acres of this spectacular warm hued wood. The Cedar Room is enhanced by a choice of pretty floral print. The most elegant is the master bedroom, with a superb half-tester bed. Of the other two rooms, one is a twin and the other a mini suite with a small sitting room.

Of necessity, dinner is served in-house; Darlington is not exactly replete with restaurants.

This guest house is licenced and the cellar features Victorian wines.

Bydowne House, 33 Parrott Street
Tel: (055) 95 1886 Fax: (055) 95 1193
Owner/contact: J.S. Fairweather
Rooms: 4
Cost: $50-$60 single, $85-$100 double

CAMPERDOWN VIC. 3260

No smoking indoors ◆ No children under 12 ◆ Dinner by arrangement

Ⓥ

Thompson's Hotel, 36 Curdie Street
Tel: (055) 95 1208
Rooms: 9
Dinner by arrangement

COBDEN VIC. 3266

Prince of Wales Guest House
Tel: (052) 31 3385
Owner/Contact: Sue & Bill Bath
Belle-Vue
Tel: (055) 97 9262
Owner/Contact: Elspeth & Lyle Buntine
Yellangip Country House, Pura Pura Road
Tel/Fax: (055) 97 9203
Owner/contact: Carmel English & Peter Judson
Rooms: 5 ensuite
Cost: $140-$180 double; Dinner $35 per person
Fully licensed ◆ No children
Rockbank Farm, R.M.B. 2/290 Bass Road
Tel: (055) 97 6626
Owner/contact: Margaret & Laweton French

COLAC VIC. 3250

Rooms: 2
Cost: $35 single, $55 double
Dinner by arrangement ◆ No smoking ◆ No children under 12
Barunah Plains, via Inverleigh

DARLINGTON VIC. 3271

Tel/Fax: (052) 87 1234
Owner/Contact: Joan & Graham Mills
Rooms: s/c quarters
Cost: $20 single
Cape Otway Cottage, R.M.B. 1590 Hordern Vale Road

BARONGAROOK VIC. 3249

Palm View Lodge, Foran Road (R.M.B. 9580, Colac, 3250)
Tel: (052) 33 8325

BIRREGURRA VIC. 3242

Bushy Park
Tel: (052) 36 2133
Owner/Contact: Greg & Dinah Farquharson
Rooms: 2
Cost: From $55 double

Elliminook, Warncoort Road
Tel: (052) 36 2080 Fax: c/- (052) 31 3424
Owner/contact: Jill & Peter Falkiner (V)
Rooms: 2
Cost: $95 double

Gannawarra, Dunlops Road (P.O. Box 9)
Tel: (052) 36 2131
Owner/contact: Prue Campbell
Rooms: 3
Cost: $40 single, $75 single full board
Child concessions

Kirewau, Princes Highway
Tel: (052) 33 6283
Owner/Contact: Kath Walsh
Rooms: 3
Cost: $55 single, $65-$75 double

Mooleric
Tel: (052) 88 9214
Owner/Contact: Sally & Angus Ramsay
Rooms: 2
Cost: $80 double, $70 single dinner bed & breakfast

Pennyroyal Raspberry Farm
Tel: (052) 36 3238
Owner/Contact: Dawn Evans & Rex Davies
Cost: $45-$50 single, $50-$60 double

CAMPERDOWN VIC. 3260

Kooraweera, R.M.B. 2235
Tel: (055) 93 8235
Owner/contact: Jill & David Deane (V)
Rooms: 2
Cost: $35 single, $60 double

COBDEN VIC. 3266

Bydowne House, 33 Parrott Street
Tel: (055) 95 1886 Fax: (055) 95 1193
Owner/contact: J.S. Fairweather
Rooms: 4
Cost: $50-$60 single, $85-$100 double
No smoking indoors ◆ No children under 12 ◆ Dinner by arrangement

Thompson's Hotel, 36 Curdie Street
Tel: (055) 95 1208
Rooms: 9
Dinner by arrangement

COLAC VIC. 3250

Prince of Wales Guest House
Tel: (052) 31 3385
Owner/Contact: Sue & Bill Bath

DARLINGTON VIC. 3271

Belle-Vue
Tel: (055) 97 9262
Owner/Contact: Elspeth & Lyle Buntine
Yellangip Country House, Pura Pura Road

Tel/Fax: (055) 97 9203
Owner/contact: Carmel English & Peter Judson
Rooms: 5 ensuite
Cost. $140-$180 double; Dinner $35 per person (V)
Fully licensed • No children

Rockbank Farm, R.M.B. 2/290 Bass Road

DERRINALLUM VIC. 3325

Tel: (055) 97 6626
Owner/contact: Margaret & Laweton French
Rooms: 2
Cost: $35 single, $55 double
Dinner by arrangement • No smoking • No children under 12

Barunah Plains, via Inverleigh

HESSE VIC. 3321

Tel/Fax: (052) 87 1234
Owner/Contact: Joan & Graham Mills
Rooms: s/c quarters
Cost: $20 single

Cape Otway Cottage, R.M.B. 1590 Hordern Vale Road

HORDERN VALE VIC. 3238

Tel: (052) 37 9256
Owner/contact: Meredith & Charles Robinson
Rooms: 2

Pilgrims Way, Simpson-Cobden Road (R.M.B. 1205, Cobden)

SIMPSON VIC. 3266

Tel: (055) 94 3220
Owner/contact: Charles & Joanna Bignold
Rooms: 2
Working dairy farm • Dinner by arrangement

TERANG VIC. 3264

Red Rattler Train Carriage, R.M.B. 6475 Pontings Road
Tel: (055) 92 5246
Owner/contact: John Charles
Rooms: 2
Cost: Unit from $50 double/day; Bed & Breakfast from $55 double

TIMBOON VIC. 3268

Inglenook Cottage, H. Robilliards Road
Tel: (055) 90 3250
Owner/contact: Carolyn Moore
Rooms: 4
Cost: $50 single, $65 double
Dinner available (3 course $15, Indonesian Feast $19.50) ◆ *Children welcomed* ◆ *Smoking on verandah*

WARNCOORT VIC. 3243

Tarndwarncoort
Tel: (052) 33 6241
Owner/Contact: Wendy & David Dennis
Rooms: s/c cottage
Cost: $65 double
Dinner by arrangement

WINCHELSEA VIC. 3241

Turnberry, Block Lane
Tel: (052) 67 2287

Great Ocean Road

Leave Geelong on the Princes Highway and within 10 km. turn left (south) onto the Surfcoast Highway to Torquay.

The farmland has a rolling coastal feel and gently leads you to Torquay 22 km. south of Geelong. This is a surfers' town with pleasant foreshore and a young feeling. Close to the town are the famous surfing beaches Bells and Jan Juc. On a good day swarms of colourful windsurfers offer excellent entertainment for the uninvolved.

The Great Ocean Road starts at Torquay and motoring through Anglesea, Aireys Inlet to Lorne is a delight, but accommodation other than in caravan parks or motel units, non-existent.

Anglesea is attractive, with a golf course that bounces with Kangaroos.

Behind the town is an open cut brown coal mine and power station which provides electricity to Alcoa aluminium refinery at Geelong. In contrast there is also access to Angahook Forest Park, an attractive reserve with walking tracks to Iron Bark Grove, Currawong Falls, Treefern Grove and Melaleuca Swamp.

A few miles further you could miss Aireys Inlet if you blink at the wrong time. Don't! Turn off for a look at the lighthouse and a walk along the beach, and if you are desperate to stay I cannot help other than to suggest knocking on the door of a local estate agent and asking for a house to let. This is always worth a try in one of these hamlets. Most of the houses are holiday homes and some are available for a night or two. Also Marc's restaurant is mentioned in the Good Food Guide.

No luck? Drive on to Lorne, you will not be disappointed.

AIREYS INLET

A hamlet of holiday homes, lovely beach and interesting lighthouse and Bark hut.

You may be able to let a holiday house at one of the estate agents, otherwise choose between the motel on the highway, with swimming pool, or Getaway Holiday Villas in a cramped gully with pool and tennis court. Otherwise Dr. McKenzie's Glen Cabins on a bare block on the wrong side of the highway, or the Light Keeper's Cottages next to the lighthouse.

Mark's Restaurant is really good, small with inventive enthusiastic skilful owners, Linda and Stewart. No lunches. Weekends only in the off season.

LORNE

Lorne, a coastal town of more substance, beautifully situated with the Cumberland Carbuncle in its neck and the superb mountain scenery of the Otway Ranges behind. From Queenscliff to Lorne the trees are scrubby or stunted, but the Otways behind Lorne are very special for anyone with a liking for forests.

Quoting from the local tourist guide:

> *Proud stands of mountain ash, messinate, blue and grey, and manna gums in the heavily forested ranges cast their long shadows over waterfalls, pristine mountain streams, impressive valleys and even rain forests like the Melba Gully near Havers Hill.*

Gosh! - but yes!

Back to Lorne - stay here if it is past lunch time. It will now become a long way between drinks.

By the way, before you get to Lorne just have a look at another caravan park with the 'best' position on the Cumberland River.

THE OTWAYS

This beautiful area needs time to walk and discover; it is a perfect place to write a book.

Do visit Melba Gully, first in daylight, and then at night have the courage to walk to Anns Falls where the glow worms are at their best.

We have combed the country between Skenes Creek and Warnambool and failed to find any B & B's of quality or charm. Greenacres at Apollo Bay has better food than most of the motels, and Muggins at Port Campbell at least offers hospitality.

PORT CAMPBELL (SHIPWRECK COAST)

Not a lot here except a pretty little sheltered beach and one good craft shop.
This is the centre of the shipwreck coast, 32 kms. long. As you leave the Otways the road comes close to the sea at Princetown. From here the many natural rock formations of the rugged coast are identified and lookouts provided. The sights include the twelve apostles and Loch Ard Gorge in the east, London bridge and The Grotto near Peterborough and the Bay of Islands and the Bay of Martyrs in the west.
The road continues to Warrnambool 66 km. beyond Peterborough.

WARRNAMBOOL (pop. 23,000)

This is a pleasant scenic coastal city with many family attractions, especially Lake Pertoke with its extensive adventure playground.
Flagstaff Hill Maritime Museum is an outstanding complex and the adjacent Mahogany Restaurant the best place, with the best view, to eat in town.
There is a viewing platform at Logans Beach where the deep water allows close observation of calving Southern Right Whales from June to October.
Scenically the area is blessed by the Hopkins and Mern Rivers, the sheltered bay and the adjacent Tower Hill Nature Reserve.

The Reserve lies between Warrnambool and Koroit and is a magnificent huge extinct volcanic crater. It is a protected home for wildlife, including emu and koalas. Do not miss it.

PORT FAIRY

The most perfect fishing village in Victoria - lots to do and see, excellent accommodation and restaurants. The wharf, with its fishing fleet and sales co-op on the sheltered estuary of the Moyne River, is the centre of bustle and activity.

There are many historic buildings in the town which you may enjoy using the Historic Walk map available from the Tourist Information Centre.

PORTLAND

Portland is famous for the Aluminium Smelter (free tours are available), but its presence does not spoil this historic town. Fawthrop Lagoon, a native reserve of permanent wetlands, is to one side of the town. The other coastal scenery varies from sand dunes to rugged cliffs.

Portland is at the start of the Great South West walk - 250 km. of scenic hiking. Day treks are available which start and finish at the town Tourist Information Centre.

Portland was one of the first settled areas of Victoria and boasts many historic buildings which are still in use today, such as the Portland Custom House built in 1849.

Also of historical importance are the three accommodation establishments to be reviewed.

MOUNT ECCLES & LAKE SURPRISE

A 6,100 ha. park enclosing bush, a crater lake and 22 caves within the biggest frozen larva flow in the state.

There is a large koala population, kangaroos and wallabies, also the rare tiger quoll has been sighted here.

This is also the site of an important aboriginal information and historical centre, Lake Condah, with stone houses and fish traps.

ACCOMMODATION

Debonaire Guest House and Hotel

Great Ocean Road, Anglesea, 3230
Tel: (052) 63 1440 Fax: (052) 63 3239
Contact: James & Tracey Hughes
Rooms: 9

This classic seaside guest house is on the last corner as you drive west out of town. It is in the final stages of a major facelift. The managers, James and Tracey Hughes, manage the comfortable bar and produce fine food with a cheerful and helpful demeanour.

There are three twin rooms, and six double, two of which are ensuite. The rest share the ladies' and gentlemen's bathrooms. They are pleasantly but simply furnished with iron beds and fitted carpets. A delightful new addition is the large sundeck where drinks and food may be served.

Swimming pool and tennis court are available. The bar and restaurant are open to the public.

Bellbrae Country Club

R.M.B. 1790, Torquay, 3228
Tel:(052) 61 3803 Fax: (052) 61 4626
Rooms: 26

This extensive complex, latterly a health resort, is now a convention centre. It is of motel design and has 26 rooms with typical motel conveniences and layout. However, it is set in 33 secluded acres, has an indoor pool and spa, tennis courts and a gymnasium. Sauna, massage and facials are available by prior arrangement. Above the norm are the executive suites, which have pleasant private rear terraces with small spa baths.

The communal room for dining or sitting is large and, at the time of my visit, seemed over-large and bare with its cathedral ceilings, but there is an open fire and plans are afoot to make this area warmer and more friendly.

Arcady Homestead

R.M.B. 1370 Barham River Road, Apollo Bay, 3233
Tel: (052) 37 6493
Contact: Ross & Marcia Dawson

Arcady Homestead is located 10 kilometres from Apollo Bay in the beautiful Barham River Valley, on the edge of the Otway forest.

The drive into this property is quite stunning - the homestead offers comfort, home cooking and the opportunity for peaceful relaxation.

The valley abounds with bird-life. Swimming, surfing, golf, horse riding, bowls and squash are within easy reach and, of course, the region is a bush walker's paradise.

If you are after a sophisticated lifestyle, this place is not for you. But, if you want a chance to stop and unwind - turn into Barham River Road and start to slow down.

Allenvale Cottages

Lorne, 3232
Tel: 052) 89 1450
Contact: Quentin Young
Rooms: 3 s/c cottages

Weekends for 2 is the only advertising regularly used for this property; how apposite. Even in the fine drizzle of a winter morning the valley and hosts exhaled a feeling of warmth and hospitality. A secluded haven.

Three charming, individual and private cottages deep among the eucalypts on the steep banks of the St. George River, close to the Phantom Falls.

One feels that Quentin Young does not do this for a living, but for a desire to share this experience with like-minded souls. The valley is a natural symphony, blending the hand of one hundred years of European settlement, shown by deciduous trees and orchards, with the natural backdrop of the Otways and the noisy river.

The owners also have an unostentatious flair married to a warm sophisticated hospitality.
A few minutes from Lorne, after an evening meal, drive carefully and do not frighten the wombats on your way home. A truly Australian experience.

Johanna Sea-Side Farm Cottages

R.M.B. 1360, Red Road, Johanna, 3238
Tel: (052) 37 4242
Contact: Joy Evans
Rooms: 3 s/c cottages
Cost: $80 per person per night
$230 - $320 per cottage per weekend
$510 - $650 per cottage per week

From Lavers Hill - Apollo Bay Road take Johanna Road to the end. Here, tucked into the sand dunes, are two simple buildings. They are of concrete block with anodized aluminium window frames, indestructible pine furniture and nylon carpet. They command a magnificent position only a hundred yards from the wild Johanna surf. The units are private, spacious and warm.
Joy Evans is a delightful, helpful proprietor, and kids would love her and the farm where there are always baby animals to feed and amazingly, also, a large heated indoor pool.

Glen Aire Log Cabins

Lavers Hill, Johanna, 3238
Tel: (052) 37 9231

Just off the Lavers Hill Apollo Bay Road, these cabins are again simple, but spacious and, again, are owned by very hospitable people.
The cabins perch on a hillside amongst tall trees through which the ocean at Apollo Bay can be seen.

Wangerrip Holiday Cottages

Blue Road, Johanna, 3238
Tel: (052) 37 4226
Contact: Wayne & Kerry Robertson
Rooms: 3 s/c lodges
Cost (weekly): $475 - $625
Weekend and daily rates available

On Johanna Blue, just around the corner from Joy, these cottages are a little more up-market and command a stunning view of the ocean. They are further away from the beach, but are situated on a 2,000 acre farm which is very picturesque with gullies, creeks and 50 waterfalls.

Three cottages are available; one 1 bedroom and two 2 bedroom, all with spacious verandahs from which to enjoy the view. They are set together in an, as yet, immature garden - a telephone and gas barbecue are available.

Muggins

R.M.B. 7615, Timboon, 3268
(Great Ocean Road, Port Campbell)
Tel: (055) 98 6329
Contact: Marnie McDowell
Rooms: 2
Cost: $70 single, $100 twin

This is on the road out to Warnambool on the right hand side. There are two simple units with disabled facilities which share a bathroom. These are separated from the tea rooms, where meals are taken, by a sheltered garden. Marnie is a very good cook and attentive hostess. Order lobster, or try her chocolate cake!

Quamby Homestead

R.M.B. 9130 Caramut Road, Woolsthorpe, 3276
Tel: (055) 69 2395
Contact: Robert Stebbing & Edna Goldman
Rooms: 7 ensuite

Quamby has recently changed hands, and format in the dining room. The accommodation remains as before and the restaurant is open to the public, but has taken on a new lease of life in taking a leaf from Clover Cottage at Berwick.

Saturday night is Banquet Night, first an entrée then soup followed by 3 main dishes, all served together at the table so you may taste and browse trying some of each.

On other nights an a la carte menu is available and this includes house wine for guests in the tariff.

A good looking mansion with an impressive drive and extensive colonial gardens, it forms an oasis in the open grazing land of the area.

Guests have the use of the drawing room, dining room and verandah, but are accommodated in the buildings nestled in the gardens fifty yards away. Seven double apartments are available, the School House and the Carriage House being spacious and particularly charming.

Between these detached buildings is a row of pretty, but basically motel style units called The Mews. These rooms are nicely furnished, all have televisions and bathrooms and open onto a sheltered verandah.

This accommodation enveloped in the old garden has a tranquil ambience shared by a diverse wild bird population which has also discovered this oasis.

Goble's Mill House

75 Gipps Street, Port Fairy, 3284
Tel: (055) 68 1118
Contact: Lorraine and Noel Adamson
Rooms: 6 ensuite
Cost (B & B): $100 The Loft, $85 other rooms

Without doubt the best place to stay on the western coast. Centrally situated at the end of Port Fairy's main street, this former flour mill has been restored with enormous loving care and attention to detail by Noel and Lorraine Adamson. There is a spacious sitting room with a large stone fireplace, huge comfy chairs and a vast sofa. A guest galley kitchen is well stocked with provisions. The interior glows in a soft yellow throughout, highlighting the polished antiques.

There are six ensuite guest rooms. At the top of the house is the large loft with its own balcony and view overlooking the Moyne River.

Breakfast is a real treat with fresh fruits in season and homemade preserves served in a delightful room with views of the river and moorings.

Dublin House Inn

57 Bank Street, Port Fairy, 3284
Tel: (055) 68 1822
Contact: Les & Wendy Ryan
Rooms: 3 double units, ensuite
Cost: $68 - $65 double

At the other end of the main street, an interesting collection of old buildings includes a double storey shop containing a restaurant which all other operators in town recognise as the best.

Les and Wendy Ryan are gentle country people who serve a cornucopia of local produce with an individual flair. The tiny dining rooms are antique rather than plush and have an ambience of quiet contented activity.

Comfortable accommodation is available at the house in 3 double units. Two open onto the rear paved courtyard garden, and one onto the street. Furnishings are comfortable country style and all units have private facilities.

The Ryans also have available a cottage and a modern apartment overlooking the bustle of the wharf, home to the fishing fleet. No children, and note that the fleet leaves for open water in the early hours of the morning.

Seacombe House

22 Sackville Street, Port Fairy, 3284
Tel: (055) 68 1082
Contact: Lou Frost
Rooms: 21 ensuite
Cost: $75 double room, $120 double s/c cottage

Situated by the motel are 3 well appointed units - delightful old whalers' cottages that have been converted into modern, warm, welcoming environments. There are few rooms in Victoria where you can have an open fire and/or a spa bath - here you can have both.

Lough Cottage

216 Griffith Street, Port Fairy, 3284
Tel: (055) 68 1583
Contact: Heather & Robert Towler
Rooms: 2
Cost (B & B): $60 double, $40 single, Dinner $20

This is the last house on the right as you leave town on Griffith Street. A sunny weatherboard cottage in a neat garden.
Heather Towler is a warm hostess offering classic B & B with one double and a twin room, sharing a bathroom. Guests are at home, but have additional access to their own dining/sitting area opening to a sunny enclosed verandah.

Tarabah

Old School Road, Tyrendarra, 3285
Tel: (055) 77 5279 or (018) 52 9827 Fax: (055) 29 5453
Contact: Michael Grimshaw
Rooms: Self contained
Cost (B & B): $120 one night, $230 three nights, $450 per week

For a piece of rural Australia near to Tyrendarra.
43 km. towards Portland from Port Fairy turn off the Princes Highway onto Old School Road to the coast. This rustic sandstone building nestles in a valley overlooking a protected lagoon. Here you are alone in coastal scenery without a house in sight.
The beach is only 1 km. away, but the short trip is a bit of an adventure since first you must cross the Fitzroy River by canoe.
The welcome is warm, log fires in the sitting room and master bedroom. Fresh flowers, a refrigerator stocked with breakfast provisions plus a side of lamb and bottle of Coonawarra red wine.
The bathroom is functional and clean with polished wooden floor, fibrous cement walls, modern plumbing - but no designer chic. The sitting room, with two couches, is cosy

with its open fires. The adjacent dining room is large and both are lined in original Baltic pine. There is a small double room and a twin. The master bedroom is spacious with two comfortable chairs and, again, an open fire.
Trees shelter the house and you may contemplate the 350 acre farm from the north facing deck which opens from the sitting room.
The enterprising owner, Michael Grimshaw, has 2 cray boats and is willing to take you on a fishing trip, if you rise early enough, or may supply you with crayfish on request.

Burswood Homestead, c.1856

15 Cape Nelson Road, Portland, 3305
Tel: (055) 23 4686 Fax: (055) 23 5293
Contact: Stephanie & Kit Oliver
Rooms: 5
Cost: $85 - $120 double, $55 single

Set in 7 acres of botanic gardens, this bluestone homestead was originally built for Edward Henty of the pioneering colonial family.
The rooms downstairs are furnished with antiques in keeping with the style and antiquity of the house. A formal drawing

room and comfy sitting room are available for guests. The double ensuite room downstairs has a four poster bed and the adjacent twin room is pleasantly furnished.
Two double rooms in the attic, servants' quarters, each ensuite, and the single room upstairs are furnished in more modest, but comfortable, cottage style. The single and twin share a bathroom.
The warmth of the host, Stephanie Oliver, is established on your arrival by a welcoming Devonshire tea. No dinner is available, but breakfast could keep you going all day with selections of juices, breads and cereal, croissant and fresh fruit platter and plunger coffee, plus a cooked breakfast supplying mushrooms, tomatoes and sausage as well as egg and bacon, all taken in the sun room overlooking the manicured gardens.

Portland Inn

4 Percy Street, Portland, 3305
Tel: (055) 23 2985
Contact: Elaine McDonald

Portland is halfway between Melbourne and Adelaide on the great Ocean Road. The region boasts waterbird sanctuaries, forest walks and beaches.
Portland Inn is one of the oldest inhabited timber buildings in Victoria. The quaint curved and angled ceilings, leadlight windows, timber lined walls and Elaine's patchwork quilts make this a truly historical place to stay.
Breakfast is served in either the kitchen or the sunny conservatory - tea and coffee are available at any time.
This is a perfect house for travellers who are looking for comfort and hosts well versed in local history.

St. Peter's Church

Bridgewater, Portland, 3305
Tel: (055) 26 7271
Contact: Joanne Kermond

Built in 1884 by Jim Hardie in an English Gothic style, this lovely building was originally owned by The Church of England. The National Trust of Australia converted it to holiday accommodation some ten years ago. It is situated 15 minutes from Portland on the Bridgewater Lakes Road.
The church sleeps 6 people and the open plan living area has a large pot belly stove. All crockery, cutlery, blankets and pillows are provided - but do take your own linen and food.
Several uncrowded beaches are an easy walk, and there is also a tennis court available for the more active.

The Shelly Beach Retreat

R.S.D. Heath Road, Portland, 3305
Tel: (055) 23 1577
Contact: Tony Horneman & Merry Abbey
Cost: Dec - March, school holidays $595 per week
After Easter - End Nov $495 per week

This modern house has stunning views over the Southern Ocean and direct access to two beaches. It is also along the Great South West Walk.
Set amongst natural bushland, the secluded hideaway sleeps six. There are 3 bedrooms, a large dining and living area with wood heater, T.V. and C.D.

Victoria House

5 - 7 Tyers Street, Portland, 3305 (P.O. Box 122)
Tel: (055) 21 7577
Contact: Lex Chalmers & Peter Stoat
Rooms: 9 ensuite
Cost (room only):$79 double, $66 single,
Breakfast $9 - $12

This is a substantial small hotel close to the sea front. A thoroughly renovated blue stone building with 9 ensuite guest rooms pleasantly and individually furnished, and two single rooms with communicating doors.

An effort has been made to offer everything found in a top motel except a swimming pool, whilst keeping the charm of a historic building offering Bed & Breakfast. Breakfast is taken in a sunny pavilion overlooking a cottage garden. Adjacent is a large friendly sitting room with an open fire.

Being very centrally positioned, there is no problem in dinner not being available. Several good restaurants are only a minute's walk away.

Great Ocean Road

ANGLESEA VIC. 3230

Debonaire Guesthouse & Motel, Great Ocean Road
Tel: (052) 63 1440 Fax: (052) 63 3239
Manager/contact: James & Tracey Hughes Ⓥ
Rooms: 11 guesthouse

Simply Blue, P.O. Box 55
Tel: (052) 63 2774
No smoking • No children

Thornton Heath, P.O. Box
Tel: (052) 63 2542
Owner/contact: Margaret Drayton

APOLLO BAY VIC. 3233

Arcady, R.M.B. 1370 Barham River Road
Tel: (052) 37 6493
Owner/contact: Ross & Marcia Dawson Ⓥ
Rooms: 4
Cost: Dinner, bed & breakfast - $55 single

Beacon Point, P.O. Box 67
Tel: (052) 37 6218

Rolling Breakers, Skenes Creek Road
Tel: (052) 37 6375
Rooms: s/c cottage and bungalow
Cost: Up to 3 nights - Cottage $300, Bungalow $250

Whitecrest, Great Ocean Road (P.O. Box 120)
Tel: (052) 37 0228 Fax: (052) 37 0245
Owner/contact: Bernie & Betty Carr
Rooms: 11 ensuite
No children at weekends

BUSHFIELD VIC. 3281

Woodfield Cottage, R.M.B. 5382
Tel: (055) 62 1927
Owner/contact: Linda Haynes
Cost: $40 single, $70 double
Meals by arrangement

DEANS MARSH VIC. 3235

Pennyroyal Valley Cottages, Pennyroyal Valley Road
Tel: (052) 36 3201
Owner/contact: Brian & Doreen Rawlings
Rooms: 3 s/c cottages
Cost: $150-$200 weekend

GRASSMERE VIC. 3282

Injemira Country House, R.M.B. 8360
Tel: (055) 65 4434
Owner/contact: Yve & Noel Bayley
Dinner available

JOHANNA (CAPE OTWAY) VIC. 3238

Glen Aire, Lavers Hill
Tel: (052) 37 9231 Ⓥ
Rooms: S/c cabins

Johanna Seaside Farm Cottages, R.M.B. 1360 Red Road
Tel: (052) 37 4242
Owner/contact: Joy Evans Ⓥ
Rooms: 3 s/c cottages
Cost: $80 person/night; Cottage $230-$320 weekend, $510-$650 week

Wangerrip, Blue Road
Tel: (052) 37 4226
Owner/contact: Wayne & Kerry Robertson Ⓥ
Rooms: 3 s/c lodges
Cost: $475-$625 weekly

LORNE VIC. 3232

Allenvale Cottages
Tel: (052) 89 1450
Owner/contact: Quentin Young Ⓥ
Rooms: 3 s/c cottages

Chalet Lorne, 4 Smith Street
Tel: (052) 89 1241
Owner/contact: Beverley & Fred Bird
Rooms: 36 ensuite
Cost: From $30-$90 person/night depending on package
All meals available

Erskine House, Mountjoy Parade
Tel: (052) 89 1209
Owner/contact: Alastair MacLean
Rooms: 80
Cost: $46-$56 single
Dinner Bed & Breakfast, and Full Board also available • *Recreation Officer for children over summer*

MOUNT RICHMOND VIC. 3305

Nioka, Nelson-Mt. Gambier Road (R.M.B. 2394, Portland)
Tel: (055) 20 2233
Owner/contact: Ruth Stanley
Rooms: 2
Cost: Dinner bed & breakfast - $20 single
Linen hire $5 per person

NELSON VIC. 3292

Contento Cottage, Cnr. Kellett & Sturt Streets
Tel: (087) 38 4161
Owner/contact: Tricia Sloan
Rooms: 8
Cost: $25-$30 single
No children ◆ Dinner available

PORT CAMPBELL VIC. 3268

Muggins, Great Ocean Road (R.M.B. 7615, Timboon)
Tel: (055) 98 6329
Contact: Marnie McDowall
Rooms: 2 (V)
Cost: $70 single, $100 twin
No children under 16 ◆ No smoking ◆ Dinner by arrangement

PORT FAIRY VIC. 3284

Clonmara, 106 Princes Highway
Tel: (055) 68 2595
Owner/contact: Julie & Rod Thomas
Rooms: s/c cottage
Cost: Bed & breakfast provisions - From $85 double

Cona
Tel: (055) 68 1000
Owner/Contact: Colleen & John Daffey

Cottages of the Port
Tel: (055) 68 1838

Dublin House, 57 Bank Street
Tel: (055) 68 1822
Owner/contact: Les & Wendy Ryan
Rooms: 3 ensuite
Cost: $58-$65 double
Dinner available in adjacent restaurant ◆ Not suitable for children

Ⓥ

Goble's Mill House, 75 Gipps Street
Tel: (055) 68 1118
Contact: Lorraine & Noel Adamson
Rooms: 6 ensuite
Cost: From $85 double
No children ◆ No smoking

Ⓥ

Hanley House, 14 Sackville Street (P.O. Box 147)
Tel: (055) 68 2709
Owner/contact: James & Marcia Gubbins
Rooms: 3
Cost: $75 double

Kilrarlen
Tel: (055) 68 7258

Lough Cottage, 216 Griffith Street
Tel: (055) 68 1583
Owner/contact: Heather & Robert Towler
Rooms: 2
Cost: $40 single, $60 double; Dinner $20
No smoking

Ⓥ

Merrijig Inn, 1 Campbell Street
Tel: (055) 68 2324
Owner/contact: Lynne Redman
Rooms: 5 ensuite
Cost: $90
Licenced restaurant ◆ *Smoking in bar only* ◆ *No children under 12*

Seacombe House Motor Inn, 22 Sackville Street
Tel: (055) 68 1082
Owner/contact: Lou Frost
Rooms: 21 ensuite
Cost: Double - Cottages $120, Motel $75 Ⓥ
Dinner available in restaurant

Seawinds
Tel: (055) 68 2709

The Old Vicarage, 23 College Street
Tel: (055) 68 1396
Owner/contact: P. Worrall & M. Brisbane
Rooms: 2
Cost: $65-$75 double

Tynemouth Villa
Tel: (03) 822 5671

PORTLAND VIC. 3305

Burswood Homestead, 15 Cape Nelson Road
Tel: (055) 23 4686 Fax: (055) 23 5293
Owner/contact: Stephanie & Kit Oliver Ⓥ
Rooms: 5
Cost: $85 - $120 double, $55 single

Portland Inn, 4 Percy Street
Tel: (055) 23 2985
Owner/contact: Elaine & Grahame McDonald
Rooms: 3 Ⓥ
Cost: $45 single, $65 twin, $75 double
No smoking ◆ *No children*

St. Peter's Church, Bridgewater
Tel: (055) 26 7271
Owner/Contact: Joanne Kermond Ⓥ
Rooms: Self-contained

The Shelly Beach Retreat, R.S.D. Heath Road
Tel: (055) 23 1577
Owner/Contact: Tony Horneman & Merry Abbey
Rooms: s/c house Ⓥ
Cost: From $495 - $595 per week

Victoria House, 5-7 Tyers Street (P.O. Box 122)
Tel: (055) 21 7577
Owner/contact: Lex Chalmers & Peter Stoat Ⓥ
Rooms: 9 ensuite
Cost: Room only - $66 single, $79 double; Light breakfast $9, inc. cooked course $12

TORQUAY VIC. 3228

Banyandah, 7 Zeally Bay Road
Tel: (052) 61 2419
Owner/contact:
Rooms: 1

Bellbrae Country Club, Cnr. Gundrys & Woodacres Roads (R.M.B. 1790)
Tel: (052) 61 3803 Fax: (052) 61 4626
Rooms: 26 Ⓥ
Sauna, massage, facials available by prior arrangement ◆
Indoor pool & spa, tennis courts, gymnasium

TYRENDARRA VIC. 3285

Quamby Park, R.M.B. 7200
Tel: (055) 29 5280
Owner/contact: Bob & Shirley Carter
Rooms: 3
Cost: Single - $20, Dinner bed & breakfast $30
Farm stay

'Tarabah', Old School Road
Tel: (055) 77 5279 or (018) 52 9827 Fax: (055) 29 5453
Owner/contact: Michael Grimshaw
Rooms: self contained Ⓥ
Cost: $120

WARRNAMBOOL VIC. 3280

Whalesway, 6 Florence Street
Tel: (055) 61 2660
Owner/contact: Pat Redden
Rooms: 3
Cost: $40 single, $60 double
Dinner by arrangement

Wollaston
Tel: (055) 62 2430
Owner/Contact: Nan Dodds

Wurroit, R.M.B. 9574 Goodwood Road
Tel: (055) 69 1501
Owner/contact: Wendy & Peter McWhinney
Rooms: 2
Cost: $45 single, $80 twin share
Dinner by arrangement

WONGARRA VIC. 3221

Wongarra Heights, Sunnyside Road (P.O. Box 159, Apollo Bay, 3233)
Tel: (052) 37 0257
Owner/contact:
Rooms: 5 (1 double/2 twin/2 family)
Cost: $50 single, $80 double/twin
Dinner by arrangement

WOOLSTHORPE VIC. 3276

Quamby Homestead, R.M.B. 9130 Caramut Road
Tel: (055) 69 2395
Owner/contact: Robert Stebbing & Edna Goldman
Rooms: 7 ensuite Ⓥ
Cost:
Dinner by arrangement

Geelong and Bellarine Peninsula

The best moment as you leave Melbourne for Geelong is looking back on the towers of the city as you cross the West Gate Bridge. The Princes Highway to Geelong is flat, industrial and frankly dull. Geelong is an industrial American-style city, unremarkable except for the Botanic Gardens and wool museum near the foreshore, but it is the gateway to the scenic delights of the South West.

The Bellarine Peninsula deserves mention, the centre of which, Queenscliff, is my favourite coastal town.

Portarlington should have been wonderful and probably still is if you own a caravan. It faces north, is sheltered and Melbourne shines in the distance, but practically the whole beach front is taken up by a caravan park.

Point Lonsdale has an enviable position, but if you can find anything moving there they are probably over 75 years of age.

BARWON HEADS

Barwon Heads is the Portsea of the west. Wonderful position at the outfall of the Barwon River and wonderful socially if you own or can rent a house for the summer season. Otherwise, besides the sea, there is little except for seaside and the pub for the tourist. Barwon Heads possesses one of the best links courses in Australia with excellent tennis courts. This Club is exclusive and has a wonderful weatherboard club house with accommodation. Again this is a private non profit-making club, but I would urge the overseas visitor to try them for accommodation with a current introduction and recommendation from their own golf club. Arrangements are best made by telephone or post before arriving in Australia, do not bowl up to the front desk!

QUEENSCLIFF

Queenscliff has everything. Quaint buildings, a marina, a ferry from Portsea to watch, diving centres, restaurants, quality accommodation, good galleries, shops and historical places of interest. It also has a beach, somewhere to buy fresh fish and crays, and even a pier!
Two more gems in Queenscliff:

Harry's Bar

Opposite Miettas in the old changing rooms in the park. A small semi-outdoor restaurant, always busy and buzzing. The menu fresh, unusual, interesting and well executed. I can never decide on an entrée so I generally browse my way through three.

Hobsons Choice Gallery

I hate galleries in tourist towns, but this has quality exhibits, and no rubbish. I enjoyed wandering around, and even spent a few dollars.

Linkside

3 Bell Street, Barwon Heads, 3227
Tel: (052) 54 2541
Contact: Robin & Neil Gubbins
Rooms: 2

This is a commodious holiday house with all mod cons and toys as well. There is available for guests a large pool, shady garden with a tennis court and a billiard room, views of the sea, only minutes away, and the famous Barwon Heads Links Golf Course literally at the doorstep.
Two bedrooms, one double, one twin, and introduction to the Golf Club on request.

Mietta's Queenscliff Hotel

16 Gellibrand Street, Queenscliff, 3225
Tel: (052) 52 1899
Contact: Patricia O'Donnell
Rooms: 22
Cost (D, B & B): From $99 single

This is to the Bellarine Peninsula what Delgany is to the Mornington Peninsula; a treasure, a haven of professional hospitality with excellent food. The two hotels are very different, and if I was made to choose between them I couldn't. Firstly at Miettas the staff are always young, but have an awareness beyond their years. I skipped from the dining room once before ordering coffee. Fifteen seconds after I had settled comfortably in front of the fire in one of the delightful sitting rooms, the young female maitre d' zoomed into the hall, surveyed me discreetly from the corner of her eye, U-turned and fifteen seconds later a waiter was at my side taking an order for coffee and bourbon. Patricia O'Donnell does remarkable things for her young staff and a stint at Miettas ensures their permanent employability in the hospitality industry. It is a grand old Australian Seaside Hotel. Lace and verandahs outside, inside exquisitely to the period with découpage screens, comfort and style and some of the most constantly perfect floral displays I have ever seen. The bar is great, the verandah better.

Patricia's champagne cocktails at six o'clock are terrific. An interesting modern menu, occasionally variable but generally excellent. There has been criticism of small rooms and lack of ensuite facilities, but honestly by the time I hit the pillow I would not care less. The four front rooms are large with open fires and the best views in Queenscliff, but I have never booked early enough to experience them. They are worth the extra tariff.

Note the tariff does assume double occupancy.

Another must do - often.

Sample Menu

First Courses

Field mushroom and grain mustard soup

Grilled scallops on sweet yellow and red peppers with balsamic vinegar

Oysters natural with crème fraiche, salmon roe and a red wine vinaigrette

Main Courses

Grilled fillet of Atlantic salmon on a bed of spinach with a lemongrass butter sauce

Roast pheasant breast and braised leg with pear and orange zest

Finely sliced venison with sautéed mushrooms and a light cracked pepper sauce

Desserts

Frozen nougat heart with kiwi fruit purée and mint Anglaise

Raspberry souffle with almond praline ice cream

Lemon tart with vanilla bean ice cream and bitter orange sauce

Choice of cheeses

Espresso Coffee with Chocolate Truffles

The Queenscliff Inn

59 Hesse Street, Queenscliff, 3225
Tel: (052) 52 3737
Contact: Gay & Gilbert Brooks
Rooms: 12
Cost: $70 - $85

Completely different, not at all up-market and you will share a bathroom with rather more people than at Miettas.

The Inn is on the main street of Queenscliff in a lovely building opposite the Vue Grand Hotel. The tariff is very reasonable but as soon as I opened the front door, I was hooked. It smelled wonderful, it looked wonderful and the hosts, Gay and Gilbert, were so incredibly nice in spite of my very inconvenient choice of moment.

What makes it so good - it feels right from the first glance; friendly, different, stylish, with fresh home baking at breakfast.

They have opened a restaurant serving light lunches and the best Devonshire teas in Queenscliff - but don't leave here until you have tried Gilbert's renowned muffins.

BARWON HEADS VIC. 3227

Linkside, 3 Bell Street
Tel: (052) 54 2541
Owner/contact: Robin & Neil Gubbins Ⓥ
Rooms: 2
Introduction to Golf Club on request

BELMONT VIC. 3216

Clydesdale Homestay, 12 Clydesdale Crescent
Tel: (052) 43 5642
Owner/contact: Pat & Geoff Hodge
Cost: $35 single, $60 double
No smoking

FRESHWATER CREEK VIC. 3216

Woodstock, 870 Dickens Road
Tel: (052) 64 5281
Owner/contact: Michael Travers
Rooms: 2 ensuite
Cost: $35 single
Dinner by arrangement ◆ *No smoking*

GEELONG WEST VIC. 3218

Langmere, 4 Aberdeen Street
Tel: (052) 29 6024 or (052) 21 2878
Owner/contact: Mrs. Maureen Sharkey
Rooms: 7
Cost: $25 single
Dinner by arrangement

Geelong and Bellarine Peninsula

HIGHTON VIC. 3216

Reads, 13 Lichen Grove
Tel: (052) 43 7773
Owner/contact: Richard & Judy Read
Rooms: 2 ensuite
Cost: $30 single, $40 double
Dinner by arrangement ◆ *No smoking*

MOUNT MORIAC VIC. 3221

Cairom Park, Cnr. Princes Hwy & Andersons Road (Postal - Gnarwarre)
Tel: (052) 66 1564
Owner/contact: Wendy & Kevin Robinson
Rooms: 3
Cost: $65 double
No smoking ◆ *No children*

QUEENSCLIFF VIC. 3225

Athelstane, 4 Hobson Street
Tel: (052) 52 1591
Rooms: 14

Mietta's Queenscliff Hotel, 16 Gellibrand Street
Tel: (052) 52 1066 Fax: (052) 52 1899
Owner/contact: Patricia O'Donnell
Rooms: 22 (V)
Cost: Dinner bed & breakfast - from $99 single

Seaview, 86 Hesse Street
Tel: (052) 52 1763
Owner/contact: Rob Brooke
Rooms: 11

The Queenscliff Inn, 59 Hesse Street
Tel: (052) 52 3737
Owner/contact: Gay & Gilbert Brooks
Rooms: 12 (V)
Cost: $70-$85
No smoking

Tasmania

Tasmania

Tasmania is Australia's smallest and oldest state. An island 200 km. south of the mainland state of Victoria, from which it is separated by the Bass Strait.

The island abounds in natural attractions, beaches, rock formations and caves. It has many temperate wilderness areas, especially the impenetrable south west and the central plateau.

There is a diverse flora and fauna blessed by no foxes and it is laced with rivers and streams. Being the first settled area of Australia, there is a rich heritage of history and buildings.

The contemporary interest in food and wine has produced a cornucopia of edibles; cool climate wines, gourmet cheese and other dairy products.

The clear, clean unpolluted ocean around the island has proved ideal for modern aquaculture; salmon, oysters and mussels are produced in abundance and to international acclaim. Crayfish and firm fleshed cold water ocean fish are also in high demand.

It is often said that Tasmania is like England. It is not – the weather is better. The island is unique, charming and user friendly, with a plethora of natural and man made attractions. History and wilderness, beauty and charm, food, wine and vistas all densely packed into a compact holiday destination.

I have based my approach on the popular fly drive concept and describe a round trip which attempts to cover the major destinations and demonstrate the variety of experience available. Kendall Airlines quickly and conveniently transported me from Melbourne to Devenport on the north of the island to collect a hire car and commence the trip covering the island anti-clockwise.

My thanks to Tourism Tasmania for their support and facilitation in accessing information.

Devonport to Stanley The North West

Devonport, and the adjacent town of LaTrobe, lie at the mouth of the Mersey river. This picturesque port is of obvious importance, with clusters of tanks and silos along the steep banks of the pretty estuary. This is the port of the Abel Tasman ferry to Melbourne.

Mersey Bluff is the favourite beach and picnic spot. This is the site of the lighthouse and the Tiagarra Aboriginal information centre.

A track follows the shore to the Don River, home of the Don River Tramway, an operating railway museum. Home Hill in Devonport was the home of Prime Minister Joe Lyons.

LaTrobe, 6 km. south of the city, is older and was originally the more important port. It has many restored old buildings of interest, especially near the wharf at Bells Parade.

The gently rolling hills around Devonport are amongst Australia's most fertile. Crops include potatoes, brassicas and pyrethrum. South are the caves of Mole Creek and the Lake Barrington international rowing venue. This is part of the Mersey-Forth Power Development Scheme and is an entry point to the central plateau of Cradle Mountain Lake St. Clair National Park.

Devonport to Stanley

Taking the coast road eastward you first pass through Ulverston, which boasts an idiosyncratic war memorial and is surrounded by rich agricultural land. To the south are limestone caves at Gunns Plains and 40 km. from Ulverstone is the beautiful Leven Canyon on the Leven River.

The next settlement is Penguin, charmingly named after its original fairy inhabitants. The town has an unusual church with keyhole windows and a neat strip of holiday homes along the beach.

Burnie is an important deep water port with an industrial foreshore. This is home to APPM, paper mills and Lactos cheese; tastings are available at the factory. There is a Pioneer Village and Museum. Natural attractions include the Upper Natone forest reserve, Guide Falls at Ridgely and Fern Glade, a pretty picnic spot on the Emu River.

Wynyard is a pretty town on the Inglis River, overlooked by Fossil Bluff. There is a pleasant drive to the Boat Harbour and Sisters Beach, with its unspoiled white sands, passing Table Cape. The Cape is colourful in October when the tulip fields are in flower.

Between Boat Harbour and Stanley is the Rocky Cape National Park, renowned for its spring flowers and aboriginal archaeological sites.

Stanley is one of Tasmania's prettiest fishing villages and third oldest town. It nestles on a promontory alongside Circular Head, a massive block of volcanic basalt which dominates Sawyers Bay and the surrounding flat landscape.

The town was the home of the Van Diemans Land Company, the original headquarters of which are currently being restored. The only remaining land holding of the company is Woolnorth. This, Australia's oldest pastoral property, is on the North West tip of the island and is open for conducted tours.

The original buildings of the town are remarkably intact with few 20th century intrusions.

There is a cable car to the top of the 'Nut' where, at nightfall, multitudes of mutton birds may be observed.

At the end of the western road lies the town of Marrawah, renowned for its surf.

ACCOMMODATION

Hawley House

Hawley Beach, 7307
Tel: (004) 28 6221
Contact: Simon Haughton

This guesthouse is conveniently situated just 20 minutes from Devonport Airport. This proximity was appreciated after a late Friday night flight from Melbourne in tempestuous winter weather.

Mansion, country house, seaside guesthouse, vineyard, chateau, a small elegant hotel, a beachside home overlooking the idyllic Rubicon Estuary - all of these.

The welcoming lights at the head of a sweeping drive and the pleasant substantial appearance of the impressive weatherboard house reflect the elegant comfort of the interior.

Your host, Simon Haughton, is an intelligent, interesting and sometimes challenging companion for a drink before dinner. He is complimented by Carlos, the talented Portugese Chef who, when out of the kitchen, has a dry wit, with just a touch of Basil Fawlty. He has a large heart and dinner was superb.

I enjoyed the huge bedroom, the capacious bathroom, the warm hospitality, the architecture, the comfortable charm and unique environment.

The house is surrounded by its own farm and vineyard, the wines from which, served at dinner, were of considerable quality.

Located on a sandy peninsula surrounded by water, the views are superb and Hawley House even enjoys its own balmy micro climate.

On a hill above the main house, there is separate accommodation in a large weatherboard cottage from which the views of the Rubicon are even more spectacular.

Breakfast is an experience enhanced by the sunny aspect of the dining room and the view over the garden.
All the rooms are large, ensuite and well appointed. It is worth the trip to Tasmania just to stay here.

Bleak House Bed & Breakfast

4 Marshall Street, Stanley, 7311
Tel: (004) 58 1428
Contact: Norma Walker

The front of this house is given over to one group of guests at a time. Your hostess, Norma Walker, lives at the back of the house.
This is a classic, comfortable B & B with a welcoming hostess.

Other accommodation in Stanley is self-contained. There are many cottages available, scattered through the town. The best area is probably The Terrace, which overlooks the bay.

- The Captain's Cottage
- Galeforth Cottage
- Harbour Master's Cottage
- Laughton House
- Monateric

At the top end of the main street is Touchwood Gift Shop and the adjacent accommodation.

- Touchwood Cottage
- The Dairy
- The Pines

The South West & Hobart

The road south to Strahan, gateway to the rugged South West, starts between Wynyard and Burnie.

The main towns on this route are Roseberry, Zeehan and Queenstown. Queenstown is famous for its naked surrounding hills, a unique spectacle at sunrise or sunset. The others are surrounded by dense mountainous bush, and any 'attractions' are related to past and present mining.

From Zeehan you may take the minor coastal road to Strahan which skirts the massive Henty Dunes for the last 20 kms.

Your first sight of water occurs as you turn into Strahan Esplanade past the gracious old private house, Ormiston.

The brilliant renovation and remaking of this quaint settlement in these spectacular surroundings has been initiated by Simon Currant, the ex-propietor of the famous Cradle Mountain Lodge. He obviously has an eye for a unique environment. The village nestles around a large protected estuary, Macquarie Harbour. Along this harbour is a continuum of historic buildings and some new developments pleasantly in keeping with the period. First there is the Customs House, occupied by Forest & Lands, Hamers Hotel and Strahan Village, a variety of newly built colonial accommodation which actually enhance the streetscape.

On the right between the road and wharf is a pleasing collection of buildings, including the interesting new visitors' centre and Morrisons Woodturners. Here also are the various cruise and seaplane booking offices.

Ocean Beach access is via an extremely rough track which thankfully is short and is worth the effort. The Strand is wild and windy and stretches miles to the north along the spectacular Henty Dunes.

Strahan's major attraction is the access it provides to the South West wilderness by the many Gordon River cruise boats. These also explore Macquarie Harbour, the second largest in Australia, from the entrance to the sea at Hells Gates, to the mirror-like Gordon River passing Sarah Island and Condemned Rock.

You may walk into the wilderness from the village or with more ease go further afield by seaplane, around Frenchman's Cap view the wild Franklin and then land on the Gordon River.

ACCOMMODATION

Hamers Hotel

Tel: (004) 71 7191

Rooms: 17

The hotel offers the usual bar facilities, but a better than average restaurant and Annabel's for cocktails. The building dates from 1930 and has recently been excellently refurbished. The rooms are reasonably priced, very comfortable, but facilities are shared. Access to tea and coffee making is also supplied communally.

Strahan Village Cottages

Tel: (004) 71 7191

Contact: Reception

Newly built in an individual variety of old styles, these supply up-market motel style accommodation in heritage vain. They include a weatherboard cottage, two storey weatherboard federation style houses, bagged and brick cottages and at the end Sarah's Stone Cottage. These all overlook a green and the water.

Franklin Manor

The Esplanade, Strahan, 7468
Tel:(004) 71 7311 Fax: (004) 71 7267
Contact: Bernadette Woods

At the top of the town, the top accommodation.
The manor is a substantial building in private grounds retaining an intimate country house feeling inside.
The excellent restaurant takes outside diners and offers Table d'hote for an extremely reasonable 28 dollars with a wide choice for each course. Enhancing the house-party feeling, an honour system operates at the bar, where you may pour your own drinks, entering them in the book. Access is available to the cellar for selection of your wine. (Tasmanian wines are rather expensive).
Bedrooms are all ensuite and pleasantly furnished with all the facilities of a four star hotel.
The sitting room is perfect with a large window overlooking the garden, lots of comfy sofas and a huge fire. Liberal use of timber throughout the building enhances the plush but rural feel of the hotel.
Professional with an excellent atmosphere.

Sample Menu - Franklin Manor

Entrée

Cream of Silverbeet Soup
Ravioli with Ocean Trout, Crayfish and Cheese Sauce
Pancetta with Shavings of Parmesan Cheese, roasted Tomatoes
Capsicum, Garlic and Onion
Fresh Octopus Salad

Main

Fillet of Beef served with Mushrooms Caps and Leek
Loin of Lamb served with Rosemary and Mung Beans
Trevalla served with Leek puree & White Cheese Sauce

Desserts

Pecan Pie
Chocolate Hazelnut Slab with lashings of Fresh Cream
Charlotte of Sundried Fruits
Poached Pears in Red Wine

Tea, Coffee & Chocolates in the Lounge

The road from Strahan to Hobart passes Queenstown in 37 kms., before entering the Franklin-Lower Gordon Wild Rivers National Park.
Wilderness surrounds you until the exit at Derwent Bridge.
Continuing to travel in forest, pass the town of Tarraleah, which services the Hydro-electric Power Station. Rolling hills and open farmland surround the towns of Ouse and Hamilton, the sheep capital of Tasmania on the Clyde River.
After Gretna turn off at Rosegarden into the lush hop gardens around Bushy Park, continue along this fertile river valley via New Norfolk to Hobart.

Derwent Bridge Chalet

Lyell Highway, Derwent Bridge, 7140
Tel: (002) 89 1125
Contact: David Fitzgibbon

This is a huge high vaulted Alpine structure with a most hospitable proprietor, David Fitzgibbon. At present the accommodation is basic motel style with 2 rooms ensuite and the other five rooms sharing two bathrooms and two lavatories. However, the wild surroundings of the place have inspired David to plan for an enormous motel/conference complex on this site.

The Guest House

Tarraleah
Contact: Mr. Lam Chau

Staying here you may enjoy all the facilities of the town, which include a pool, golf, tennis, badminton and squash.
The house is large, clean and bright. Lots of rooms, but only one ensuite. Your host is the charming Mr. Lam Chau.

"Over The Back" Holiday Cottage

Curringa, P.O. Box 39, Hamilton, 7140
Tel: (002) 86 3230 Fax: (002) 86 3318
Contact: John & Sue Parson
Rooms: s/c cottage
Cost: From $80 double

John and Sue invite you to spend a little time at their delightful holiday retreat. They promise you a warm welcome, a hearty breakfast and every home comfort. The secluded cottage is "Over the Back" of their 300 hectare farm, tucked away on the shore of picturesque Lake Meadowbank, which is safe for swimming, boating and fishing. There is a dinghy and fishing tackle (in season) for your use.

The spacious pine cottage has two bedrooms (one queen, three singles), a large living area and kitchen, bathroom, separate toilet and laundry, and boasts a log fire, large fridge and electric stove, microwave, electric blankets, doonas, linen, colour T.V., books, games, wheelchair access and a barbeque.
The farm is extensively irrigated and they carry sheep and cattle and grow various fodder and cash crops.
4 km. west of Hamilton, 80 km. from Hobart and close to Mt. Field National Park, this is an ideal base for your Tasmanian holiday.

The Cottage Collection

'Uralla', Main Road, Hamilton, 7140
Tel: (002) 86 3270
Contact: Judy Madden

For historic charm a selection of stone cottages furnished with antiques. George's, Edward's and Victoria's. All have open fires and beautiful cottage gardens. Breakfast supplies attract an extra charge.

The Hamilton Inn

Hamilton, 7140
(Licensed 1838)

Terry, your host, is the soul of enthusiastic hospitality. Hearty breakfasts and night tours of the extensive cellars.
Excellent varied accommodation. Four ensuite rooms in the attic at $65 double B & B. Two ensuite rooms and a family room on the floor below at $58 double B & B, and two double sharing a bathroom at only $45.

Hawthorn Lodge

(c. 1869)

Glenora Road, Bushy Park, 7140

Tel:(002) 86 1311 Fax: (002) 86 1311

Contact: Faye Gregory

Rooms: 4

Cost (B & B) $80 double

A neat weatherboard house in large grounds hidden in the hop gardens near to the Styx River. The vista is enhanced by the charming historic kilns built in 1867 by Ebenezer Shoobridge, the original proprietor of the Lodge.

Your hostess, Faye Gregory, a consummate professional of the bed and breakfast industry, offers 2 double rooms ensuite downstairs, each with half tester beds. There are two more double rooms upstairs which share a bathroom on the ground floor.

Deep amongst the bright green hops, this high quality establishment takes on a magical feeling in the summer time.

Redlands

R.M.B. 5075, Plenty, 7140
Tel: (002) 61 1122
Contact: Richard & Lynne Page

Have you ever driven along a road and looked down into a valley and thought 'wouldn't it be wonderful to go in there'? This was the overwhelming feeling I had when I first saw Redlands.

This property is a living museum - glorious old homestead, a terrace of workers' cottages, large barns and hop kilns, a smithy and even a shop - all evidence that the estate was once a completely self-contained village. Now it is a working property.

One comfortable suite is available in converted outbuildings adjacent to the homestead. All provisions are provided for a cooked breakfast.

The garden is part of Tasmania's Open Garden Scheme - a real country garden; huge trees, hollyhocks and roses. There is a tennis court and the grounds slope gently down to the river and its swimming holes.

Don't drive past - go in and stay.

Glen Derwent

Lyell Highway, New Norfolk, 7140
Tel: (002) 61 3244
Contact: Barbara & Malcolm Lewena

A very professional guest house offering a variety of high quality accommodation. There are 4 ensuite rooms in the main house, all spacious and comfortable and with open fires, along with the 'Servants' quarters', which has a sitting room and double & twin bedrooms and bathroom.
Outside are 2 double storey cottages, The Tank Room and The Master Stables, offering a unique ambience. A large swimming pool dominates the front garden.

Tynwald

Willow Bend Estate, P.O. Box 57 (Lyell Highway), New Norfolk, 7140
Tel: (002) 61 2667
Contact: Garry Roohan & Patricia Kelsall
Rooms: 5

This property has a grand facade and wide verandahs. The rooms downstairs are ensuite, the two double bedrooms upstairs share a bathroom. There is a large drawing room with an open fire, a tennis court and swimming pool. Furnishings are genuinely antique and the surrounding garden pleasant. The view across the lush green flats to the river is exceptionally pretty.

HOBART

A city of perfectly accessible size, hills and stunning waterways. The scenery pushing into the city is breathtaking and the centre, especially at Battery Point and Salamanca Place, a delightful human scale collection of charming old buildings, Georgian, Regency and Victorian. The Saturday Salamanca Market is colourful and interesting and the warehouses fronting the 'Place' bulge with arts and crafts interspersed with hotels, cafés and restaurants. There are easy and interesting day trips in all directions; North to Richmond or New Norfolk, South to the Tasman Peninsular with Cape Pillar and the historic, pretty but sinister Port Arthur. A ferry from the delightful waterfront hamlet of Kettering goes to Bruny Island. Another interesting route is to Huon, the apple centre of the Apple Isle, also the Huon National Park, Hastings Cave and Thermal Pool. For unforgettable views of Hobart go to Mt. Nelson.

Most of the interesting Guest Houses are in Battery Point. Take Kelly's steps from Salamanca Place and browse in the antique shops of Hampton Street.

Richmond, site of the oldest bridge in Australia is one of Tasmania's most famous historic towns. Prime amongst the many attractions are the bridge 1823, St. Luke's Anglican Church and the rectory, and the gaol built in 1825. The gaol predates Port Arthur by five years and a visit provokes deep emotion. The solitary cells 7ft. by 3ft., the flogging yard, the cell with its stout iron ring to which new prisoners were chained are in ironic juxtaposition to the charming stone quadrangle shaded by a gentle old almond tree.

ACCOMMODATION

Colonial Battery Point Manor

13 Cromwell Street, Battery Point, 7004
Tel: (002) 24 0888 Fax: (002) 31 0972
Contact: Freddy Forstner (the star attraction!)
Rooms: 8

Top of the hill, top of the range with a top view, this substantial Georgian Guest House, built in 1834, is spacious and welcoming. There are 7 huge rooms with all the facilities of a 5 Star hotel. There is a guest sitting room with video, an guest lounge and a garden with an additional 9½ sq. family cottage.
Breakfast and dinner are offered in the Bavarian 'Dungeon' downstairs.
The accommodation is very reasonably priced for the quality offered in such a convenient and prestigious position.

Ascot Guest House

Colville Street, Battery Point, 7004
Tel: (002) 24 2434
Contact: Margaret Chalkley

Hospitality is giving and greeting; the hostess, Margaret Chalkley, does both naturally. Two ensuite rooms are available well furnished with both T.V. and bar fridge. No smoking. The sun room is a bonus in the winter.

Avon Court

4 Colville Street, Battery Point, 7004
Tel: (002) 23 4837

Avon Court is a clean good value motel at the centre of Battery Point. The large suites offer good family value.

Panache Restaurant

Salanarra Place, Hobart, 7000

At the far end of Salanarra Place, a bright and breezy restaurant with bright and breezy staff seems to be always open.
Reasonable prices for an extensive variety of fresh food for the vegetarian or carnivore, the pasta lover or sophisticate with a jaded palate desperate to try something new.
Try it. Not fine dining, but satisfaction guaranteed.

Crabtree House

(c.1879)
Crabtree Road, Crabtree, 7109
Tel: (002) 66 4227
Contact: Peter & Gianna Gavagna
Rooms: 3

South of Hobart, on the edge of the Huon Valley, this house is a simple large white weatherboard heated by slow combustion fires, and has built a reputation on the excellent Northern Italian food offered. Only 3 rooms, two doubles ensuite and a twin with its own bathroom.
Breakfast on the verandah in Summer is a peaceful delight, dinner a gourmet affair.

Sample Menu - Crabtree House

Gianna comes from the Veneto region in Northern Italy and her food is typically Venetian, using the freshest of ingredients. Depending on market availability, the menu might be:

Entrée

Risotto with Tasmanian Scollops & Rosemary

or

Minestrone with a dash of Chilli and Pesto

Main

Grain fed Chicken with Basil and Sun Dried Tomatoes

or

Trevalla with Herbs and extra Virgin Olive Oil

Main course served with fresh garden vegetables Venetian style

Dessert

Tiramisu

or

Fresh berries in season with cold Sabayon Sauce

Coffee

Pre-dinner drinks - Tasmanian wines - ports, liqueurs, etc. are available

Prospect House

Cambridge Road, Richmond, 7025
Tel:(002) 62 2207 Fax: (002) 62 2551
Contact: Mike Buscombe
Rooms: 11
Cost, Double: $96 room only, $116 bed & breakfast

As Richmond is entered from Hobart, an imposing residence is encountered on the left at the edge of town.

This Georgian building is one of Tasmania's best guest houses and is approached from the highway over a rickety wooden bridge. Its reputation is based on the superb cuisine of the restaurant and the ambience of the house. Three intimate dining rooms, a bar and reception occupy the ground floor; upstairs are staff quarters. Guests are accommodated in the converted buildings behind the house.

These buildings surround the sheltered courtyard with its pergola covered in Glory vine. The stables are two storey and each suite has double doors either to the courtyard or, upstairs, to a verandah.

The rooms are lined in pine and have private facilities. Brass beds and televisions are in every suite. One family cottage is also available. Downstairs is a kitchen with slate floor and pot-belly stove and the bathroom. Upstairs the accommodation comprises of one double room and a large twin.

Sample Menu - Prospect House

Soup of the day

Entree

Shaslik of Mussels bacon and nori served on fried spinach leaves with a Mediterranean style sauce of sundried tomatoes garlic vermouth and red onion

Main Course

Eye Fillet of Beef wrapped in Jarlsberg Cheese Spinach and Crispy Bacon oven baked placed on a Swiss crouton then complimented by a rich red wine and wild mushroom stock sauce

Dessert

Chocolate Cherry and Walnut Marquis - Rich chocolate cream cherries and walnuts are combined to make a delicious dessert served with rum macerated oranges and coffee Anglaise

Daisy Bank Cottages

Daisy Bank, Richmond, 7025
Tel: (002) 62 2390
Contact: Dinky Jones
Rooms: 2 s/c cottages
Cost (B & B): $95 double, $20 each extra person

Behind Prospect House, two units in a converted 1830 sandstone barn. A very comfortable and spacious environment with slow combustion heaters. Extras include free breakfast provisions, T.V., a microwave and a very jolly helpful hostess. The two bedrooms are upstairs with views over Richmond and the Coal River Valley.

Laurel Cottage

(c.1830)
15 Wellington Street, Richmond, 7025
Tel: (002) 62 2250 or (002) 62 2357
Contact: Sandra Barwick

Just beyond the town over the old bridge, this house has been fastidiously decorated and supplies two bedrooms. The floor boards groan on cue and the open fires give a friendly flickery warmth. The garden is a secluded haven, with a laurel tree, and a private tennis court is available.
Breakfast provisions are supplied.

The Dispensary

Edward Street, Richmond, 7025
Tel: (002) 62 2226
Contact: Mrs. Starr Oclee
Rooms: 3
Cost (B & B) $115 double, $20 each extra person

Off the main road on Edward Street leading to St. Lukes. A one bedroom sandstone cottage with a pretty deck overlooking the garden, the Cole River and open country. This garden is shared with the rectory 50 secluded metres away. Tennis court available.

The East Coast to Launceston

The route now takes the east coast road to St. Mary's before turning inland to Launceston.

From Richmond to Buckland, investigate the old Buckland Inn and arrive at the coast at Orford after crossing the Prosser River by the timber bridge. The road on to Swansea is 60 kms. of rural coastal pleasure, through farmland and forest with glimpses of sea and islands. Travelling is easy on this well made road.

Swansea is a pretty little town of just 500 people and is dominated by Morris's General Store. Of interest is Morey's Mill, a restored black wattle bark mill. Spikey Bridge and Spikey Beach. Crayfish and restaurants here.

From Swansea the road passes the Freycinet Vineyard before the turn to Coles Bay. The vineyard makes a superb Pinot Noir and Chardonnay plus an unusual Riesling blend. Coles Bay settlement is no picturesque fishing village and is in itself a disappointment, but the natural beauty of the Freycinet National Park and Wine Glass Bay are unsurpassed in Tasmania.

Bicheno, a small fishing village, is the next settlement to the north. The granite coastline offers wonderful views, a blow hole, and the Diamond Island nature reserve, which is home to Fairy Penguins.

From St. Mary's it is an easy drive to Launceston via Longford.

The North east corner of Tasmania is sparsely settled, but worth a detour for its scenery and the Pipers Brook Vineyard.

ACCOMMODATION

Holkham House & Miranda's Cottage

Tasman Highway, Orford, 7190
Tel: (002) 25 1248
Contact: Anne Saunders
Rooms: s/c cottage (sleeps up to 14)
Cost (B & B): $95 double, $25 each extra adult
$12.50 children under 14

Set on ten acres next door to the golf club and opposite a pleasant beach, both houses offer self contained accommodation.

Holkham, the larger, is furnished in simple country style and will accommodate fourteen people if the bunks in the games room are utilized.

Miranda's is smaller with just a double and a twin.

Tennis court available and breakfast provisions supplied.

Lester Cottages

Gordon Street, Swansea, 7190
Tel: (002) 57 8494
Contact: Dianne Sinclair
Rooms: s/c cottage
Cost (B & B) $95 - $110 double

These units are set in a broad open expanse of garden close to the beach, with an uninterrupted view of Coles Bay and the Freycinet National Park.

Peter and Helen Morey offer five self contained units of varying design and size, with small dry stone walled gardens and plenty of wood for the slow combustion stoves.

Pine Cottage and Cedar each have 2 bedrooms. The Hay Loft is small with a charming balcony looking out to sea. Oak is a 'duplex' containing a large and a small apartment.

Schoulens House

1 Waterloo Road, Swansea, 7190
Tel: (002) 57 8564
Contact: Terry Fidler

This offers excellent value and is the closest accommodation to the beach. Terry Fidler is very friendly and naturally welcoming and claims he is an innovative and experienced chef (reports, please) with an inclination to French cuisine with an Asian influence.
There are four rooms ensuite, one with a sea view. Refrigerators, T.V. and coffee making facilities.
Terry has made great efforts to provide a pleasant, comfortable environment with, I suspect, little cash and we wish him success to match his enthusiasm.

Meredith House

(c.1853)
15 Noyes Street, Swansea, 7190
Tel: (002) 57 8119
Contact: Clive Olbery
Rooms: 5
Cost: $75 double, $55 single

Peacefully situated on the hill of the town, this gracious Georgian house built of mellow handmade bricks affords stylish accommodation.
Downstairs is a sitting room and dining room with a country house feeling and one suite. The suite has its own sitting room with T.V., two bedrooms, a bathroom and access to the back verandah. Upstairs rooms 1 & 6 are ensuite, 2 has a double and single bed and there is one further double and two twin rooms. Bedroom furnishings are comfortable, but

without the genuine antique 'style' of the ground floor. The bathrooms are grouped at one end of the house.
All is clean and bright as a new pin and the housekeeping is excellent. Dinner is offered by arrangement and you have the choice of two menus:

1. Taste of Tasmania includes oysters, salmon and local berries.
2. Farmhouse roasts and wholesome country fare.

Redcliffe House

Tasman Highway, Swansea, 7190
Tel: (002) 57 8557
Contact: Doug & Jocelyn Stugle
Rooms: 3

Slightly out of town to the north, this two storey weatherboard is a true haven, quiet and secluded in a shady garden. Jocelyn and Doug are lovely people and the furnishings are an eclectic mix of taste and objét trouvée. Jocelyn is a little shy about her cooking, but will supply an excellent dinner if persuaded.
There are 3 main bedrooms, all ensuite with electric blankets and T.V.'s. The double room upstairs has, in addition, a comfortable sitting area. There is also a sitting room, dining room and verandah, available to guests downstairs.
It all comes together with a warm ambience.

Bicheno Hideaway

87 Harveys Farm Road, Bicheno, 7215
Tel: (003) 75 1312 Fax: (003) 75 1312
Contact: Helmut & Danijela Rademacher
Rooms: 3 s/c chalets
Cost: $69 double, $15 each extra adult, $5 each child

Before reaching Bicheno, 3 kms. south a beachside property offers three unique chalets in six acres of waterfront bushland.

Of unusual semi-circular design, they have large windows and broad raised verandahs to enhance the enjoyment of the ocean vistas.

These chalets are fully self-contained; one sleeps four people and the others accommodate six.

The surrounding bush is home to owls, possums, bandicoots, wombats, wallabies and Tasmanian Devils.

Diamond Island Resort

69 Tasman Highway, Bicheno, 7215
Tel: (003) 75 1161
Contact: Liz Brown

Arriving late on a winter's night 'ghost hosted' properties do not offer easy access, so I was lucky to find this welcoming well run motel. There is lots of garden area, a swimming pool, tennis court and it is right on the beach. The food was generous, simple and well cooked. A good value establishment, especially with kids. It has an uninterrupted view over the ocean. Waking up to watch the sunrise over the ocean is the best way to start anyone's day. Stay in the "Wessex" studio apartment.

The Old Rosary

Longford Hall, Longford, 7301
Tel:(003) 91 1662
Contact: Rose Falkiner

The Old Rosary at Longford Hall, an old monastery, is a conversion of the buildings previously used as stables and bakery.

This is top drawer accommodation, spacious and open plan with lovely antique furnishings.

The open tread stairs lead up to the two bedrooms and a balcony, again beautifully furnished. The bathroom is central on this floor and most elegantly presented with hand-painted flowers decorating the walls.

Fresh eggs and fruit are supplied ad-lib in season, and the proprietor, Rose Falkiner, allows use of the tennis court.

Rose is a keen and knowledgeable gardener and organises garden tours in the area.

Brickendon Historic Cottages

Wellington Street, Longford, 7301
Tel:(003) 91 1251 Fax: (003) 91 2073
Contact: Louise Archer
Rooms: 2 s/c cottages
Cost: $88 and $98 double, $20 each extra adult

This impressive estate dates from 1823. It boasts a large country house surrounded by an English garden - a small park with mature specimen trees. In addition it has its own village on the property with a chapel and shop, barns, shearing shed, dairy, smithy and farm cottage.

Two self contained cottages are available in the garden/park around the homestead.

Coachmans is close to the main house and sleeps five people. Open fires and lots of timber, beams, shiny floor boards and creaky stairs. Two bedrooms are upstairs and one down. The kitchen has all modern appliances and the cottage is set in its own pretty garden.

A little way off on the fringe of the 'park' is the charming secluded Gardener's Cottage. This has been brilliantly renovated and it is impossible to detect that the interior is mostly new. Comprising a double bedroom and small sitting

room with an open fire, a well equipped kitchen and great bathroom with old brass fittings. Amazingly the roof has its original iron over perfectly preserved shingles.
Breakfast provisions are supplied and a hamper may be provided for dinner. There are three good restaurants in the area, though none of these are in Longford, 3 kms. away.

Racecourse Hotel

(c.1840. Now delicensed)
114 Marlborough Street, Longford, 7301
Tel: (003) 91 2352 Fax: (003) 91 2430
Contact: Mary & Doug Rutledge
Rooms: 5
Cost: $65 single, $90 double, $25 each extra person

This is an attractive, well established top quality guest house, large and professionally operated. two sitting rooms downstairs with T.V.
Breakfast only is served in the dining room, so again there is that drive to a 'local' restaurant for dinner.
All rooms are ensuite and the tariff includes full cooked breakfast.

LAUNCESTON

On the north coast, first settled in 1865. This is a substantial city on another of those beautiful Tasmanian estuaries, providing perfect protected anchorage.
The city lies on the Tamar River 50 kms. from the open sea at the confluence of the North and South Esk Rivers.
If you can drag yourself away from the casino and golf club, the main natural attraction of the town only a few minutes from the centre is the Cataract Gorge. Here the South Esk River spills down into the Tamar. There is a natural park, and views of this and the gorge are facilitated by a chair lift. Charming old buildings like the Customs House on the esplanade abound. The small human scale of Launceston makes sightseeing an easy pleasure.

ACCOMMODATION

The Shambles

121-127 Balfour Street, Launceston, 7250
Tel: (003) 34 2231 Fax: (003) 34 2696
Contact: Helen Poynder
Rooms: 4 s/c cottages
Cost (B & B) $115 double, $25 each extra person

In a small garden off the road, a row of five connected cottages on the edge of the city centre. All are snug with fires, four poster beds and individual décor. They comprise a sitting room, bedroom and large bathroom with a central bath.
They are named according to style; English, Scottish, Welsh, etc.

The Old Bakery Inn

(c.1870)
Cnr. York & Margaret Streets, Launceston, 7250
Tel:(003) 31 7900 Fax: (003) 31 7756
Contact: Miss Rhana Crago
Rooms: 21
Cost: $55 single, $65 double/twin,
$10 each extra person

Sixteen individually designed rooms with antique furnishings and private facilities. Some rooms have balconies and some overlook a garden courtyard.
A separate self contained cottage known as Bakers Cottage is available.
Breakfast not included, but is served in the dining room, which is a fully licensed restaurant in the evening.

York Mansions

9 - 11 York Street, Launceston, 7250
Tel: (003) 34 2933 Fax: (003) 34 2870
Contact: Mike Angell & Christine Jones
Rooms: 5 s/c apartments
Cost (B & B): $115 single/double/twin,
$25 each extra person

In the city, five lavish apartments - 3 two bedroom and 2 three bedroom. Sleeping areas are all situated at the quiet rear of the building. There is access and use of the garden and summer house.
The Duke of York, Duchess of York, the Countess and Baroness are all extremely grand. We loved Gamekeepers, tucked into the base of the house with its low ceilings, rustic feel and direct access to the garden.
Breakfast provisions supplied.

Alice's Place

17 York Street, Launceston, 7250
Tel: (003) 34 2231 Fax: (003) 34 2696
Contact: Helen Poynder
Rooms: s/c cottage
Cost (B & B): $115 double, $25 each extra person

A special, romantic experience. Eccentric antique furnishings embellish a charming cottage in an English garden near the city centre. Two bedrooms, one with four poster. Breakfast provisions supplied.

Freshwater Point

56 Nobelius Drive, Legana, 7277
Tel: (003) 30 2200
Contact: Laurie Thomas
Rooms: 3 self contained cottages

Travel north along the western side of the Tamar to Freshwater Point and our favourite house in Tasmania. A house full of sunshine and warmth. A house of style reflecting confident taste with a disregard for interior designer themes. An eclectic mix of loved objects chosen by people of natural talent with an eye for quality. Full, but not fussy. Sophisticated, but comfortable. Damask covered sofas and a comfortable cat.

Accommodation in the house is of two double rooms which share a huge bathroom.

There are three tasteful, comfortable, attractively designed cottages in the grounds. Fully self contained down to the T.V. and microwave. The Stables has a king size bed and a twin room.

Dinner for all accommodation by arrangement, the view has already been arranged.

Tasmania

BARRINGTON TAS. 7306

Glencoe, Sheffield Main Road
Tel: (004) 92 3267

BEAUTY POINT TAS. 7270

Irrewarra, 61-67 West Tamar Highway
Tel: (003) 83 4372

BEECHFORD TAS. 7252

Wendy's Beach House, 4 The Esplanade
Tel: (003) 82 2235
Holm Lodge, 24 Victoria Esplanade

BELLERIVE TAS. 7018

Tel: (002) 44 3656
Contact: Desmond & Miriam Cooper
Rooms: 3, all ensuite (all Q/size beds)
Cost: Bed & Breakfast - From $65 double, $50 single, $25 each additional person. Dinner $18 per head
Special family rates • *Please enquire re. children*

BERRIEDALE TAS. 7011

Villa Vera, 14 Maritana Place
Tel: (002) 49 2759

BICHENO TAS. 7215

Andali House, 25 Tribe Street
Tel: (003) 75 1146

Bicheno Berries, Tasman Highway (P.O. Box 34)
Tel: (003) 75 1481
Contact: Dianne & David Williams
Rooms: s/c suite, sleeps 4
Cost: $60-$75 double

Bicheno Gaol House, Cnr. James & Burgess Streets
Tel: (003) 75 1430 or (003) 75 1250
Contact: Arthur Pearce

Bicheno Hideaway, 87 Harveys Farm Road
Tel: (003) 75 1312 Fax: (003) 75 1312
Contact: Helmut & Danijela Rademacher (V)
Rooms: 3 s/c chalets
Cost: Per night - $69 couple, $5 per child extra, $15 per extra adult

Coombend Cottage, Coombend (RSD 14, Swansea, 7190)
Tel: (002) 57 8256 Fax: (002) 57 8484
Contact: John & Jo Fenn-Smith
Rooms: s/c cottage, sleeps 6
Cost: $85 double

Diamond Island Resort, 69 Tasman Highway
Tel: (003) 75 1161 (V)
Contact: Liz Brown

Greenlawn Cottage, Tasman Highway
Tel: (003) 75 1114
Contact: Mrs. Julie Lyne
Rooms: s/c cottage - 3 rooms
Cost: $75 for 2 adults, $20 per extra adult. 25/12/93 - 30/4/93 $85 for 2 adults, children $10
Provisions for full breakfast provided

Tasmania

BLACK RIVER TAS. 7321

Gateforth Cottage, Gateforth
Tel: (004) 58 3230 Fax: (004) 58 3237
Contact: Mrs. Christine Medwin
Rooms: 2 s/c cottages
Cost: Bed & Breakfast per couple per night - $95, additional adult $35, additional child $20
Full kitchen facilities in cottages • Several restaurants 10 mins. drive

BLACKWALL TAS. 7275

The Old School House, 103 Blackwall Road (RDE 56, Deviot, 7275)
Tel: (003) 94 4969
Contact: Mrs. Caroline Bartlett
Rooms: s/c cottage with 2 bedrooms and private bathroom
Cost: $70 per couple, $15 extra adults, $10 extra children

BOAT HARBOUR TAS. 7321

Country Garden Cottages, RSD 815 Port Road
Tel: (004) 45 1233

Killynaught Cottages, Bass Highway
Tel: (004) 45 1041 Fax: (004) 45 1041
Contact: Ruth & Glenn Deans
Rooms: 3 s/c cottages, each sleep 4-5
Cost: $88 double

Nanmay Cottage, Bass Highway
Tel: (004) 45 1184

BOTHWELL TAS. 7030

Bothwell Grange, Alexander Street
Tel: (002) 59 5556 Fax: (002) 59 5556
Contact: Paul & Anne Hensall
Rooms: 7 ensuite
Cost: $65/double room only, $7 per head continental breakfast, $12 per head cooked breakfast
A-la-carte dinner menu • no children • no smoking in dining rooms or bedrooms

Mrs. Woods Farmhouse, Dennistoun
Tel: (002) 59 5612 Fax: (002) 59 5567
Contact: Felicity & Henry Edgell
Rooms: s/c cottage, sleeps 8
Cost: $65 double
Wheelchair access

Whites Cottage, Queen Street
Tel: (002) 59 5651 Fax: (002) 59 5718
Contact: Jenny G. Denholm
Rooms: s/c cottage, sleeps 6
Cost: $85 double, $20 each extra adult
Breakfast ingredients supplied

BREADALBANE TAS. 7258

Greycliffe, RSD 527 Midlands Highway
Tel: (003) 44 7667
Contact: Jo & Tony Bilton
Rooms: s/c cottage, sleeps 5
Cost: $80 double

BRIDPORT TAS. 7262

Bridairre Modern B & B, Frances Street
Tel: (003) 56 1438

Jensenvilla Host Farm, Waterhouse Road
Tel: (003) 56 1179

BRIGHTON TAS. 7030

Stonefield, Broadmarsh Road
Tel: (002) 68 1385 or (002) 68 1902

The Cottage, Bonorong Wild Life Park, Briggs Road
Tel: (002) 68 1184 Fax: (002) 68 1811
Contact: Barbara Jones

BRUNY ISLAND TAS. 7150

Aventure Bay Holiday Home, Quiet Corner, Adventure Bay
Tel: (002) 43 6169

Barnes Bay Villas, Lot 1, Barnes Bay
Tel: (002) 34 6840

Christopher Lumsden Cottage, Great Bay
Tel: (002) 25 2250

Coolangatta Cottage, Cloudy Bay Road, Lunawanna
Tel: (002) 93 1164

Horizons Seaside Accommodation, Main Road, Adventure Bay
Tel: (002) 93 1325

Karana Holiday Farm, Barnes Bay
Tel: (002) 25 1383

Kelly's Lookout, Bull Bay Road, Dennes Point
Tel: (002) 60 6212

Lyndenne Cottage, Barnes Bay
Tel: (002) 60 6264
Contact: Ted Mann
Rooms: s/c holiday cottage
Cost: $65 per couple, $5 each additional person (maximum 5 adults & 1 baby)
Cot supplied ◆ Dinner available on request (adjacent to restaurant)

Mavista Cottages, Adventure Bay
Tel: (002) 93 1347

Mill Cottage, Cloudy Bay Road, Lunawanna
Tel: (002) 93 1156

Rosebud Cottage, Lorkins Road, Adventure Bay
Tel: (002) 93 1156

The Cosy Corner, Adventure Bay
Tel: (002) 93 1347

The Shed, 'Morella', Adventure Bay
Tel: (002) 93 1131

BURNE TAS. 7320

Glen Osborne House, 8 Aileen Crescent
Tel: (004) 31 9866

BUSHY PARK TAS. 7140

'Hawthorn Lodge' Colonial Accommodation, Glenora Road
Tel: (002) 86 1311 Fax: (002) 86 1311
Contact: Fay & Brian Gregory
Rooms: 2, both ensuite
Cost: Bed & Cooked Breakfast - $80 per couple Ⓥ
Dinner by arrangement on arrival ◆ no children ◆ no smoking

Tasmania

CAMBRIDGE TAS. 7170

Barilla House, RSD 216 Denholms Road (P.O. Box 18, Rosny Park, 7018)
Tel: (002) 48 5654 Fax: (002) 48 5677
Contact: Ron & Nalda Limb
Rooms: 2 room suite, sleeps 5
Cost: Bed & Breakfast - $75-$85

CAMPANIA TAS. 7026

Elmshurst, Cnr. Estate & White Kangaroo Roads
Tel: (002) 62 4209
Contact: Lindsay & Marilyn Richley
Rooms: 2, ensuite
Cost: Bed & Breakfast - $50 single, $70 double
No smoking

CAMPBELL TOWN TAS. 7210

Baskerville Hall, 206 Macquarie Road
Tel: (003) 81 1116
Contact: Henry & Kay Jacobs
Rooms: 4
Cost: Double - B & B $85, D.B & B $155. Children under 9 - $15 plus meals

The Broadwater on Macquarie, 'Barton'
Tel: (003) 98 5114 Fax: (003) 98 5170
Contact: Melissa Youl
Rooms: 3 (bathroom, bedroom & living with bed)
Cost: Per night - $60 double, $10 each extra person. Breakfast requirements extra - $5 continental, $7 full
Great fishing

The Gables, 35 High Street
Tel: (003) 81 1347

CARRICK TAS. 7291

Hawthorn Villa Guest House, Bishopsbourne Road
Tel: (003) 93 6150

CASTLE FORBES BAY TAS. 7116

Castle Forbes Bay House, Meredith Road
Tel: (002) 97 1610

CHUDLEIGH TAS. 7304

Alum Cliffs Homestead, "Elton-Vale", Mersey Hill Road
Tel: (003) 63 6149

Bentley Cottage, RSD 3010 Mole Creek Road
Tel: (003) 63 6131
Contact: Valerie Cramp
Rooms: s/c cottage - 2 bedrooms (sleep 5)
Cost: $55 double, $15 per extra person, $8 children under 12
Breakfast provisions included ◆ *No smoking* ◆ *Dinner by arrangement*

COLES BAY TAS. 7215

Coles Bay Holiday Villas, Coles Bay Road, Hepburn Point
Tel: (002) 57 0102

Freycinet Camping Ground, Freycinet National Park
Tel: (002) 57 0107

Jessie's Cottage, Esplanade
Tel: (002) 57 0143

Swan River Cottages, Swanwick
Tel: (002) 57 0216

Tasmania

CRABTREE TAS. 7109

Crabtree House, Crabtree Road
Tel: (002) 66 4227 ⓥ
Contact: Peter & Gianna Gavagna

CYGNET TAS. 7112

Lower Bagot Farm, RSD 1117 Wolfes Road, Gardners Bay
Tel: (002) 95 1615

The Deepings, RSD 868 Nichols Rivulet
Tel: (002) 95 1398
Contact: Roslyn & Adrian Hunt
Rooms: 1 s/c cottage, 1 s/c suite, each sleeps 4-6
Cost: $72-76 double

Wilfred Lodge, 22 Channel Highway
Tel: (002) 95 1604

DELORAINE TAS. 7304

Bonneys' (Farm), Off Weetah Road (P.O. Box 24)
Tel: (003) 62 2122 Fax: (003) 62 3566
Contact: James A. Bonney
Rooms: 3 s/c units, 1 Guest house unit with ensuite
Cost: Bed & Breakfast - $60 double, $17 each extra person.
All meals available

Bonney's Inn, 17 West Parade
Tel: (003) 62 2974

Bowerbank Mill, Bass Highway
Tel: (003) 62 2628 Fax: (003) 62 3586
Contact: Jane Maxwell
Rooms: 2 cottages, ensuite
Cost: $90 double, including continental breakfast. Dinner, $30 per person

Granada, RSD 1053 Mole Creek Road
Tel: (003) 62 2621

Millers Cottage, Bass Highway
Tel: (003) 62 2628 Fax: (003) 62 3586
Contact: Jane Maxwell

The Chimney House, Bass Highway
Tel: (003) 62 2628 Fax: (003) 62 3586
Contact: Jane Maxwell

Tierview Cottage, 125 Emu Bay Road
Tel: (003) 62 2377

DERWENT BRIDGE TAS. 7140

Derwent Bridge Chalet, Lyell Highway
Tel: (002) 89 1125 (V)
Contact: David Fitzgibbon

DESOLATION BAY TAS.

Huon Charm Cottage, Esperance Coast Road
Tel: (002) 97 6314

DEVONPORT TAS. 7310

Daisy Cottage, 16 Mersey Road
Tel: (004) 27 2267
Contact: Chris Gurr
Rooms: 2 cottages (both 2 bedrooms)
Cost: With continental breakfast provisions - $68 double, $15 extra person, $6 child
Cooking facilities available in cottages

Rosalie Cottage, c/o Post Office, Don, 7310
Tel: (004) 24 1560 or (004) 24 5797
Contact: Heather & Maureen Rawding

Trelawney, 6 Chalmers Lane
Tel: (004) 24 3263
Contact: Bronwen Dickinson
Rooms: 1 suite (2 bedrooms, 1 lounge, 1 kitchenette, 1 bathroom
Cost: Including cooked breakfast - $45 single, $68 double, $22 extra adult, $12 child, $5 cot
Dinner by prior arrangement

DILSTON TAS. 7252

Rostella, RSD 915 Rostella Road
Tel: (003) 28 1237

DOUGLAS RIVER TAS. 7215

Douglas River Cabin, Tasman Highway
Tel: (003) 75 1164

DOVER TAS. 7117

Island Holiday Apartments, Jetty Road
Tel: (002) 98 1396

DUNALLEY TAS. 7177

Fulham Shearers Quarters, "Fulham"
Tel: (002) 53 5247 Fax: (002) 53 5247
Contact: Penny & Sandy Gray
Rooms: s/c cottage, sleeps 8
Cost: $70 double

ELIZABETH TOWN TAS. 7304

Ashgrove Farmhouse, RSD 272
Tel: (003) 68 1137
Contact: Connie Bennett
Roome: 3 bedrooms/lounge/sunroom/kitchen/bathroom/toilet/laundry
Cost: $60 per double per night, $10 each extra person

ELLENDALE TAS. 7140

Hillcrest Holiday Cabins, Dillons Road
Tel: (002) 88 1199

Hopfield Cottages, Main Road
Tel: (002) 88 1223 Fax: (002) 88 1207
Contact: Anne & John Trigg
Rooms: 2 s/c cottages
Cost: Bed & Cooked Breakfast - $80 double
Cottages 100 years old, fully restored

EVANDALE TAS. 7212

Coral Cottage, 6 Nile Road
Tel: (003) 91 8376

Greg and Gill's Place, 35a Collins Street
Tel: (003) 91 8248

Solomon Cottage, High Street
Tel: (003) 91 8331

FLINDERS ISLAND TAS. 7255

Boat Harbour Beach House, Boat Harbour
Tel: (003) 59 9709

Carnsdale Holiday Home, Memana
Tel: (003) 59 9718 or (003) 59 9752

Emita Beach Cottage, Lot 10 Elliott Street, Emita
Tel: (003) 59 4539

Felicity's Cottage, Holloway Street, Lady Barron
Tel: (003) 59 3641

Greenglades Host Farm, Fairhaven Road, Emita
Tel: (003) 59 8506

Lady Barron Holiday House, Franklin Parade, Lady Barron
Tel: (003) 59 3555

Lisa's Cottage, Whitemark
Tel: (003) 59 6530

FLOWERDALE TAS. 7325

Alcheringa, RSD 62A
Tel: (004) 45 4255

FORT TAS. 7310

The Wattles, Pumping Station Road
Tel: (004) 28 2242
Contact: Rob & Dot Tuck
Rooms: 2
Cost: $55 double, $35 single
Dinner on application ◆ *No smoking*

FRANKFORD TAS. 7275

Fernhill Host Farm, Holwell Road
Tel: (003) 96 1283

FRANKLIN TAS. 7113

Franklin Lodge, Main Road
Tel: (002) 66 3506

GEEVESTON TAS. 7116

Hartz Cottage, Arve Road
Tel: (002) 97 1724 Fax: (002) 97 1117
Contact: Adriana Burgess
Rooms: 5 and s/c
Cost: $60 per double, $10 each extra person, $5 each child under 13
No smoking

Tasmania

GEORGE TOWN TAS. 7253

The Grove/Nanna's Cottage, P.O. Box 68
Tel: (003) 82 1336
Contact: Mrs. Chlo Martin
Rooms: s/c unit
Cost: $55 double off season, $65 double in season, $10 each extra adult, $5 each child
No smoking

GLEBE TAS. 7000

Wellington Lodge, Scott Street
(002) 31 0614

GOLDEN VALLEY TAS. 7304

Anglers Inn, RSD 945 Lake Highway
Tel: (003) 69 5280
Contact: David & Kerry McMeniman
Rooms: s/c cottage, sleeps 4-6
Cost: $70-$80 double

GRETNA TAS. 7140

Norton Mandeville, Lyell Highway
Tel: (002) 86 3209

HAGLEY TAS. 7292

Hagley House, Station Lane
Tel: (003) 92 2366

HAMILTON TAS. 7140

McCauley's Cottage, Main Road
Tel: (002) 34 1158 or (002) 78 2868

Old School House, Lyell Highway
Tel: (002) 86 3292

Over the Back Holiday Cottage, Lyell Highway (P.O. Box 39)
Tel: (002) 86 3230
Contact: John & Sue Parson (V)

The Cottage Collection (Edward's, Emma's, George's, Victoria's), 'Uralla', Main Road
Tel: (002) 86 3270 (V)
Contact: Judy Madden

HAWLEY BEACH TAS. 7307

Bardon Holiday Flats, 16 Dumbleton Street
Tel: (004) 28 6744

Hawley House
Tel: (004) 28 6221
Contact: Simon Houghton (V)

HOBART TAS. 7000

Ascot House Guest House, Colville Street, Battery Point, 7004
Tel: (002) 24 2434
Contact: Margaret Chalkley (V)

Avon Court Holiday Apartments, 4 Colville Street, Battery Point, 7004 (V)
Tel: (002) 23 4837

Barrack Street Colonial Cottage, 55 Barrack Street (P.O. Box 851)
Tel: (002) 25 4235 Fax: (002) 25 0317
Contact: Chris Downie

Barton Cottage, 72 Hampden Road, Battery Point, 7004
Tel: (002) 24 1606

Battery Point Guest House, 7 McGregor Street, Battery Point, 7004
Tel: (002) 24 2111 Fax: (002) 24 2111
Contact: Jeff Gordon
Rooms: 5 ensuite
Cost: Bed & Breakfast - $95 double, $75 single, $20 each extra adult, $15 child under 3/cot
No Smoking

Brooker Cottage, 327 Brooker Avenue
Tel: (002) 23 6181

Central City Backpackers, 138 Collins Street
Tel: (002) 24 2404

Colonial Battery Point Manor, 13 Cromwell Street, Battery Point, 7004
Tel: (002) 24 0888 Fax: (002) 31 0972
Contact: Zsa Zsa Beauchamp & Freddie Forstner
Rooms: 8, all ensuite Ⓥ
Cost: Bed & Cooked Breakfast - $105 single, $20 each additional person
No smoking ◆ *Dinner available upon request*

Colville Cottage, 32 Mona Street, Battery Point, 7004
Tel: (002) 23 6968

Cove Cottage Penthouse, 7 Murray Street
Tel: (002) 23 3553

Cromwell Cottage, 6 Cromwell Street, Battery Point, 7004
Tel: (002) 23 6734

Crows Nest, 2 Liverpool Crescent
Tel: (002) 34 9853

Islington Private Elegant Hotel, 321 Davey Street
Tel: (002) 23 3900

Jane Franklin Hall, 6 Elboden Street, South Hobart, 7004
Tel: (002) 23 2000 Fax: (002) 24 0598
Contact: Mrs. E. A. Humes
Rooms: 180
Cost: Bed & Breakfast - $28 single, $10 extra person
Dinner available if pre-booked

Lenna of Hobart, 20 Runnymede Street, Battery Point, 7004
(002) 32 3900

Memory Lane Cottages, 130-132 Brisbane Street
Tel: (002) 54 1264

Montrose House, 76 Montrose Road
Tel: (002) 72 2264

Portsea Terrace, 54-62 Montpelier Retreat, Battery Point, 7004
Tel: (002) 34 1616
Contact: Mr. F.E. Smith
Rooms: 10 s/c apartments, all ensuite
Cost: $65 single, $75 double

The Lodge on Elizabeth, 249 Elizabeth Street
Tel: (002) 31 3830

The Star Inn, 63 Goulburn Street
Tel: (002) 43 9017

Warwick Cottages, 119-121 Warwick Street
Tel: (002) 54 1264

HOWDEN TAS. 7054

Kesterkin Lodge, 420 Brightwater Road
Tel: (002) 67 2344

JERICHO TAS. 7030

Commandant's Cottage, "Park Farm"
Tel: (002) 54 4115 Fax: (002) 54 4137
Contact: Graeme & Jill Salmon
Rooms: s/c cottage (up to 9 persons)
Cost: $85 per couple, $20 each additonal person

Ellesmere Cottage, Ellesmere Road
Tel: (002) 54 4140 Fax: (002) 54 4134
Contact: Mary & Greg Taylor
Rooms: s/c cottage, sleeps 6
Cost: $65 double

Rose Hill QuarterS, "Rose Hill"
Tel: (002) 54 4141
Contact: Clare Headlam
Rooms: s/c colonian cottage (sleeps 6)
Cost: $75 double, $15 each extra person

KEMPTON TAS. 7030

Wilmot Arms Inn, Main Road
Tel: (002) 49 1272

KETTERING TAS. 7155

Herons Rise Vineyard, Saddle Road
Tel: (002) 67 4339
Contact: Gerry & Sue White
Rooms: 2 double, both ensuite
Cost: $50 single, $65 double
No smoking • Dinner available

Old Kettering Inn, Ferry Road
Tel: (002) 67 4426 Fax: (002) 67 4884
Contact: Sandra Baldwin
Rooms: 2 (1 ensuite, 1 private bathroom)
Cost: $69 double, including full cooked breakfast
No smoking • Dinner by prior arrangement

KING ISLAND TAS. 7256

Devil's Gap Retreat, Charles Street, Currie
Tel: (004) 62 1180

Yarra Creek Host Farm, RSD 49, Yarra Creek
Tel: (004) 61 1276
Contact: Graeme & Margaret Batey
Rooms: 2
Cost: Bed & Breakfast - $50 double, $40 single
No smoking • Dinner available

KINGSTON BEACH TAS. 7050

Tranquilla, 30 Osborne Esplanade
Tel: (002) 29 6282

KOONYA TAS. 7187

'Cascades' Colonial Accommodation, RMB 1355
Tel: (002) 50 3121 Fax: (002) 50 3121
Contact: Sue Clark
Rooms: 4 s/c cottages (2 people per cottage)
Cost: $80, including continental breakfast provisions

Port Arthur Convict Out Station, Nubeena Road
Tel: (002) 50 3121

LALLA TAS. 7267

The Pear Walk, Lalla Road
Tel: (003) 95 4226

Tasmania

LATROBE TAS. 7307

Erica Cottage, 35 Gilbert Street
Tel: (004) 24 4735 Fax: (004) 23 1832
Contact: Chris West
Rooms: s/c cottage (3 bedrooms)
Cost: Including provisions for full breakfast - $65 single, $85 double, $15 each extra person

Frogmore, Mersey Main Road
Tel: (004) 26 1620

LAUNCESTON TAS. 7250

Agnew House, 23 Welman Street
Tel: (003) 34 3485

Airlie Dorset Terrace, 138 St. John Street
Tel: (003) 34 2162

Alice's Place, 17 York Street
Tel: (003) 34 2231 Fax: (003) 34 2696
Contact: Helen Poynder (V)
Rooms: s/c cottage
Cost: Bed & Breakfast, per night - $115 double

Annsbrae House, 4 High Street
Tel: (003) 34 2654

Antiquity Lodge, 45 Elizabeth Street
Tel: (003) 34 5651

Bass Villas, 1 Casino Rise
Tel: (003) 34 7259

Brickfields Terrace, 64 Margaret Street
Tel: (003) 30 1753 Fax: (003) 34 1693
Contact: Sarah Lebski

Camellia Cottage, 32 Welman Street
Tel: (003) 34 2231 Fax: (003) 34 2696
Contact: Helen Poynder
Rooms: s/c cottage (3 bedrooms, sleeps 6)
Cost: Bed & Breakfast, per night - $115 double

Canning Cottage, 28 Canning Street
Tel: (003) 34 7388

Glebe Cottages, 41 Cimitiere Street
Tel: (003) 34 0934

Hillview House, 193 George Street
Tel: (003) 31 7388
Contact: June & Jock Carmichael

Hunter Cottage, 12 Hunter Street
Tel: (003) 24 3555

Ivy Cottage, 17 York Street
Tel: (003) 34 2231 Fax: (003) 34 2696
Contact: Helen Poynder
Rooms: s/c cottage (2 bedrooms, sleeps 4)
Cost: Bed & Breakfast, per night - $115 double, $25 each extra person (including children)

Molecombe Cottage, Mt. Leslie Road (23 Kenyon Street)
Tel: (003) 31 1355
Contact: Megan England

Partridge Cottage, 129 Balfour Street
Tel: (003) 34 2231 Fax: (003) 34 2696
Contact: Helen Poynder
Rooms: s/c cottage (2 bedrooms, sleeps 4)
Cost: Bed & Breakfast, per night - $115 double, $25 each extra person (including children)

Penny Royal Watermill Motel, 145-147 Paterson Street
Tel: (003) 31 6699

Penny Royal Village, 145-147 Paterson Street
Tel: (003) 31 6699

Prince Albert Inn, Cnr. William & Tamar Streets
Tel: (003) 31 1931

Riverside Hotel/Motel, 407 West Tamar Highway
Tel: (003) 27 2522

Rose Lodge, 270 Brisbane Street
Tel: (003) 34 0120

The Cottage on the Park, 29 Lawrence Street
Tel: (003) 34 2238 Fax: (334) 34 5061
Contact: Mrs. Suzanne Edginton
Rooms: s/c cottage (2 bedrooms, sleeps 4)
Cost: Per night, including breakfast provisions - $110 double, $20 each additional person
After 24th December 1993: $115 double, $25 additional person
No smoking • No children under 12

The Edwardian, 227-229 Charles Street
Tel: (003) 31 4089

The Old Bakery Inn, Cnr. York & Margaret Streets
Tel: (003) 31 7900 Fax: (003) 31 7756
Contact: Miss Rhana Crago Ⓥ
Rooms: 21, all ensuite
Cost: $55 single, $65 double/twin, $10 each extra person
Fully licensed restaurant

The Shambles, 121-127 Balfour Street
Tel: (003) 34 2231 Fax: (003) 34 2696
Contact: Helen Poynder
Rooms: 4 s/c cottages (1 queensize bedroom, ensuite) Ⓥ
Cost: Bed & Breakfast, per night - $115 double, $25 each extra person (including children)

York Mansions Colonial Accommodation, 9-11 York Street
Tel: (003) 34 2933 Fax: (003) 34 2870
Contact: Mike Angell & Christine Jones
Rooms: 5 s/c apartments (2 or 3 bedrooms)
Cost: Including full breakfast provisions - single/twin/double $115 per night, Additional people sharing $25 per person. Ⓥ
After 24th December 1993: $125 plus $25 per extra person
Tasmanian Tourism Awards winner 1992 and 1993 ◆ No smoking ◆ No children under 12

LEGANA TAS. 7277

Freshwater Point, 56 Nobelius Drive
Tel: (003) 30 2200 Ⓥ
Contact: Laurie Thomas

LILYDALE TAS. 3140

Hawkspur, Doaks Road
Tel: (003) 95 1268
Contact: Robert & Amanda Laing
Rooms: s/c cottage, sleeps 11
Cost $70 double
No smoking

Plovers Ridge Host Farm, Lalla Road
Tel: (003) 95 1102
Contact: Carol & Colin Cook
Rooms: s/c cottage and s/c suite, sleep 4 and 5
Cost: $72-$86 double
No smoking

LINDISFARNE TAS. 7105

Orana Accommodation, 20 Lowelly Road
Tel: (002) 43 9017
Contact: Brian & Claire Marshall
Rooms: 5, ensuite
Cost: Including full breakfast - $69 double/twin, $20 each extra person, $12 each child
No smoking

LONGFORD TAS. 7301

Brickendon Historic Cottages, Wellington Street
Tel: (003) 91 1251 Fax: (003) 91 2073
Contact: Louise Archer (V)
Rooms: 2 s/c cottages (sleep 5 and 2)
Cost: Gardeners Cottage $88 double, Coachmans Cottage $98 double, $20 each additional person
Dinner hamper by arrangement

Kingsley House, Wellington Street
Tel: (003) 91 2318

The Old Rosary, Longford Hall
Tel: (003) 91 1662 (V)
Contact: Rose Falkiner

The Racecourse Private Hotel, 114 Marlborough Street
Tel: (003) 91 2352 Fax: (003) 91 2430
Contact: Mary or Doug Rutledge (V)
Rooms: 5, ensuite
Cost: $65 single, $90 double/twin, $25 each additional person
No smoking • No children under 12

LOW HEAD TAS. 7253

Belfont Cottages, 178 Low Head Road
Tel: (003) 82 1841 Fax: (003) 82 1304
Contact: Graham Neilson & Ian Littlejohn

LOWER BARRINGTON TAS. 7306

Stonehaven, Lower Barrington Road
Tel: (004) 92 3338
Contact: Jean & Terry Pool
Rooms: 3
Cost: Bed & Breakfast - $80-$90 double
No smoking

MIDDLETON TAS. 7163

Holly Tree Farm, Channel Highway
Tel: (002) 92 1680

MOLE CREEK TAS. 7304

Blackwood Park, Alum Cliff Road (RSD 645 Deloraine, 7304)
Tel: (003) 63 1208
Contact: Karin Butschek
Rooms: s/c cottage (2 bedrooms)
Cost: $60-$65 double, extra person and children $15, including full breakfast provisions
No smoking • Dinner by arrangement

Rosewick Cottage, Alum Cliff Road
Tel: (003) 63 1354 Fax: (003) 63 1354
Contact: Michael & Sallie Scott
Rooms: s/c cottage (3 bedrooms)
Cost: $45 double, $15 each extra person, $5 children 5-14 yrs., including breakfast provisions
Children very welcome (owners operate dairy farm) • Children under 5 free • Free cot

Tasmania

MOUNT NELSON TAS. 7007

Signalman's Cottage, 685 Nelson Road
Tel: (002) 23 1215

NATIONAL PARK TAS. 7140

Mount Field National Park YHA Hostel, Main Road
Tel: (002) 88 1369

NEW NORFOLK TAS. 7140

Friendship Lodge, 5 Oast Street
Tel: (002) 61 1171 Fax: (002) 61 3872
Contact: Rosalie & Colin Wood
No Smoking

Glen Derwent, Lyell Highway
Tel: (002) 61 3244 Ⓥ

Rosie's Inn, 5 Oast Street
Tel: (002) 61 1171 Fax: (002) 61 3872
Contact: Colin & Rosalie Ward
Rooms: 16 (4 ensuite, 12 shared facilities)
Cost: Double - $55 shared facilities, $70 ensuite
No smoking ◆ *No children under 5*

"**Tynwald**", Willow Bend Estate, Lyell Highway (P.O. Box 57)
Tel: (002) 61 2667 Ⓥ
Contact: Garry Roohan & Patricia Kelsall
Rooms: 5

NIETTA TAS. 7315

Kaydale Lodge, Luck Road
Tel: (004) 29 1293

OATLANDS TAS. 7120

Amelia Cottage, 104 High Street
Tel: (002) 54 1264
Rooms: s/c cottage, sleeps 9

Forget-Me-Not Cottage, 17 Dulverton Street
Tel: (002) 54 1264
Rooms: s/c cottage, sleeps 5

Oatlands Lodge, 92 High Street
Tel: (002) 54 1444

Waverley Cottage & Croft, "Waverley Lodge", Bowhill Road
Tel: (002) 54 1264
Rooms: s/c cottage, sleeps 6

ORFORD TAS. 7190

Holkham House (Colonial Accommodation), Tasman Highway
Tel: (002) 25 1248 Fax: (002) 31 1529
Contact: Anne Saunders
Rooms: s/c cottage (sleeps up to 14) Ⓥ
Cost: $95 first 2 adults, $25 each extra adult, $12.50 children under 14, including full breakfast provisions

Lulling Cottage, Rheban Road
Tel: (002) 57 1234

Miranda Cottage, Tasman Highway
Tel: (002) 57 1248 Ⓥ
Contact: Anne Saunders

OUSE TAS. 7140

Rosecot, "Millbrook"
Tel: (002) 87 1222

Tasmania

PENGUIN TAS. 7316

Broadacres, RSD 280 Nine Mile Road, West Pine
Tel: (004) 37 5267

Mabroonca, 196 Main Street
Tel: (004) 37 2147

Neptune Grand Hotel, Main Street
Tel: (004) 37 2406

Watercress Valley, Browns Lane (P.O. Box 230)
Tel: (004) 37 1145 Fax: (004) 37 1308
Contact: Mike & Judi Walker
Rooms: 1 s/c cabin
Cost: Bed & Breakfast - $70 double, $60 single
No smoking ◆ *No children* ◆ *Dinner by arrangement*

PLENTY TAS. 7140

Redlands Cottage, R.M.B. 5075
Tel: (002) 61 1122 Ⓥ
Contact: Richard & Lynne Page

POLICE POINT TAS. 7116

Huon Delight Holiday Cottage, Lot 8 Esperance Coast Road
Tel: (002) 97 6336

PONTVILLE TAS. 7030

Kuringal House, Midlands Highway
Tel: (002) 68 1295

The Barracks, Midlands Highway
Tel: (002) 68 1665
Contact: Richard Giddings
Rooms: 3 s/c terraced cottages (each with 2 bedrooms, etc.)
Cost: $80 first person, $10 second person, $15 each extra person
Children under 3 years free

RICHMOND TAS. 7025

Churchill Cottage, Colebrook Road (P.O. Box 92)
Tel: (002) 62 4194
Contact: Olaf & Laura Hedbert
Rooms: s/c cottage, sleeps 5-7
Cost: $19-100 double

"Daisy Bank" Cottages, "Daisy Bank"
Tel: (002) 62 2390
Contact: Dinky Jones Ⓥ
Rooms: 2 s/c cottages, sleep 3 and 4 (cots available)
Cost: $95 double, $20 each extra person, including provisions for full country breakfast

Emerald Cottage, 23 Torrens Street
Tel: (002) 62 2136 Fax: (002) 62 2610
Contact: Tom Smith
Rooms: s/c cottage, double bedroom, etc.
Cost: $90 double per night, including substantial breakfast provisions
Children free - folding bed and/or cot available

Laurel Cottage, 15 Wellington Street
Tel: (002) 62 2250 or (002) 62 2357 Ⓥ
Contact: Sandra Barwick

Lavender Cottage, 27 Bridge Street
Tel: (002) 62 2400
Contact: Lesley Bick

Prospect House, Cambridge Road
Tel: (002) 62 2207 Fax: (002) 62 2551
Contact: Mike Buscombe
Rooms: 11, all ensuite
Cost: Double - $96 room only, $116 Bed & Breakfast Ⓥ
Licensed restaurant

Richmond Cottages, 12 Bridge Street
Tel: (002) 62 2561 Fax: (002) 62 2668
Contact: Ian Fry

Richmond Country Bed & Breakfast, "Morville House", Prossers Road
Tel: (002) 62 4238 Fax: (002) 62 4423
Contact: Robyn Mendham
Rooms: 2
Cost: Including continental breakfast - $35 single, $55 double, $18 each extra person, $12 children 3-12 yrs., $8 cot
Non-smokers preferred

The Dispensary, Edward Street
Tel: (002) 62 2226
Contact: Mrs. Starr Oclee Ⓥ
Rooms: 3, ensuite
Cost: $115 double, $20 each extra person, including full breakfast

The Leys, Fingerpost Road
Tel: (002) 62 4378 Fax: (002) 62 4416
Contact: K & M Avery
Rooms: 3 double/twin, all ensuite
Cost: Bed & Breakfast - $90 double, $60 single

ROSEBERY TAS. 7420

Miners Cottages, 12 & 16 Karlson Street
Tel: (004) 73 1796 Fax: (004) 73 1796
Contact: Barry & Marriett Yewen
Rooms: 2 s/c cottages
Cost: Including breakfast - $45 single, $65 double, $15 each extra person, children negotiable
Outside smoking preferred • Dinner by arrangement • Pets by arrangement

ROSEVEARS TAS. 7277

Tamar House, Rosevears Drive
Tel: (003) 30 1744 Fax: (003) 30 2035
Contact: Ray Oxford
Rooms: 3, ensuite
Cost: Per night - $76 double, $20 each extra person, including cooked breakfast
No smoking • Dinner by prior arrangement

ROSS TAS. 7209

Apple Dumpling Historic Cottage, Bridge Street (Reception in Church Street)
Tel: (003) 81 5354 Fax: (003) 81 5408
Contact: Tim & Sue Johnson
Rooms: s/c cottage, 2 bedrooms, etc. (sleeps 4)
Cost: $90 double, $20 each extra person, $15 cot charge first night only
Dinner available within village

Church Mouse Cottage, High Street (Reception in Church Street)
Tel: (003) 81 5354 Fax: (003) 81 5408
Contact: Tim & Sue Johnson
Rooms: s/c cottage: 1 bedroom, 1 living/kitchen
Cost: $90 double, $15 cot charge first night only
No smoking • No children unless in cot • Dinner available within village

Hudson Cottage, Church Street
Tel: (003) 81 5354 Fax: (003) 81 5408
Contact: Tim & Sue Johnson
Rooms: s/c cottage, 2 bedrooms, etc. (sleeps 4)
Cost: $90 double, $20 each extra person, $15 cot charge first night only
Dinner available within village

The Elms Inn, Church Street
Tel: (003) 81 5246
Contact: Ken & Sue Elvidge
Rooms: 4, ensuite
Cost: $70 double/twin, $20 extra person
No smoking in bedrooms • No children under 12

SANDY BAY TAS. 7005

Amberley House, Sandy Bay Road
Tel: (002) 25 1005

Christ College, College Road
Tel: (002) 23 5190

Red Chapel House, 27 Red Chapel Avenue
Tel: (002) 25 2273
Contact: Beverley & Ivan Colev
Rooms: 8, sleep 20
Cost: Bed & Breakfast - $50-55 single, $65-85 double, $25 extra person
No smoking • Child concession

SCAMANDER TAS. 7215

Home for Tea, Tasman Highway
Tel: (003) 72 5112
Contact: Ruth Coughlan
Rooms: 2
Cost: $45 double, $28 single, $17 extra person. 3 course dinner (guests only), $15

SCOTTSDALE TAS. 7260

Anabel's of Scottsdale, 46 King Street (Tasman Highway)
Tel: (003) 52 3277 or (003) 52 2144
Contact: Andrea Blake
Rooms: 2 s/c units, can accommodate 4 comfortably
Cost: $70 double, unit only
Dining on property in National Trust home • Non-smokers preferred

SHEFFIELD TAS. 7306

Badgers Host Farm, Nook Road (P.O. Box 47)
Tel: (004) 91 1816
Contact: Barbara & Bob McArthur
Rooms: s/c suite, sleeps 6
Cost: $85 double, including breakfast
No smoking

Bonnie Doon, RSD 201
Tel: (004) 91 1485
Contact: Barbara Jacobs
Rooms: 3, ensuite
Cost: $60 double, $45 single, $20 children
No smoking • No children under 10

Carinya Farm, Staverton Road
Tel: (004) 91 1593
Contact: Chris & Garry Sutton
Rooms: 2 s/c units, sleep 3 and 5
Cost:$65 single, $80 double, $20 each extra person, $15 child 3-14, $8 cot
No smoking • Dinner upon request

Gnome Home, RSD 613 Staverton Road
Tel: (004) 91 1560

The Granary Accommodation, RSD 615 Staverton Road
Tel: (004) 91 1689
Contact: Alan Sainsbury
Rooms: 3 s/c cottages, each sleep 8
Cost: $35 single, $60 double, $15 each extra person
Children under 3 free

SOUTH ARM TAS. 7022

Lennaville, 118 Bezzants Road
Tel: (002) 39 9243 Fax: (002) 39 9243
Contact: Darilyn Dowding
Rooms: s/c cottage, sleeps 4
Cost: $80 double, $16 each extra person, including breakfast provisions
C.1892 • Dinner by prior arrangement

ST. HELENS TAS. 2716

Cecilia House, 78 Cecilia Street
Tel: (003) 76 1723
Contact: Jim & May Fillmore
Rooms: 3
Cost: $40 single, $60 double
No smoking • Dinner by arrangement

Cockle Cove Beachfront, 234 St. Helens Point Road, Steiglitz
Tel: (003) 76 3036
Contact: Gabrielle Carlier
Rooms: 2, plus s/c cottage
Cost: Cottage $66-$70 double, Bed & Breakfast $55-$60 double

Warrawee Guest House, Kirwans Beach
Tel: (003) 76 1987
Contact: Eric & Barbara Lawson
Rooms: 7 (4 double, 1 twin, 2 single)
Cost: $55 double, $70 double ensuite, $30 single, $50 single ensuite
Smoking outside only • Dinner by prior arrangement

Wybalenna, Tasman Highway
Tel: (003) 76 1611
Contact: Charles & Joan Scott
Rooms: 3
Cost: Including full breakfast - $50 double/twin, $65 double ensuite

STANLEY TAS. 7331

Bleak House, 4 Marshall Street
Tel: (004) 58 1428 (V)
Contact: Norma Walker

Captain's Cottage, 30 Alexander Terrace
Tel: (004) 58 1109

Harbour Master's Colonial Cottage, 42 Alexander Terrace
Tel: (004) 58 1209 Fax: (004) 58 1209
Contact: Lee & Warren Bulloch
Rooms: s/c cottage (3 bedrooms)
Cost: $85 double, $20 each extra person
No smoking • Reduced weekly rate on application

Pol & Pen Holiday Cottages, 8 Pearse Street
Tel: (004) 58 1334

Ride Cottage, 12 Pearse Street
Tel: (004) 58 1315
Contact Jann Brauer
Rooms: s/c house (2 bedrooms)
Cost: $70 double, $10 each extra adult, $5 children under 5, cot free
No smoking

Touchwood Cottage, 33 Church Street
Tel: (004) 58 1348
Rooms: sleeps 6

Wistaria Cottage, 3 Victoria Street
Tel: (004) 58 1186 Fax: (004) 58 1286
Contact: Tracey Jacobs
Rooms: s/c unit, sleeps 4
Cost: $70 double, $60 single, $20 each extra adult, $10 child under 15, including continental breakfast
No smoking

STRAHAN TAS. 7468

Bay View Cottages, Ocean Beach Road
Tel: (004) 71 7142
Contact: B & L Gardiner
Rooms: s/c cottage
Cost: $60 double, $15 each extra person, including breakfast

Franklin Manor, The Esplanade
Tel: (004) 71 7311 Fax: (004) 71 7267
Contact: Bernadette Woods (V)
Rooms: 13

Gull Cottages, The Esplanade
Tel: (004) 71 7227

Hamers Hotel
Tel: (004) 71 7191 (V)
Contact: Reception
Rooms: 17

Strahan Colonial Cottages, c/o General Store, The Esplanade
Tel: (004) 71 7263
Contact: Bernadette Woods & Peter Genders

Strahan Village Cottages
Tel: (004) 71 7191 (V)
Contact: Reception
Rooms: 12

Strahan Wilderness Lodge, Ocean Beach Road
Tel: (004) 71 7142
Contact: B & L Gardiner
Rooms: s/c lodge
Cost: $40 double, $30 single, $10 each extra person 13 yrs. & over, $8 child, $5 cot, including breakfast

SWAN ISLAND TAS.

Swan Island Guest House, c/o P.O. Gladstone
Tel: (003) 57 2211 Fax: (003) 57 2211
Contact: Jill & Ron Harris
Rooms: s/c house (3 bedrooms)
Cost: Room only - $140 double, $20 each extra person
Special family rates available

SWANSEA TAS. 7190

Hollyhock Cottage, Tasman Highway
Tel: (002) 57 8494 or (002) 57 8267
Contact: Dianne Sinclair
Rooms: s/c cottage
Cost: $95 double, $15 each extra person

Keefers Cottage, Tasman Highway
Tel: (002) 57 8494 or (002) 57 8267
Contact: Dianne Sinclair
Rooms: s/c cottage
Cost: $95 double

Lester Cottage, 412 Gordon Street
Tel: (002) 57 8105
Contact: D. Trethowan
Rooms: 4 Ⓥ
Cost: Bed & Breakfast - $95 - $110 double
No smoking

Meredith House, 15 Noyes Street
Tel: (002) 57 8119
Contact: Clive Olbery Ⓥ
Rooms: 5
Cost: $75 double, $55 single
No smoking

Oyster Bay Guest House, 10 Franklin Street
Tel: (002) 57 8110
Contact: Suzanne Williamson
Rooms: 10
Cost: Bed & Breakfast - From $55 double to $70 double ensuite
No children under 10

Redcliffe House, Tasman Highway
Tel: (002) 57 8557 (V)
Contact: Doug & Jocelyn Stugle
Rooms: 3

Schoulens House, 1 Waterloo Road (V)
Tel: (002) 57 8564
Contact: Terry Fidler

Swansea Cottages, 43 Franklin Street
Tel: (002) 57 8328

The Shepherd's Cottage, "Lisdillon Estate", Tasman Highway
Tel: (002) 57 7567

Wagners Cottage, Tasman Highway
Tel: (002) 57 8494 or (002) 57 8267
Contact: Dianne Sinclair
Rooms: s/c cottage
Cost: $95 double, $15 each extra person

TABLE CAPE TAS. 7325

Cape House, Scenic Road
Tel: (004) 45 1317

TARANNA TAS. 7180

Norfolk Bay Convict Station, RMB 956 Arthur Highway
Tel: (002) 50 3487

Taranna House, Off Arthur Highway
Tel: (002) 50 3161

TAROONA TAS. 7053

Hillgrove Colonial Accommodation, Opposite Shot Tower, 269 Channel Highway
Tel: (002) 27 9043
Contact: Mrs. E.A. McMahon
Rooms: s/c suite
Cost: $82 double, $20 each extra person, $10 children to 14, $50 cot, including full breakfast provisions

TARRALEAH TAS. 7140

Tarraleah Chalet Resort
Tel: (002) 89 3128 Fax: (002) 89 3177
Contact: Izzy Munoz
Rooms: 12
Cost: Room only - $30 single, $48 double/twin, $12.50 extra person. Breakfast - continental $5, cooked $7

The Guest House Ⓥ
Contact: Mr. Lam Chau

TUNNACK TAS. 7120

Pine Hill Cottage, "Gettington", Square Road (P.O. Box 19)
Tel: (002) 54 7211
Contact: Greg & Sue Scott
Rooms: s/c cottage, sleeps 6
Cost: $70 double

ULVERSTONE TAS. 7315

Ocean View Guest House, 1-3 Victoria Street
Tel: (004) 25 5401
Contact: Jenny & Jeff Foster

UPPER ESK 7214

Upper Esk Host Farm (P.O. Mathinna, 7214)
Tel: (003) 77 1153
Contact: Barry & Jenny McGuire
Rooms: s/c cottage, sleeps 6-8
Cost: $70 double

VERONA SANDS TAS. 7112

Wombat Cottage, Lot 29 Vincent Avenue
Tel: (002) 27 8695

WEST CALDER TAS. 6325

Emerald Valley, RSD 437 Bassetts Road
Tel: (004) 38 4160

WESTBURY TAS. 7303

Egmont, 922 Birralee Road
Tel: (003) 93 1164 or (003) 62 3586
Contact: Virginia Greenhill

Old Bake House, 52 William Street
Tel: (003) 93 1140
Rooms: s/c cottage, sleeps 6

Westbury Inn, 1 Bass Highway
Tel: (003) 93 1627
Contact: Vicki & John Lont
Rooms: 2
Cost: Bed & Breakfast - $70 double/twin, $55 single
Dinner available

WESTERWAY TAS. 7140

The Haven Tea Garden, Gordon River Road
Tel: (002) 88 1120

Tasmania

WILMOT TAS. 7310

Antill Apartments, Narrawa Road
Tel: (004) 92 1473 Fax: (004) 92 1109
Contact: Kaye & Arv Suna
Rooms: 2 s/c cottages, sleep 4 and 2
Cost: $75-$80 double

WILTSHIRE TAS. 7321

Myrtle Brook, 'Myrtle Brook', P.O. Forest, 7330
Tel: (004) 58 3174
Contact: Hazel V. Langridge
Rooms: 3 (6 people)
Cost: $65 double, $45 single, $12 children 3-14
No smoking ◆ Dinner available if booked at least day before

WOODBRIDGE TAS. 7162

Honeywood Cottage, Pullens Road
Tel: (002) 67 4550

Melaleuca, Lot 3 Pullens Road
Tel: (002) 67 4877

WYENA TAS. 7254

Red Rooster Host Farm, Burns Road (P/O Lebrina)
Tel: (003) 95 6181
Contact: R & S Jensen
Rooms: 2 bedrooms, 1 kitchen, toilet, shower
Cost: Per night - $40 double, $30 sing,e - concession, children
No smoking

WYNYARD TAS. 7325

Alexandria Guest House, Table Cape Road
Tel: (004) 42 2094
Contact: Roy Alexander
Rooms: 4, ensuite
Cost: $75-$80 double, $60 single, including full breakfast
No smoking in bedrooms ◆ Dinner by arrangement

Valgury Vista Guest House, 87 Scenic Drive, East Wynyard
Tel: (004) 42 2886 or (004) 42 2391

ZEEHAN TAS. 7469

Hotel Cecil, Main Road (P.O. Box 84)
Tel: (004) 71 6221 Fax: (004) 71 7366
Contact: Vicki & Graham Appleby

South Australia

THE BUSINESS OF B & B

A professional newsletter for owners and operators of B & B's and country inns in Australia and New Zealand was started in September 1992. The newsletter provides information on a wide range of topics and current issues and also serves as a forum for the exchange of ideas between hosts. Feedback and letters from hosts in the business are a vital part of the newsletter's success.

Editor and publisher, Carol Glen, came from California in 1981 and established one of the first upmarket B & B inns in New Zealand, catering for the overseas tourist market. Today she is editor and publisher of **The Business of B & B**.

For a complimentary copy of the newsletter, write to Carol Glen, **The Business of B & B**, Box 407, Nelson, New Zealand.

Subscription fees are $45 per year, and back issues are available on request.

Adelaide

Adelaide, once dubbed the City of Churches, is one of the best planned capitals of the world. Designed by architect Colonel William Light, the city centre retains its attractive Victorian and Edwardian homes which were the cornerstone of the early plans begun in 1836.

There's so much to see and do in this modern, vibrant city. Or else make it a base to visit the differing regions that make South Australia such an unusual state.

Adelaide is situated on the Adelaide Plains, a fertile corridor of land enriched by the Mediterranean climate. The South Australian capital has some of Australia's best restaurants, well serviced by locally produced premium wines.

Once you have sampled the delights the city has to offer, it may be time to move on to explore the rest of South Australia. Adelaide truly is the ideal getaway.

Adelaide

BLACKWOOD S.A. 5051

Somerset House, 14 Hillside Road
Tel: (08) 278 6063
Owner/Contact: June & Ian Will
Rooms: 2
Cost: $60 single, $70 double/twin, $20 children
Dinner by arrangement • No smoking • No children under 5 years

DARLINGTON S.A. 5047

Platter-Puss, 25 Hyland Avenue
Tel: (08) 296 1669
Owner/Contact: Maurice & Beverley Friline
Rooms: 2
Cost: $45 single, $65 double, dinner $10-$20

HENLEY BEACH S.A. 5022

Meleden Villa, 268 Seaview Road
Tel: (08) 235 0577 Fax: (08) 353 3579
Owner/Contact: Mel Dennett
Rooms: 6
Cost: $45 - $55 double
Dinner by arrangement • No smoking inside

MITCHAM S.A. 5062

Nee-Rim, 6 Playford Road
Tel: (08) 271 4904
Owner/Contact: Pauline Henningsen
Rooms: 2
Cost: $40 single, $60 double

NORTH ADELAIDE S.A. 5006

Buxton Manor Mansion, c/o 109 Glen Osmond Road, Eastwood, 5063
Tel: (08) 272 1355 Fax: (08) 272 6261
Rooms: s/c apartments
Cost: $120 single/2 nights
No children • *No smoking inside*

Adelaide Hills

Just 20 minutes from the heart of Adelaide and you are in another world. Once the summer retreat for the city's leading families, the "enchanted hills", as architect Colonel William Light described them, are full of tourist attractions.

With a distinct German flavour, particularly around the pretty towns of Hahndorf and Birdwood, the hills are an ideal escape from the city haste. Birdwood is home to the National Motor Museum, which houses the largest collection of vintage cars in the Southern Hemisphere.

At Hahndorf, the German past has been lovingly recreated in a railway exhibition and, if you are into clocks, take time out to view the Antique Clock Museum, which features the world's biggest cuckoo clock.

Relax in the peace and quiet of the Warrawong Wildlife Sanctuary at Mylor, where rare nocturnal animals such as the bandicoot, potoroo and bettong can be observed.

At Gumeracha, there's the world's biggest rocking horse (it stands 18.3 metres high).

The Fairyland Village at Lobethal should also be on your "must do" schedule, especially if you have a young family.

Apple Tree Cottage/Gum Tree Cottage

P.O. Box 100, Oakbank, 5243
Tel: (083) 88 4193 Fax: (083) 88 4733
Owner/Contact: Brendan & Gai Adcock
Rooms: s/c cottages
Cost: $140 double
Winner of S.A. Tourism Awards 1992 and 1993

These delightful fully self contained cottages are owned by Brendan and Gai Adcock. Both are approximately 30 minutes from Adelaide and 7 minutes from historic Hahndorf.

Apple Tree Cottage is a beautifully restored two-storeyed cottage with a private lake overlooking rolling countryside and orchards. There are 2 bedrooms upstairs, both with queen-sized beds – linen is provided. The house is air conditioned and has an open fire for the winter months.

Gum Tree Cottage is an early Australian-style stone building with a pretty garden and surrounded by a post and rail fence. The house is filled with antiques and fresh flowers. Again, linen is provided.

Lavender Fields

P.O. Box 100, Oakbank, 5243
Tel: (083) 88 4193 Fax: (083) 88 4733
Owner/Contact: Brendan & Gai Adcock
Rooms: s/c cottage
Cost $200 a night for the cottage

This is an idyllic and luxurious country retreat for those seeking a sense of seclusion.

The provincial style cottage has thick stone walls, beams and natural mellowed walls. The 2 bedrooms have queen size beds and private bathrooms.

Other features include an open log fire, underfloor heating, air conditioning and barbecue facilities.
This is the ultimate cottage experience.

Wattlebark Cottage

P.O. Box 177, Echunga, 5153
Tel: (08) 388 8076 Fax: (08) 388 2200
Owner/Contact: Heather & Peter Adcock
Rooms: s/c cottage
Cost: $120 double

This recently renovated early Australian style cottage has already won the 1992 State Bank South Australian Tourism Award, so the Adcocks must be doing something right!
There are 2 romantic bedrooms – one with a four-poster. The other has a draped canopy and they share a bathroom.
The house has air conditioning, a log fire and stabling for your own horses. With "Coomaba" being situated in lovely rolling countryside and only 15 kms. to the Heysen Trail, good riding is assured.
All linen and breakfast provisions are provided.

Bush Tree Tonica

P.O. Box 226, Upper Sturt, 5156
Tel: (08) 339 2117
Owner/Contact: Pauline McPharlin
Rooms: 1
Cost: $80

This modern sculptural architecture set on 4 hectares of bushland should not be missed.
There is just one large guest room with windows on 3 sides and one private bathroom.
Pauline McPharlin enjoys serving beautiful food.
A unique experience.

St Githa's Cottage

12 Rosewater Crescent, Bridgewater, 5155
Tel: (08) 339 1264
Owner/Contact: Sandie & Laurie Cousin
Rooms: s/c cottage

Originally built in 1890, the charming stone cottage was relocated and rebuilt within a private section of St. Githa's Garden in 1993. Retaining many of the original features and incorporating modern luxury facilities, the cottage provides accommodation for 2 – 4 guests. The lounge has a large stone fireplace and is furnished with antiques. Breakfast goodies for a hearty meal are left in the fully equipped kitchen. There is also a laundry for your convenience.

For those with a yearning towards beautiful gardens, this National Award winning garden must be one spot not to miss.

If being self-contained is not your style, St. Githa's House has just one guest room. Sandie is a marvellous cook and the house is licensed.

Uraidla Aristologist

Cnr. Greenhill & Basket Range Roads, Uraidla, 5142
Tel: (08) 390 1995
Owner/Contact: Jennifer Hillier & Michael Symons
Cost From $70

Built in 1870, these stone buildings have been refurbished to provide travellers with a reasonably priced base. There are 4 bedrooms and a former police stable and cell which have both been converted into a separate suite.

There are large chestnut trees and wonderful rambling roses, but the real reason that people flock to Uraidla Aristologist is for the exceptional food – traditional Italian and French cooking with a wine list featuring local vineyards (B.Y.O. also possible).

Georgia Mews

31 - 33 Wakefield Street, Kent Town, 5067
Tel: (08) 362 0600 Fax: (08) 373 3802
Owner/Contact: Di Guerin & Judy Hassam
Cost: From $85

Originally built in 1869 as a pair of terraced houses and separate coach house, Georgia Mews has been converted into six spacious apartments.

Located in a quiet tree-lined street in Kent Town only minutes from the city centre, these apartments offer excellent self-contained accommodation. There are one or two bedrooms, a fully equipped kitchen with dining area, queen size beds and a living room with colour T.V.

Laundry and ironing facilities are available and your hosts live on the property.

Deansgate Cottage

70 Tusmore Avenue, Tusmore, 5065
Tel: (08) 31 4643 Fax: (08) 373 3802
Owner/Contact: Diane & Noel Guerin
Cost: $80 double

This charming little cottage can accommodate up to 4 people. Originally built in the 1930's as lodgings for the housekeeper, it has been carefully restored to retain the charm of the building.

The open plan ground floor area has a well equipped kitchen, dining area and sofa bed.

The air conditioned bedroom upstairs and modern bathroom have views over the garden. It is only eight minutes from the city centre and has off-street parking.

Highly recommended.

ALDGATE S.A. 5154

"Aldgate Lodge", 27 Strathalbyn Road
Tel: (08) 370 9337 Fax: (08) 339 4899
Owner/Contact: Roxley Greenwood & Don Lord
Rooms: 3
Cost: $65 double, $45 single, dinner $15 each

"Chippings Cottage" Bed & Breakfast, 32 Ludgate Hill Road
Tel: (08) 339 1008 Fax: (08) 374 0505
Owner/Contact:
Rooms: suite of 4 rooms
Cost: $80 double, $65 single
No children

ASHTON S.A. 5137

Debney Hill Bed & Breakfast, 53 Debneys Road (P.O. Box 357)
Tel: (08) 390 1660
Owner/Contact: G.N. & J.M. Bungey
Rooms: 2
Cost: $70-$75 double, $50-$60 single
Dinner by arrangement ◆ *No smoking inside*

BASKET RANGE S.A. 5138

Babi's Stud Farm, P.O. Box 236
Tel: (08) 390 3225 Fax: (08) 390 1264
Owner/Contact: Sue & John Babi
Rooms: 2, ensuite
Cost: $100 double, $15 child under 12
Dinner by arrangement

Babi's Rose Cottage, P.O. Box 236
Tel: (08) 390 3225 Fax: (08) 390 1264
Owner/Contact: Sue & John Babi
Rooms: S/C Cottage
Cost: Bed, breakfast & lunch, double - 1 night $175, 2 nights $300, 3 nights $415
Dinner by arrangement ◆ No children over 12 months

Tetratheca Retreat, Main Road
Tel/Fax: (08) 390 3469
Owner/Contact: Isabel Bishop
Rooms: s/c house
Cost: $90 double, $25 extra person
No smoking

BEAUMONT S.A. 5066

"**Hunterbury**", 10 Bayview Crescent
Tel: (08) 379 3960 or 376 1100 Fax: (08) 376 0918
Contact: Joanne McLaren
Rooms: 2
Cost: $65 twin, $40 single
No smoking indoors

BRIDGEWATER S.A. 5155

St. Githa's Cottage, 12 Rosewarne Crescent
Tel: (08) 339 1264
Owner/Contact: Sandie & Laurie Cousin
Rooms: s/c cottage
Cost: $120 double (V)
No smoking

St. Githa's Garden, 12 Rosewarne Crescent
Tel: (08) 339 1265
Owner/Contact: Sandie & Laurie Cousin
Rooms: 1 Ⓥ
Cost: $100 double
Dinner by arrangement ◆ No smoking ◆ No children

BURNSIDE S.A. 5066

"Leafy Glade", 18 Queens Avenue
Tel: (08) 332 3001
Owner/Contact: Janet Dutton
Rooms: 2
Cost: From $75 twin, $60 single
Dinner by arrangement ◆ No smoking ◆ No children

CHERRYVILLE S.A. 5134

The Cherryville Lofts, Cherryville Road
Tel: (08) 390 1375
Rooms: s/c cottage
Cost: $105 single/2 nights
No children

CRAFERS S.A. 5152

Mount Lofty House, Summit Road
Tel: (08) 339 6777 Fax: (08) 339 5656
Cost: From $295 single/2 nights
Dinner available ◆ No children

ECHUNGA S.A. 5153

Hazelmere Park, Meadows Road
Tel/Fax: (08) 388 8385
Owner/Contact: Ron & Pat Smith
Rooms: s/c cottage and lodge
Cost: $80 - $95 double, $25 extra person
No smoking ◆ No children

Wattlebark Cottage, Pocock Road (P.O. Box 177)
Tel: (08) 388 8076 Fax: (08) 388 2200
Owner/Contact: Heather & Peter Adcock
Rooms: s/c cottage (V)
Cost: $120 double, $30 extra person
No smoking

GLENALTA S.A. 5052

Nottinghamway, Nottingham Way
Tel: (08) 278 7732
Rooms: 3
Cost: From $80 single/2 nights
No children ◆ No smoking in bedrooms

HAHNDORF S.A. 5245

Elderberry Cottage, Old Mount Barker Road
Tel: (08) 388 7997 Fax: (08) 388 1242
Rooms: s/c cottage
Cost: From $50 single/2 nights

KENT TOWN S.A. 5067

Georgia Mews, 31-33 Wakefield Street
Tel/Fax: (08) 362 0600
Owner/Contact: Di Guerin & Judy Hassam (V)
Rooms: 4 apartments and 1 coach house
Cost: Apartment $85 double, Coach House $95 double

KERSBROOK S.A. 5231

Maidstone House, Main Road
Tel: (08) 389 3061
Owner/Contact: Neil Spearritt & Chris Parham
Rooms: Private wing, 4 persons
Cost: $85 double, Dinner $30-$35
No smoking in bedrooms ◆ No children

LEABROOK S.A. 5068

Leabrook Lodge, 314 Kensington Road
Tel: (08) 331 7619 Fax: (08) 364 2638
Owner/Contact: Mrs. Barbara Carter
Rooms: 4
Cost: $50 single, $65 - $85 double/twin
Dinner by arrangement

LENSWOOD S.A. 5240

Monte Bello Villa, Harris Road
Tel/Fax: (08) 389 8504
Owner/Contact: Gaetano Ceravolo
Rooms: 5
Cost: From $90
Dinner by arrangement ◆ *No children* ◆ *No smoking*

MT. LOFTY S.A.

Hoppy's Nest, Summit Road (P.O. Box 95, Crafers, 5152)
Tel: (08) 370 9767
Owner/Contact: Suzy Gilbert
Rooms: 2
Cost: $80 double
Dinner by arrangement ◆ *No children* ◆ *No smoking*

NORTON SUMMIT S.A. 5136

Drysdale Cottage - The Barn, P.O. Box 44
Tel: (08) 390 1652
Owner/Contact: Mary Playford Snarskis
Rooms: s/c accommodation
Cost: $95 double
No smoking inside ◆ *No children*

Norton Summit Holiday Cottage, Crescent Drive (P.O. Box 72)
Tel: (08) 390 1329 Fax: (08) 390 3663
Owner/Contact: Jane Fergusson
Rooms: 1, ensuite
Cost: $80 double
No children • No smoking

OAKBANK S.A. 5243

Apple Tree Cottage, P.O. Box 100
Tel: (08) 388 4193 Fax: (08) 388 4733
Owner/Contact: Mrs. Gai Adcock
Rooms: s/c cottage ⓥ
Cost: $140 double, $30 extra person
No smoking • No children under 5

Gum Tree Cottage, P.O. Box 100
Tel: (08) 388 4193 Fax: (08) 388 4733
Owner/Contact: Mrs. Gai Adcock ⓥ
Rooms: s/c cottage
Cost: $140 double, $30 extra person
No smoking • No children under 5

"Lavender Fields", P.O. Box 100
Tel: (08) 388 4193 Fax: (08) 388 4733
Owner/Contact: Mrs. Gai Adcock
Rooms: s/c luxury cottage ⓥ
Cost: $200 per night/cottage
No smoking • No children

ROSSLYN PARK S.A. 5072

Mary Penfold Panorama, 17 Mary Penfold Drive
Tel: (08) 332 6684
Owner/Contact: Bruce & Marian Jennings
Rooms: 2
Cost: $85 double/twin, $75 single
Dinner by arrangement • No smoking

SPRINGFIELD S.A. 5062

Wharfedale House, 55A Delamere Avenue
Tel: (08) 379 1935
Owner/Contact: Mrs. R. Dawson
Rooms: 3
Cost: $80 double
Dinner by arrangement • No smoking • No children

STIRLING S.A. 5152

Mrs. May's Cottage, P.O. Box 767
Tel: (08) 339 5876 or (08) 339 5410
Owner/Contact: Jenny & Alan Rumsby, Val & Bob Daws
Rooms: s/c cottage
Cost: $90 double, $5 child
No smoking

Olivet House, 46 Ayers Hill Road
Tel: (08) 339 6544 Fax: (08) 370 9866
Owner/Contact: Dianne Barron-Davis & Howard Davis
Rooms: 3

Panorama Lodge, 35 Garrod Crescent
Tel: (08) 339 1898
Owner/Contact: Barbara Metzger
Rooms: s/c unit
Cost: From $65 double/twin
No smoking • No children

The Croft B & B, 43 Snows Road
Tel: (08) 339 3902
Owner/Contact: Helen & Michael Pierce
Rooms: 1, ensuite
Cost: From $85
No smoking indoors ◆ No children under 14

The Keep, Glenside Lane
Tel: (08) 339 6748 Fax: (08) 370 9950
Rooms: 1, ensuite spa bath
Cost: $195 single/3 nights
No children

Thorngrove Manor, 2 Glenside Lane
Tel: (08) 339 6748 Fax: (08) 370 9950
Owner/Contact: Kenneth Lehmann
Rooms: 4, ensuite spa baths
Cost: $130 - $370 double
Dinner by arrangement ◆ No children

TUSMORE S.A. 5065

Deansgate Cottage, 70 Tusmore Avenue
Tel: (08) 31 4643 Fax: (08) 373 3802
Owner/Contact: Di Guerin
Rooms: s/c cottage (V)
Cost: $80 double, $25 extra person

UPPER STURT S.A. 5156

Bush Tree Tonica, P.O. Box 226
Tel: (08) 339 2117
Owner/Contact: Pauline McPharlin (V)
Rooms: 1
Cost: $80

URAIDLA S.A. 5142

Uraidla Aristologist, Cnr. Greenhill & Basket Range Roads
Tel: (08) 390 1995
Owner/Contact: Jennifer Hillier & Michael Symons
Rooms: 5 Ⓥ
Cost: $70 - $90
Smoking & Children discouraged

WISTOW S.A. 5251

Jubilee Retreat, c/o P.O., Nairne, 5252
Tel: (08) 388 0337 Fax: (08) 389 7434
Rooms: s/c cottage
Cost: $95 single/2 nights
No children

WOODFORDE S.A. 5072

Adelong Hideaway, Norton Summit Road
Tel: (08) 331 7485
Rooms: s/c accommodation
Cost: $190 single/2 nights
No children ◆ No smoking in bedroom

Flinders Ranges

Divided into three, the Flinders Ranges are part of a mountain chain which extends for 430 kilometres.

The Ranges are arguably Australia's most under-rated natural attraction. They are only four hours drive from Adelaide and roads are well maintained.

The Ranges comprise the southern, central and northern regions and are abundant in wildlife, in particular wedge-tailed eagles, emus, colourful parrots and the rare yellow-footed rock wallaby.

The best known feature of these vastly different Ranges is the Wilpena Pound. This amazing structure typifies the variety of the area. The only entrance is a narrow gorge through which a creek sometimes flows.

In the south, there is the Mount Remarkable National Park where climatic changes have created interesting natural phenomena. There are also important Aboriginal heritage sites spread throughout the Ranges.

Other attractions worth a look to the north include Willow Springs Lookout and the Great Wall of China.

The Captain's Cottage

Mine Road, Blinman, 5730
Tel/Fax: (086) 48 4894
Owner/Contact: Jane Fargher

The Captain's Cottage at Blinman is a delightfully restored pug and pine cottage which is fully self contained and fitted with all modern conveniences. Built in the 1860's in the copper mining town on the edge of the flinders Ranges, it retains a link with its past, through the attention to period detail and antique furniture.

It is large, with 3 bedrooms – 2 double and a twin.

Breakfast provisions are provided on the first day.

Oratunga Station

Blinman, 5730
Tel: (086) 48 4863
Owner/Contact: Ian & Di Fargher
Rooms: Shearers' Quarters
Cost: $10 adult, $6 child, ($50 nightly minimum)

The shearers' quarters on this station have been thoroughly revamped to provide quality budget accommodation. There are 14 beds. Crockery, cutlery, etc., is provided – B.Y.O. linen and food.

At $10 an adult and $6 a child with a nightly minimum of $50 it is a remarkably economical way to experience this unique part of Australia.

Flinders Ranges

BLINMAN S.A. 5730

Historic Mine Manager's Residence
Tel: (086) 48 4894

The Captain's Cottage, Mine Road
Tel/Fax: (086) 48 4894
Contact: Jane Fargher
Rooms: s/c cottage
Cost: From $64 single/2 nights
Ⓥ

Emohrou
Tel: (086) 48 6282
Contact: Marion & Peter McInnis
Rooms: 2 bedroomed cabin

Oratunga Station
Tel: (086) 48 4863
Owner/Contact: Ian & Di Fargher
Ⓥ

Wilderness Cabin
Tel: (086) 48 6438
Owner/Contact: Ben & Susan Carn

Windana Cottage
Tel: (086) 48 4136
Owner/Contact: Peg & Phil Duffield

Wonoka Holiday Cottage
Tel: (086) 48 6282
Contact: Marion & Peter McInnis

HAWKER S.A. 5434

Mount Little Station
Tel: (086) 48 4260
Owner/Contact: Julie Henschke

Yappala Station Holiday Units, Box 35
Tel: (086) 48 4164
Owner/Contact: Rodney & Shirley Smith

MURRAYTOWN S.A. 5481

Vondon Homestead, Murraytown via Melrose
Tel: (086) 66 4209 Fax: (086) 66 2152
Rooms: 3
Cost: $75 single/2 nights

PARACHILNA S.A. 5730

The Prairie Hotel, West Terrace
Tel: (086) 48 4895 Fax: (086) 48 4894
Rooms: 6
Cost: From $35 single
Dinner available

QUORN S.A. 5433

Blossom's Cottage, Bruce via Quorn
Tel/Fax: (086) 48 6344
Rooms: s/c cottage
Cost: From $100 single/2 nights
No smoking in bedrooms

Barossa Valley

Australia's most famous wine-growing area is just 55 kilometres north of Adelaide.

Although it is so close, don't just cast it aside as a day-trip attraction. There's a lot more to the Barossa than that!

It was named in 1837 by Colonel Light in memory of Barossa in Spain where he had fought a major battle in 1811. The spelling was never corrected.

There is a definite Germanic "feel" to the area based on the early German settlers.

Some of the most famous wineries based in the Barossa are Yalumba, Orlando, Penfolds and Seppelts. Original family members still operate some of these wineries.

There is more to sample than just wine, although the area does produce more than half Australia's quality wine.

There is the splendid avenue of date palms leading to Seppeltsfield with its historic towns and villages.

Why not enjoy some award-winning food with the local wine at the numerous top restaurants in the area?

The Dairy

P.O. Box 391, Lyndoch, 5351
Tel: (085) 24 4507
Owner/Contact: Tom Twopenny & Sonia Laidlaw
Cost: $95 (surcharges apply)

This romantic, delightfully converted dairy sleeps only 2 lucky people. The view from the loo must be one of the best in Australia!!

This idyllic spot should be a must for anyone feeling the stress that '93 caused – relax and enjoy The Dairy in '94.

P.S. Tom and Sonia, to complete that relaxation, can arrange for a masseuse to visit you at either The Dairy or Warrenda.

Warrenda Cottage

Menzel Road, Lyndoch, 5351 (P.O. Box 391)
Tel: (085) 24 4507
Owner/Contact: Tom Twopenny & Sonia Laidlaw
Cost: From $105 for 1 couple to $205 for 3 couples

Warrenda Cottage is situated on a wonderful undulating 600 acre property in the Barossa Valley. This dear stone house has been faithfully restored and beautifully furnished to provide restful accommodation for up to 6 people. There is a fully equipped kitchen and goodies are provided for a wonderful breakfast.

Sonia is a great cook – and given notice when you make your reservation, will deliver to your door a superb dinner.

Hillview Guest House

12 Hill Street, Angaston, 5353
Tel: (085) 64 2761
Owner/Contact: Wendy & Kym Rohrlach
Rooms: 2, ensuite
Cost: From $120

Originally a private girls' grammar school, Hillview is a late 1800's two-storey home which has recently been renovated with elegance and furnished with fine antiques.

The ground floor of the house offers 2 bedrooms with ensuite bathrooms. There is a guest lounge, heated pool and spa. It is also fully licensed.

Hillview makes a good base from which to explore the Barossa Valley, and Wendy and Kym are more than happy to provide you with local information.

Lawley Farm

Krondorf Road, Tanunda, 5352 (P.O. Box 103)
Tel/Fax: (085) 63 2141
Cost: From $99

Lawley Farm offers a genuine heritage experience. The original settlers' farm buildings (circa 1852) have been attractively restored to form suite accommodation. Choose from Brittany, Para, Jacobs or Langmeil.

Breakfast is served in the dining room of the homestead. There is a hot tub spa and a games room, but it is the tranquillity of the gardens that appealed to me.

Each suite has a shady verandah. With a glass of local wine and a book you wouldn't need to venture far – except for dinner at Crackeré Restaurant in Tanunda.

The Lodge Country House

R.S.D. 120, Seppeltsfield, 5355
Tel: (085) 62 8277 Fax: (085) 62 8344
Owner/Contact: Aaron Penley & Graham Butler
Rooms: 4
Cost: From $175

The Lodge Country House, once part of the Seppelt Estate in the Barossa Valley, has a superb setting surrounded by vineyards and a creek. A glorious 3 acre garden, complete with a lawn tennis court and swimming pool, makes this one of the finest country houses in Australia.

The house itself is of generous proportions. The 4 bedrooms are individually designed with bay window seats and private bathrooms. The place has real style.

The food is important too – home grown fruit and vegetables, and a cellar stocked with premium Barossa wines for you to select from ensure a fine night's dining.

This is truly elegant and warm country hospitality.

Sample Menu

Champagne and Hors d'oeuvre

Tomato Onion & Basis Soup – Country Style
with Parmesan Toast Fingers

Grilled Baby Spatchcock (Poussin) with our own
Mild Chilli Plum Sauce and
Vegetable Stir Fry in Coconut Cream
and Jasmine Rice

Hot Passion Fruit Soufflé

Coffee, etc., by the fire

The Miner's Cottage

Goldfields Road, Cockatoo Valley, 5351
Tel: (085) 24 6213 Fax: (085) 24 6650
Owner/Contact: Brenda Gardiner

My choice for the most romantic spot in South Australia. This delightfully restored stone miner's cottage is just 45 minutes from Adelaide and set in a rural landscape of huge green trees and a billabong. There is also a swimming pool and barbecue facilities.

The cottage has just one double bedroom with ensuite with bath. It is air conditioned for summer comfort and has an open fire for the chillier winter nights and that soft romantic flicker.

Brenda is a superb cook, providing picnic hampers and three course dinners delivered to your door – but only by prior arrangement.

Winner of 'Overall Excellence' Barossa Tourist Industry Award 1991.

The Lanzerac Estate Country Inn

Menge Road, Tanunda, 5352 (P.O. Box 153)
Tel: (085) 63 0499 Fax: (085) 63 3652
Rooms: 4, ensuite

Indulgence is the word that comes to mind when I think of the Lanzerac. Situated on the outskirts of historic Bethany, surrounded by vineyards, this property provides four ensuite rooms, all beautifully decorated, with period furniture. The beds are large and comfortable. The fully licensed restaurant has an enviable reputation – even the white fantail pigeons are plump and well cared for!

If you are searching for somewhere for a night or two, this is a haven only 71 km. from Adelaide.

Winner, 'Best Restaurant' – Tourism Awards 1993.

ANGASTON S.A. 5353

Collingrove Homestead, Eden Valley Road
Tel/Fax: (085) 64 2061
Owner/Contact: Patsy Taylor & Kerry Hall
Rooms: 4
Cost: From $100 double/twin
Dinner by arrangement ◆ No smoking

Hill House Bed & Breakfast, Lindsay Street
Tel: (085) 64 2023
Rooms: Private suite
Cost: From $105 single/2 nights
Dinner by arrangement ◆ No children ◆ No smoking indoors

Hillview Guest House, 12 Hill Street
Tel/Fax: (085) 64 2761
Owner/Contact: Wendy & Kym Rohrlach
Rooms: 2, ensuite
Cost: From $120 (V)
Dinner by arrangement ◆ No smoking

Talyala Lodge, 43 North Street
Tel: (085) 64 2147
Owner/Contact: Sandra Johnston
Rooms: s/c unit
Cost: $80 double
No smoking ◆ No children

Wroxton Grange, Flaxman's Valley Road
Tel: (085) 65 3227
Owner/Contact: Josephine & Ian Zander
Rooms: 1
Cost: $70 double
No smoking ◆ No children

BETHANY S.A.

Barossa Bush Retreat, Rifle Range Road, via Bethany
Tel: (08) 378 7975 Fax: (085) 63 0032
Rooms: s/c cabin
Cost: From $30 single/2 nights

High Wycombe Wines/Lodge, Bethany Road (Box 259 Tanunda, 5352)
Tel: (085) 63 2776
Owner/Contact: Angela Davis
Rooms: 5 ensuite units
Cost: $75 double, $15 extra person
Dinner by arrangement

The Landhaus, Bethany Road
Tel: (085) 63 2191
Cost: $113 single
No children • No smoking indoors

BIRDWOOD S.A. 5234

Birdwood Bed & Breakfast, 38 Olivedale Street
Tel/Fax: (085) 68 5444
Owner/Contact: Pam Thoday
Rooms: self contained
Cost: From $65 double, $15 extra adult, $10 child
Dinner basket available • No smoking inside

COCKATOO VALLEY S.A. 5351

The Miner's Cottage, Goldfields Road (Box 28)
Tel: (085) 24 6213 Fax: (085) 24 6650
Owner/Contact: Brenda & Godfrey Gardiner
Rooms: s/c unit Ⓥ
Cost: From $105 double
Dinner by arrangement

EDEN VALLEY S.A. 5235

"The Honey-Room", L. Pumpas Road
Tel: (085) 65 3256
Owner: Nicky & Richard Sage
Rooms: s/c cottage
Cost: $85 double
No smoking indoors ♦ *No children*

GREENOCK S.A. 5360

Sophie's Cottage, Frederick Street
Tel/Fax: (085) 62 8084
Owner/Contact: Mr. & Mrs. M.N. Schluter
Rooms: s/c cottage
Cost: $100 double, $80 without breakfast
No children

LAMEROO S.A. 5302

Meranwyney Host Farm, P.O. Box 51
Tel: (085) 76 5215
Owner/Contact: Kay & Doug Day
Rooms: 3
Cost: Single - $45, $15 dinner, $90 full board
No smoking

LIGHT PASS S.A.

"Lebenwohl", Light Pass Road
Tel: (085) 62 2843
Contact: Mrs. Lois McMillan
Rooms: s/c house
Cost: $250
No children

Light Pass Farmhouse
Tel: (085) 62 1641 or 62 1129 Fax: (085) 62 3410
Owner/Contact: Brian & Jan Linke
Rooms: s/c accommodation
Cost: $75 double

LYNDOCH S.A. 5351

Barossa Country Cottages, 55 Gilbert Street (P.O. Box 291)
Tel: (085) 24 4426 Fax: (085) 24 4931
Owner: Valerie & John Arnold
Rooms: s/c cottages
Cost: $90 double, $30 extra person, $15 children

The Dairy, P.O. Box 391
Tel: (085) 24 4507
Owner/Contact: Tom Twopenny & Sonia Laidlaw (V)
Rooms: s/c cottage
Cost: From $95

Warrenda, Menzel Road (P.O. Box 391)
Tel: (085) 24 4507
Owner/Contact: Tom Twopenny & Sonia Laidlaw
Rooms: s/c cottage (V)
Cost: From $105 double

Woodlands of Lyndoch, Cnr. Barossa Valley Way & Altona Road
Tel/Fax: (085) 24 4511
Rooms: 2 s/c suites
Cost: From $80 single/2 nights

Barossa Valley

MARANANGA S.A.

Marananga Cottage, Seppeltsfield Road
Tel: (085) 63 3494 Fax: (085) 63 3556
Rooms: s/c cottage
Cost: From $110 single/2 nights
No children • No smoking indoors

The Hermitage of Marananga, Seppeltsfield Road
Tel: 008 088 806 Fax: (085) 62 3133
Rooms: Mini suite
Cost: $160 single/2 nights
No children • Dinner available

MOUNT PLEASANT S.A. 5235

Holmes Estate Cottage, Burns Road (P.O. Box 59)
Tel: (085) 68 2319
Owner/Contact: Leonie Holmes
Rooms: s/c cottage
Cost: From $60 double, from $10 extra person
Dinner by arrangement

SEPPELTSFIELD S.A. 5355

The Lodge Country House, R.S.D. 120
Tel: (085) 62 8277 Fax: (085) 62 8344
Owner/Contact: Graham Butler & Aaron Penley
Rooms: 4, ensuite (V)
Cost: $210 double, $175 single, dinner $50
No children • No smoking

TANUNDA S.A. 5352

Barossa Junction Resort, Barossa Valley Way
Tel: (085) 63 3400 Fax: (085) 63 3660
Cost: $111 single/2 nights

Barossa Valley

Barossa House, Barossa Valley Way (Box 339)
Tel: (085) 62 2716
Owner/Contact: Bee & Joe Spencer
Rooms: 3, ensuite
Cost: $50 double

Blickinstal Hillside B & B, Rifle Range Road
Tel: (085) 63 2716
Owner/Contact: John & Alicia Gerkens
Rooms: 4 s/c units
Cost: From $80 double
No children

Langmeil Cottages, 89 Langmeil Road
Tel: (085) 63 2987
Owner/Contact: Cynthia & Colin Spehr
Rooms: 4 s/c units
Cost: $90

Lanzerac Country Accommodation, Menge Road (P.O. Box 353)
Tel: (085) 63 0499 Fax: (085) 63 3652
Owner/Contact: Mr. Wyndham House Ⓥ
Rooms: 4, ensuite
Cost: $285 single, all inclusive, 2 nights

Lawley Farm, Krondorf Road (P.O. Box 103)
Tel/Fax: (085) 63 2141
Owner/Contact: Sancha & Bruce Withers
Rooms: 6, ensuite Ⓥ
Cost: From $99
Dinner by arrangement

Naimanya Cottage, P.O. Box 544
Tel: (085) 65 3275
Owner: Mary & Roger Bryson
Rooms: s/c cottage
Cost: $85 double, $25 extra person
No smoking inside

Norma's Place, 12 John Street
Tel/Fax: (085) 63 0100
Owner/Contact: Loris & Leon Pullen
Rooms: 2
Cost: $95 double, $30 extra person

Stonewell Cottages, Stonewell Road (P.O. Box 96)
Tel: (085) 63 2019
Owner/Contact: John & Yvonne Pfeiffer
Rooms: 3, with private spas
Cost: From $106 double
No children

Veritas Cottage, Stelzer Road (P.O. Box 126)
Tel: (085) 63 2330 or 63 0535
Owner/Contact: Mrs. F. Binder
Rooms: s/c cottage
Cost: $70 double
No smoking • Children not recommended

WILLIAMSTOWN S.A. 5351

"Tungali"
Tel: (085) 24 6251
Owner/Contact: Doug & Elizabeth Gordon
Rooms: s/c cottage
Cost: $80 double, $25 extra person, $10 child
Dinner by arrangement

The Mid North

This region has an amazing blend of history in mining and agriculture.
Some of Australia's best known pastoral properties are here - along with some fascinating pioneer stories relating to the discovery of copper in the 1840s. This created a flurry of action, similar to the gold rush days, with miners from Cornwall, Wales and Scotland coming out to extract the precious ore. There are plenty of examples of that copper fever at towns such as Kapunda and Burra.
The region is also famous for its merino studs such as Bungaree near Clare.
Nature lovers should head for the hills (the bottom of the Finders Ranges, actually) near Crystal Brook. The landscape changes quickly from open grassland to scenic gorges and rolling hills.

ACCOMMODATION

Thorn Park Country House

College Road, Sevenhill, 5453
Tel: (088) 43 4304 Fax: (088) 43 4296
Owner/Contact: David Hay & Michael Speers
Rooms: 6
Cost: From $105 per person

Thorn Park offers genuine country house hospitality. Set in sixty acres of undulating farmland in the Clare Valley, close to the historic Sevenhill Cellars and Church of Saint Aloysius, the 1850's homestead offers the most inviting accommodation. There are six beautifully appointed bedrooms, each with private facilities, a spacious drawing room, library and splendid dining room – all fitted with fine antiques and David & Michael's art collection.

Food here is a focal point. Utilising fresh produce in an imaginative way ensures that dining here will be an essential ingredient of your stay. The house is also fully licensed.

Sample Menu

Blue Cheese Custards served with a tomato & orange sauce

Boned Loin of Lamb on a bed of puréed eggplant
with a rosemary glaze,
Baby potatoes and a salad

Candied Citrus and pine nut tart, with rich cream

Miss Mabel's Cottage

2 Penglawdd Street, Burra, 5417
Tel: (08) 362 3306 Fax: (08) 362 6142
Owner/Contact: Jan Davis

Owned by Jan Davis, this B & B is one of the best. Lived in by Miss Mabel until her death at the grand age of 100 years, it has been operating as a self contained cottage for about 8 years.
It is a time warp – valve radios – in fact little has changed since Miss Mabel's day. But Jan has added so much charm and all modern comforts. The kitchen is stocked with beautifully cooked goodies and there is always a 'Welcome' bottle of wine to greet you.
Sitting in the delightful garden of herbs, olives, walnuts, pistachios and old fashioned roses makes it a difficult place to leave.
I hear that a sumptuous refit is planned for early 1994, so make sure you book to avoid disappointment.

Oliver's at Ford House

80 Main Street, Kapunda, 5373
Tel: (085) 66 2280
Owner/Contact: Gerri Nelligan & Oliver Portway
Rooms: 4, ensuite

Built in the 1860's, Ford House is a two-storey stone building with a balcony. Recently restored and refurbished, it now offers extremely comfortable accommodation. There are 4 upstairs bedrooms, all with ensuite facilities.
Oliver is a racing cyclist and Gerri cooks the most marvellous food, so if you are planning a few days away the Heritage town of Kapunda is a good base to do the wine districts of the Barossa and Clare Valleys.
Oliver's also houses a licensed restaurant and Gerri is happy to put together picnic baskets.
Go with some friends, book the house out and have fun.

Tooralie Homestead

Hallett, 5419
Tel: (088) 94 2067
Owner/Contact: Sylvia & Brian Pohlner

This 2100 ha. property has been held by the Pohlner family since 1873. They run 23 Micron Merinos and crop wheat and oats.

Here you have a choice of accommodation. You can either stay in The Lodge, which is a fully contained house that sleeps up to 15 people – bed, bath and kitchen, linen provided – at a remarkable $25 B & B, dinner $15 or a barbecue at $12.

Or you can choose to sleep in the Homestead, where there are 3 comfortable bedrooms, share bathroom. A cooked breakfast and evening meal are provided at $75 per person, or if you prefer to be just B & B it will cost $40 per person.

Tooralie is close to the famous Heysen Trail that stretches from the Parachilna Gorge to the Flinders Ranges and named after Sir Have Heysen.

Daisy Manor

King Street, Auburn, 5451
Tel: (088) 49 2134
Owner/Contact: Maureen Robb & Colleen Keane
Cost:$75 Monday - Thursday, $85 Friday - Sunday

Auburn is a pretty town in the Clare Valley, with historic buildings and an attractive main street with a few antique shops and restaurants. This is also C.J. Dennis country.

Tucked away down King Street is a real find – Daisy Manor. It is owned by two happy and helpful people, namely Maureen & Colleen. They have created a quiet haven for B & B lovers. A separate guest entrance, double bedroom with ensuite bathroom and a delightful little sitting room – there is a stereo system (take your own CD's and tapes).

Barbecue facilities are available in the pretty garden, and if this isn't enough for you they will provide a cooked breakfast to

your room and pack you up a picnic hamper to tour the Clare Valley.
Go to Sevenhills, or one of the other many other vineyards – buy a bottle and find a shady tree. This is pretty, pretty countryside.

Paxton Square Cottages

Burra, 5417
Tel: (088) 92 2622
Contact: The Manager
Cost: 2 room (bedsit & kitchen) $40
3 room (bedroom, kitchen & lounge) $45
4 room (2 bedrooms, kitchen & lounge) $50

Copper was discovered in Burra Creek by Thomas Pickett in 1845. By 1850 Burra was the largest mine in Australia and today is on the Register of the National Estate and many buildings are listed on the State Heritage Register.
Paxton Square Cottages survive from those times. They are situated near the pretty Burra Creek and a short walk from the centre of town.
There are 33 carefully restored self-contained cottages that offer accommodation for up to eight people. Barbecue and laundry facilities are available. It is B.Y.O. linen and food, but for a very modest $3 per person linen can be hired. Breakfasts are available and in winter firewood may be purchased.
The best cottages are Nos. 12—22.

Craigs Hill & Settlers Cottage

Clare & Sevenhill, 5453

Tel: (08) 379 5595 or (08) 379 7404

Owner/Contact: Mary or Rachel Kennedy

No chapter on the Clare Valley would be complete without mentioning the Kennedys' delightful self-contained properties.

Craig Hill is the larger, sat on 30 hectares of natural bushland with rose and herb gardens. This gracious century-old stone homestead sleeps up to 3.

Settlers Cottage nestles amongst the vines in Sevenhills – close to the famous Jesuits Vineyard. With rambling roses and a cottage garden, Settlers sleeps up to 6.

The Kennedys provide all linen, a country breakfast, supper and a welcoming bottle of Clare Valley wine – what else. Take your own fruit and vegetables!! And if you must, some good friends.

Tarlee Antiques & Motel

Main Road, Tarlee, 5411

Tel: (085) 28 5328 Fax: (085) 28 5326

This is a real surprise! I stopped here because I can't resist antique shops – and is this an antique shop! Five rooms filled to capacity with genuine antiques, Edwardiana and bric-a-brac.

Behind the antiques there is a tea room and licensed restaurant. Walk through that into the garden, and there are 4 motel style units – but with a difference. Antique brass beds and cedar chests, T.V.'s and electric blankets.

The hospitality is warm and friendly. If you buy large pieces of furniture they are happy to arrange delivery.

The Mid North

AUBURN S.A. 5451

Daisy Manor, King Street
Tel: (088) 49 2134 (V)
Owner/Contact: Maureen Robb & Colleen Keane
Cost: From $75

Koonowla Cottage, Saddleworth Road
Tel: (088) 49 2080 Fax: (088) 49 2293
Rooms: s/c cottage
Cost: From $80 single/2 nights
No children • No smoking in bedrooms

Rising Sun Mews, Main North Road
Tel: (088) 49 2015 Fax: (088) 49 2266
Cost: From $65 single
No smoking in bedrooms

Stonehurst Country Style B & B, Lot 12 Main North Road
(P.O. Box 61)
Tel: (085) 22 5865
Owner/Contact: Julie M. Butler
Rooms: 3
Cost: $85 double
No smoking • No children

Tateham's Restaurant & Guest House, Main North Road
Tel: (088) 49 2030 Fax: (088) 49 2020
Cost: From $65 single
No children

BOWER S.A. 5374

Glenbower Cottage
Tel: (085) 81 0586
Rooms: s/c cottage
Cost: From $45 single/2 nights
No smoking indoors

BURRA S.A. 5417

Bon Accord Cottage, Railway Terrace
Tel: (088) 92 2519
Contact: Joan de Metris
Rooms: s/c cottage
Cost: $75 double, $20 extra person

Burra Heritage Cottages, Truro Street
Tel: (088) 92 2461
Rooms: s/c cottages
Cost: From $58 single/2 nights

Burra View House, 7 Mt. Pleasant Road
Tel: (088) 92 2648 Fax: (088) 92 2150
Owner/Contact: Avian & Freda Pink
Rooms: 5
Cost: $80 double, $50 single, $20 children under 10
Dinner by arrangement ◆ *No smoking*

Coppervilla, 10 Paxton Terrace
Tel: (088) 92 2648 Fax: (088) 92 2150
Owner/Contact: Avian & Freda Pink
Rooms: s/c cottage
Cost: $70 double, $20 extra person
No smoking

Ellen's Cottage, 8 Paxton Terrace
Tel: (088) 92 2648 Fax: (088) 92 2150
Owner/Contact: Avian & Freda Pink
Rooms: s/c cottage
Cost: $70 double, $20 extra person
No smoking

Miss Mabel's Cottage, Penglawdd Street
Tel: (08) 362 3306 Fax: (08) 362 6142
Owner/Contact: Jan Davis, 13 The Parade, Norwood, 5067 Ⓥ
Rooms: s/c cottage
Cost: $95 double
moking on verandah • Children & pets by arrangement

Paxton Square Cottages
Tel: (088) 92 2622
Owner/Contact: The Manager
Rooms: 32 s/c cottages Ⓥ
Cost: From $40

Penhaligon's Country House, 6 Chapel Street
Tel: (088) 92 2259
Owner/Contact: Mrs. Susan Roche
Rooms: 4
Cost: $65 single, Dinner $35
No children

Wildildie, Box 135
Tel: (088) 92 2394
Owner/Contact: Robert Heading
Rooms: 3

CLARE S.A. 5453

Bruce Hill Country Lodge, Warenda Road
Tel: (088) 42 2925
Rooms: 4 s/c apartments
Cost: $125 single/2 nights
No children • No smoking

Bungaree Station, Box 231
Tel: (088) 42 2677 Fax: (088) 42 3004
Owner/Contact: Sally Hawker
Rooms: s/c cottages & quarters
Cost: From $15 single, from $10 child, Dinner $15
Dinner available • No smoking inside

Craigs Hill, c/o 9 Austin Crescent, St. Georges, 5064
Tel: (08) 379 5595 or (08) 379 7404
Owner/Contact: Mary Kennedy Ⓥ
Rooms: s/c house
Cost: $60 single
moking on verandah

Maggies Farm Cottage, c/o 10 Day Terrace, Croydon, 5008
Tel: (08) 346 3953
Rooms: s/c cottage
Cost: From $80 single/2 nights
No children • No smoking

Mundawora, Box 9905 Mundawora
Tel: (088) 42 3672
Owner/Contact: Peter & Natalie Pratt
Rooms: 4 cottage suites
Cost: $80 double
Dinner by arrangement

The Palms B & B, 25 Victoria Road
Tel: (088) 42 3911
Owner/Contact: John & Fiona Cockington
Rooms: 2
Cost: $40 single
Dinner by arrangement • No smoking

HALLETT S.A. 5419

Tooralie Homestead
Tel/Fax: (088) 94 2067
Owner/Contact: Sylvia Pohlner
Rooms: 3 Ⓥ
Cost: $40 single
Dinner available • No smoking • No children

KAPUNDA S.A. 5373

Oliver's at Ford House, 80 Main Street
Tel: (085) 66 2280
Owner/Contact: Ms. Gerri Nelligan & Mr. Oliver Portway Ⓥ
Rooms: 4, ensuite
Cost: $80 double, $60 single
Dinner available • No smoking indoors

MINTARO S.A. 5415

Martindale Hall, Manoora Road
Tel: (088) 43 9088 Fax: (088) 43 9082
Rooms: 9
Cost: $200 single/2 nights
No children under 15 • No smoking indoors

Miller's House, c/o 22 Weemala Drive, Mitcham, 5062
Tel: (08) 271 6601
Rooms: s/c cottage
Cost: From $80 single/2 nights

Mintaro Hideaway, Burra Street
Tel: (088) 43 9011
Rooms: s/c cottage units
Cost: From $100 single/2 nights
No smoking in bedrooms

Mintaro Mews, Burra Street
Tel: (008) 43 9001 Fax: (008) 43 9002
Cost: From $183 single/2 nights
No children • No smoking indoors

Mintaro Pay Office Cottages, Hill Street
Tel: (088) 43 9026
Rooms: s/c cottages
Cost: From $95 single/2 nights

Oldfields, The Old School House, Young Street
Tel: (088) 43 9038
Rooms: s/c cottage
Cost: $95 single/2 nights
No children • No smoking in bedrooms

PORT PIRIE S.A. 5540

Sampson's Cottage, 66 Ellen Street (c/o 184 Balmoral Road)
Tel: (086) 32 2272
Contact: Nancy Wood
Rooms: s/c cottage
Cost: $90 double, $25 extra person
Dinner by arrangement • No smoking

SEVENHILL S.A. 5453

Miss Nobels Cottage, Quarry Road
Tel: (088) 43 4326 or (088) 43 0020
Rooms: s/c cottage
Cost: From $42 single/2 nights
No smoking indoors

Nedslea Lodge, Mintaro Road, Polish Hill River
Tel: (088) 43 4292
Rooms: s/c holiday house
Cost: From $60 single/2 nights
No smoking in bedrooms

Nykiels, Polish Hill River Road
Tel: (088) 43 4292
Rooms: s/c holiday house
Cost: From $73 single/2 nights
No smoking in bedrooms

Settlers Cottage, c/o 9 Austin Crescent, St. Georges, 5064
Tel: (08) 379 5595 or (08) 379 7404
Owner/Contact: Mary Kennedy
Rooms: s/c cottage
Cost: $60 single (V)
moking on verandah

Thorn Park Country House, College Road
Tel: (088) 43 4304 Fax: (088) 43 4296
Owner/Contact: David Hay & Michael Speers
Rooms: 6
Cost: From $105 per person, dinner $40 (V)

Windermere Cottage, Skillogalee Road
Tel: (088) 43 4270
Rooms: s/c cottage
Cost: From $75 single/2 nights
Pets by arrangement

TARLEE S.A. 5411

Ryelands Farm Retreat
Tel: (085) 28 5262
Rooms: s/c holiday house
Cost: From $25 single/2 nights

Tarlee Antiques, Main Road
Tel: (085) 28 5328 or (018) 83 6543 Fax: (085) 28 5326
Owner/Contact: The Manager
Rooms: Guest cabins
Cost: From $55 double ⓥ
Dinner available

The Murraylands

As the name suggests, Australia's largest river, the Mighty Murray, is at the heart of this region.

Being the lifeblood of the region, it's not hard to realise things revolve around the river. From watersports to irrigation for farming, the Murray is vital.

Paddle steamers are a perfect way to view some of the more inaccessible spots, but if you stick to the beaten tracks there's still plenty to see and enjoy.

The waterway provides a natural environment for birds and sunset can provide some spectacular sights with the day's final rays dancing over the water.

Industry is thriving in the region with agriculture leading the way, as it has for more than 150 years.

The Murray area was also a communications centre during the Victorian gold rush days of the 1850s and remnants of that difficult past are worth a look.

ACCOMMODATION

Mill Park

Box 15, Meningie, 5264
Tel/Fax: (085) 75 6033
Owner/Contact: Peter & Serena Watson
Cost: $110 double, $20 each extra person

This is how a self-contained homestead should be operated. It is sparklingly clean, extremely comfortable and wonderfully situated for the Coorong National Park. Three attractively furnished bedrooms, open fireplaces – fire lit prior to your arrival – fresh flowers and thoughtful provisions left in the pantry. There is even a spa bath to relax in after you have wandered over the heath and coastal Mallee.

Mill Park is within sight of Lake Albert and only 15 minutes drive to the Coorong – surely one of the most interesting areas for bird watchers.

Acacia Cottage

Box 15, Meningie, 5264
Tel/Fax: (085) 75 6033
Owner/Contact: Peter & Serena Watson
Cost: $60 double, $20 each extra person

Also owned by Peter and Serena, this is a more modest style of accommodation in a bushland setting. There is sleeping for six in 3 bedrooms. Similar caring touches to Mill Park, just a different environment.

The choice is yours.

CLAYTON S.A. 5256

Waterfront Lodge, c/o Lakes & Coorong Restaurant Complex
Tel: (085) 37 0177
Rooms: s/c units
Cost: From $130 single/2 nights

COONALPYN S.A. 5265

No smoking indoors
Bayree Farm, Venning Road (P.O. Box 36)
Tel: (085) 71 1054 Fax: (085) 71 1222
Owner/Contact: Geoff Kuehne
Rooms: 4
Cost: $45

GOOLWA S.A. 5214

Dinner available ◆ *No smoking*
Goolwa Cottage, 3 Hays Street
Tel: (085) 55 1021
Owner/Contact: Alan & Helen Jones
Rooms: 2
Cost: $65
No smoking

Holiday Cottages - Goolwa, 14–16 Hutchinson Street
Tel: (085) 55 3601
Owner/Contact: David Sinclair or John Morfesse
Rooms: 3 s/c cottages

MANNUM S.A. 5238

Cost: $80 double, $20 extra person
Mannaroo Farm, East Front Road
Tel/Fax: (085) 69 1646
Owner/Contact: Bobbie & Ian Mann
Rooms: 2
Cost: $65 double, $50 single, $10 children

MENINGIE S.A. 5264

Dinner available
Acacia Cottage, Box 15
Tel/Fax: (085) 75 6033 Ⓥ
Owner/Contact: Peter & Serena Watson
Rooms: s/c cottage
Cost: $60 double, $20 extra person

Mill Park, Box 15
Tel/Fax: (085) 75 6033
Owner/Contact: Peter & Serena Watson Ⓥ
Rooms: s/c cottage

MURRAY BRIDGE S.A. 5253

Cost: $110 double, $20 extra person
Hy-am Home, 43 Parish Crescent
Tel: (085) 32 1174
Owner/Contact: Bert & Nita Hyam
Rooms: s/c unit
Cost: $60 double, $15 children

PALMER S.A. 5237

No smoking
Astrid's, Adelaide Road
Tel: (085) 69 4105
Owner/Contact: Astrid Keiman
Rooms: 1
Cost: $80 double

PINNAROO S.A. 5304

Dinner available • No children
Alcheringa Host Farm, Bordertown Road
Tel: (085) 76 6171
Cost: $90 single, full board
No smoking indoors

RENMARK S.A. 5341

The Gables Bed & Breakfast, c/o 7 Telopea Drive, Athelstone, 5076
Tel: (08) 337 6100 or (085) 86 4186 Fax: (08) 336 9880
Rooms: s/c holiday house
Cost: From $65 single/2 nights
No smoking indoors

TAILEM BEND S.A. 5260

Poltalloch Station, Narrung
Tel: (085) 74 0043 Fax: (085) 74 0065
Contact: Annie & Les Davis-Ross
Rooms: 4 s/c cottages
Cost: From $10 single
Dinner available

Fleurieu Peninsula

Just half an hour's drive from Adelaide and you are in one of the state's most spectacular regions, complete with ocean views. It's only a tiny area, stretching from O'Halloran Hill for about 90 kms to Cape Jervis, but it is crammed full of magnificent scenery.

Fleurieu is bounded by water on three sides - Gulf St Vincent, the Southern Ocean and the River Murray - so it is no surprise that it is a Mecca for water lovers.

There are more than 20 conservation and national parks through which walking tracks, including the spectacular Heysen Trail, meander.

The surf beach at Victor Harbor is a must for swimmers, while keen anglers should try Goolwa, which is also the starting point for paddle wheeler cruises up the Murray.

History has also left its special mark in the region, with much of the early architecture remaining.

For steam train enthusiasts, a steam train journey on the Southern Encounter from Adelaide to Victor Harbor is a splendid way to travel to the Encounter Coast. The journey passes through the Adelaide Hills via Mount Lofty, Mount Banker, Strathalbyn, Goolwa, Middleton, Port Elliott and into the station at Victor Harbor.

The Cockle Train line extends from Goolwa to Victor Harbor and operates on Sundays from September to November and May to June.

Whale Watching

The Encounter Bay coast is ideally suited for whale watching activities. Victor Harbor is the site of 3 old whaling stations, and Encounter Bay is the play and nursery grounds of the majestic Southern Right Whale. They are in this area from June to September, courting, mating and giving birth to their young.

ACCOMMODATION

The Whalers Inn

The Bluff, Encounter Bay, Victor Harbor, 5211
Tel: (085) 52 4400 Fax: (085) 52 4240
Rooms: s/c apartments

The Whalers Inn is built on the old whaling station site, which was the first industry of the colony of South Australia. There is a plaque depicting the meeting of the French ship commanded by Baudin and the English ship commanded by Flinders.

The spacious, luxurious two-storey apartments all have balconies overlooking the bay. The kitchens are equipped with stoves, microwaves and dishwashers. Downstairs there are queen sized beds and double spas.

There is also a 'settlers cottage', now used as a honeymoon suite. This unique experience would definitely be something to remember.

Old Cape Jervis Homestead

c/o Post Office, Delamere, 5204
Tel: (085) 98 0233 Fax: (085) 98 0271
Owner/Contact: Sandi & John Hill
Rooms: 2

This grand homestead is constructed of local stone with walls two feet thick. Built 150 years ago by Frederick Ramsford, the Old Cape Jervis Homestead offers peace and tranquillity amid the rolling landscape of the Fleurieu Peninsula.

There are 2 double bedrooms with French doors opening onto a large verandah with a magnificent Moreton Bay fig tree close by. One room has an ensuite.
A large living room with open fireplace enables guests to relax after the ferry trip back from Kangaroo Island.
Dinner is also available.

Leonards Mill

Cape Jervis Road, Second Valley, 5204
Tel: (085) 98 4184 Fax: (085) 98 4110

Nestled amongst the rolling hills of the southern Fleurieu coastline, Leonards Mill is a restored bluestone flour mill of 1849, combining heritage cloth with the comforts and quality of modern facilities.
There are 7 cottage rooms with ensuites and pot belly stoves. There are also motel style rooms on the other side of the road – try to avoid these. There is a games room, tennis court and restaurant where the food is good and they have a good list of regional wines.

Anchorage Guest House

Flinders Parade, Victor Harbor, 5211
Tel: (085) 52 5970 Fax: (085) 52 1970

For those with a yearning to paint – what better way to spend a day or two than under the guidance of an experienced artist using either watercolour, oils, acrylic or wash.
The Anchorage Guest House is a heritage listed building with a licensed restaurant. The bedrooms have a choice of ensuite or shared facilities.

ALDINGA BEACH S.A. 5173

"Illawara" Bed & Breakfast, 19 Morgan Street
Tel/Fax: (085) 57 7740
Owner/Contact: John & Diny Warmer
Rooms: 2, ensuite
Cost: From $98
Dinner by arrangement ◆ *No children* ◆ *No smoking inside*

ASHBOURNE S.A. 5157

Kondoparinga Homestead
Tel: (085) 36 6111 Fax: (085) 36 6206
Owner/Contact: Melanee Vournard or David Tredrea
Rooms: 8
Cost: $190 double, dinner bed & breakfast
No smoking inside

CAPE JERVIS S.A. 5204

Old Cape Jervis Homestead, c/o Post Office, Delamere, 5204
Tel: (085) 98 0233 Fax: (085) 98 0271
Owner/Contact: Sandi & John Hill
Rooms: 2 Ⓥ
Dinner available

CLARENDON S.A. 5157

Old Clarendon Winery, Main Road
Tel: (08) 383 6166 Fax: (08) 383 6487
Cost: From $45 single

ENCOUNTER BAY S.A. 5211

The Whalers Inn, The Bluff
Tel: (085) 52 4400 Fax: (085) 52 4240 Ⓥ
Rooms: s/c apartments
Cost: From $70 single/2 nights

HINDMARSH ISLAND S.A. 5007

Narnu Park Homestead, Batson Parade
Tel: (085) 55 2010 Fax: (085) 55 1450
Cost: From $125 single/2 nights, including dinner
No smoking inside

McLAREN VALE S.A. 5171

McLaren Vale Bed & Breakfast, 56 Valley View Drive
Tel: (08) 323 9351 or (018) 803 379
Owner/Contact: Bev Mitchell
Rooms: 2
Cost: $70 double, $50 single
Dinner by arrangement ◆ No smoking ◆ Children negotiable

Samarkand Bed & Breakfast, Branson Road (P.O. Box 322)
Tel/Fax: (08) 323 8756
Owner/Contact: Annette & Dick Inwood
Rooms: Suite of rooms
Cost: $75 single, $90 double, $40 extra adult
No smoking

Southern Vales Bed & Breakfast, 13 Chalk Hill Road
Tel: (08) 323 8144
Owner/Contact: Mrs. Helen Tilley
Rooms: 5
Cost: $70 double, $55 single
No smoking indoors ◆ No children

MIDDLETON S.A. 5213

Mindacowie Guest House, 48 Goolwa Road
Tel: (085) 54 3243 Fax: (085) 54 2438
Owner/Contact: John Elliott & Julie Churches
Rooms: 4
Cost: From $85
Dinner available ◆ No smoking indoors ◆ No children

MOUNT COMPASS S.A. 5210

Compass Country Cabins, Cleland Gully Road
Tel: (085) 56 8425
Rooms: 2 s/c cabins
Cost: From $60 single/2 nights

NORMANVILLE S.A. 5204

Dunes Cottage, c/o The Island Travel Centre, Gresham St., Adelaide, 5000
Tel: (08) 212 4550 Fax: (08) 231 1785
Rooms: s/c cottage
Cost: From $80 single/2 nights
No children

PORT ELLIOT S.A. 5212

Trafalgar House Accommodation, 25 The Strand
Tel: (085) 54 2483
Owner/Contact: Denise Darling
Rooms: 3 + s/c cottage & s/c flat
Cost: From $68 double
No smoking

SECOND VALLEY S.A. 5204

Leonards Mill, Cape Jervis Road
Tel: (085) 98 4184 Fax: (085) 98 4110 (V)
Cost: From $125 single/2 nights
No children

SELLICK'S BEACH S.A. 5174

Sellicks-on the-Sea, 21 The Esplanade
Tel: (085) 56 3273
Owner/Contact: Mark & Sharon Prance
Rooms: 1, ensuite
Cost: From $90 double
No children ◆ *No smoking*

VICTOR HARBOR S.A. 5211

Anchorage Guest House, Flinders Parade
Tel: (085) 52 5970 Fax: (085) 52 1970 (V)
Cost: $180 single
No children

Beken House, 46 White Crescent
Tel: (085) 52 4955
Owner/Contact: Betty & Ken Viney
Rooms: 2, ensuite
Cost: $75 double, $60 single, $15 dinner
No smoking ◆ *No children*

Huntworth, Cnr. Battye Rd. & Kirby St., Encounter Bay (P.O. Box 615)
Tel: (085) 52 4671
Owner/Contact: Margaret & Neil Wilkinson
Rooms: Self contained
Cost: $70 double, $50 single
Dinner by arrangement ◆ *No smoking indoors* ◆ *No children*

"Riverhouse", Waggon Road (P.O. Box 72, Norton Summit, 5136)
Tel: (08) 390 1329 Fax: (08) 390 3663
Owner/Contact: Jane Fergusson
Rooms: 3
Cost: $80 double, $20 extra person
No smoking

Villa Victor Bed & Breakfast, 59 Victoria Street
Tel: (085) 52 4258
Owner/Contact: Lyn Butcher
Rooms: 4 + s/c cottage
Cost: From $55 double, $35 single
No smoking

WILLUNGA S.A. 5172

Kurianda Cottage, c/o 3 Baykai Grove, West Lakes, 5021
Tel: (08) 268 4471
Rooms: s/c cottage
Cost: From $55 single/2 nights
No smoking indoors

Moo's Cottage, R.S.D. Meadows Road, Hope Forest
Tel: (085) 56 7292
Owner/Contact: Kerry Rochford
Rooms: s/c cottage
Cost: $80 per night for cottage
Dinner by arrangement

Willunga House B & B, 1 St. Peter's Terrace
Tel: (085) 56 2467
Owner/Contact: Rosie & Kingsley Knott
Rooms: 3
Cost: $90 double
No smoking • No children

Kangaroo Island

If you want natural beauty at its finest, Kangaroo Island is the place for you.

I travelled there at the beginning of December and it left me breathless. Off the tourist track, except for the month of January, the island is a wilderness refuge, one of the last true unspoilt areas.

The joy of standing metres from massive sea lions who totally ignore your presence was quite amazing. Not to be outdone, New Zealand fur seals join in the fun in their own salt rock pools.

Many plants and animals found on the island are no longer found on the mainland.

Kangaroo Island is Australia's third largest island - about 145 kilometres long and 60 kms wide.

Apart from the seals and sea lions, the island has an unusual throwback to yesteryear. Honey bees, introduced in 1881, are now in demand with mainland hives.

The eucalyptus oil distilling industry has now returned after an absence of nearly a century. A visit to a still is worthwhile.

For bird watchers, Kangaroo Island has the last surviving Glossy Black cockatoos in South Australia.

Admirals Arch and the Remarkable Rocks are two gems of nature in the Flinders Chase National Park.

The Settlement

North Coast Road, Middle River (R.S.D. 26, Kingscote, 5223)
Tel: (084) 83 6237 Fax: (084) 83 6260
Owner/Contact: Belinda Hannaford
Rooms: 2 s/c cottages
Cost: $100 a day, base, plus $10 per adult

Certainly the best place to stay on Kangaroo Island and in the best position. Take your pick from The Beach House or Settlers Cottage.

Perfectly positioned, these limestone cottages have enormous living space, polished floor boards and beautiful oak furniture. The Settlers is the larger of the two, with sleeping for 6 and two huge bathrooms. The Beach House is lighter and all the bedrooms face the sea.

Kitchens have all mod cons and breakfast provisions can be provided. Belinda is an amazing cook and 'some' catering may be arranged – but generally these cottages are self catering.

It is advisable to book 4 months in advance!

Koala Lodge Bed & Breakfast

Cygnet River via Kingscote, 5223
Tel: (084) 82 9006

Situated at Cygnet River and just 10 minutes from Kingscote, Koala Lodge offers comfortable accommodation with friendly warm hospitality.

The bedroom has an ensuite and guests have a private entrance.

The area is renowned for its large population of Koalas and abundant wildlife.

Kangaroo Island Wilderness Accommodation

Rocky River Headquarters, Flinders Chase National Park
(PMB 246 via Kingscote, 5223)
Tel: (084) 83 7235 Fax: (084) 83 7268
Rooms: 8 cottages
Cost: From $22.50 at Mays Cottage to $60 at Flinders Keep

There are 8 cottages under the care of the National Parks and Wildlife Services. They are in near original condition and available for rent year round. All except Mays Cottage have kitchen, running water, electric or gas stove, refrigerator, bathroom, sinks, hot showers and toilet. All have basic cutlery, crockery, saucepans, etc. You will need to take your own linen, bedding, pillows, toilet paper and food supplies.

All revenue collected is used to restore and maintain these historic lodgings.

Flinders Keep is a large and roomy stone residence that sleeps 6.

Hartley Hut is the modern prefabricated relieving keepers quarters – sleeps 4.

The Old Rocky River Homestead is a four roomed stone cottage with low-pitched corrugated iron roof. It has 2 bedrooms and sleeps 6.

Parndana and Karatta Lodge are classic ex-lightkeepers' houses, large and rooms, built around 1910. Three bedroomed, each sleeps 6. Stay here and spend hours watching the New Zealand black fur seals at Admiralty Arch.

Lightkeepers Cottages 1 and 2. On the easternmost point of the island, these rusticated asbestos-clad cottages form part of the lightkeepers settlement of Cape Willoughby. Each cottage sleeps 8 people comfortably.

Mays Cottage is a one room stone hut equipped with two double bunk beds, a table and chairs, a small fridge and a wood stove (wood is provided). The cottage is next to the Old Homestead, closer by the Rocky River Headquarters.

Kangaroo Island

AMERICAN RIVER S.A. 5221

Wanderers Rest of Kangaroo Island, Bayview Road
Tel: (084) 83 3140 Fax: (084) 83 3282
Owner/Contact: Pat & Geoff Wright
Rooms: 8, ensuite
Cost: $120 double/twin, $110 single
Dinner available ◆ No children

CYGNET RIVER S.A. 5223

Koala Lodge (via Kingscote)
Tel: (084) 83 1233 or (084) 82 9006 Fax: (084) 83 1190
Contact: Eastern Cove Ferry Services (booking service) Ⓥ
Cost: $54 double, $10 extra person
No smoking

EMU BAY S.A.

Emu Bay Holiday Homes, Bayview Road
Tel: (084) 89 6083
Rooms: s/c holiday houses
Cost: From $45 single/2 nights
No smoking indoors

GOSSE S.A.

Roo Lagoon Cottage, Roo Lagoon
Tel: (084) 83 1233 Fax: (084) 83 1190
Contact: Eastern Cove Ferry Services (booking service)
Rooms: 1, ensuite
Cost: $60/night
Dinner available ◆ No smoking ◆ No children

HANSON BAY S.A.

Hanson Bay Cabins, c/o 10 McKenna Street, Kensington Park, 5068
Tel: (08) 333 0646 Fax: (08) 331 3969
Rooms: s/c cabins
Cost: From $72 single/3 nights

Kangaroo Island

KARATTA S.A.

Attarak Homestead, Mt. Taylor Road
Tel: (084) 83 7202 A.H.
Owner/Contact: Val or Roger Borgmeyer
Rooms: 4
Cost: $50 double, $30 single, $20 children
Dinner available • No smoking

KINGSCOTE S.A. 5223

"**Amberlee, Kingscote**", 33 Kohinoor Road (Box 15, Parndana, 5220)
Tel: (084) 83 7239
Owner/Contact: Don & Heather Latty
Rooms: s/c house
Cost: $70 double, $15 extra person
No smoking indoors

MIDDLE RIVER S.A. 5223

The Settlement, North Coast Road (R.S.D. 26, Kingscote, 5223)
Tel: (084) 83 2636-7 Fax: (084) 83 6260
Owner/Contact: Belinda Hannaford
Rooms: 2 s/c cottages (V)
Cost: $100 per cottage/night + $10 per adult
Dinner by arrangement

PARNDANA S.A. 5220

Coora Cottage, P.O. Box 43
Tel: (084) 89 6027 Fax: (084) 89 6080
Rooms: s/c holiday house
Cost: From $70 single/3 nights

PENNESHAW S.A. 5222

Cape View Cottage, P.O. Box 435, Kingscote, 5223
Tel: (084) 82 2390
Rooms: s/c cottage
Cost: From $75 single/5 nights

Muggleton-Moles B & B
Tel: (084) 83 1233 Fax: (084) 83 1190
Contact: Eastern Cove Ferry Services (booking service)
Rooms: 2
Cost: $75 double, $40 single, Dinner $15 each
No smoking

ROCKY RIVER S.A. 5223

Kangaroo Island Wilderness Accommodation, Rocky River Headquarters, Flinders Chase National Park (P.M.B. 246, via Kingscote 5223)
Tel: (084) 83 7235 Fax: (084) 83 7268
Rooms: 8 s/c cottages (V)
Cost: From $22.50 - $60

The South East

There's plenty of variety in landscape and scenery in this region.

Rugged coasts, with ancient caves, extinct volcanoes, forests and vineyards and beautiful beaches are just some of the attractions waiting to be discovered, if you plan properly.

The fishing industry still thrives in old seaports such as Robe and Beachport.

The area between Kingston and Port MacDonnell is known as the "crustacean coast" because of the giant lobsters caught there at certain times of the year.

Mount Gambier is worth a visit for its volcanic attractions, most notably the famous Blue Lake crater.

Penola should also be on your route because of its heritage buildings and its closeness to the Naracoorte Caves.

The Bool Lagoon near Naracoorte is a special wetlands region teeming with different species of birds.

ACCOMMODATION

Grey Masts

1 Smillie Street, Robe, 5276
Tel: (087) 68 2303
Owner/Contact: Raimon Aplin & Andrew Reid
Rooms: 4

Built in 1853, originally as a wool store, this glorious old weatherboard building has been given a new lease of life under the ownership of Raimon Aplin and Andrew Reid.

Four double bedrooms, redecorated with great attention to detail, share two bathrooms. There is a small sitting room with an open fireplace, the surrounds of which took 8 layers of paint stripper to expose the soft, mellow wood. But it is in the feeling of Grey Masts, from the moment you walk onto the warm timbered flooring of the dining room, that you know you have arrived somewhere quite special.

Sure, the view of that famous Robe bay helps – this must be the bluest water in South Australia.

The food in the restaurant relies heavily on local produce, with an abundance of fresh fish and crays in season.

The service comes with a smile and a chat, and the chef is usually hovering somewhere to ensure all is well.

The atmosphere reflects a relaxed seaside mood, but nonetheless that is a feeling of quality – from the lovely china and cutlery to the generous wine glasses begging to be filled with some of South Australia's finest wines from the impressive (if slightly expensive) wine list.

Don't miss this one!

The Lakeside

Main Road, Robe, 5274
Tel: (087) 68 2042 Fax: (087) 68 2485
Owner/Contact: Mel & Peter Riseley
Rooms: 3
Cost: $95 - $115

Built in 1882 of local stone, Lakeside is one of the grand old residences of Robe on the foreshores of Lake Fellmongery.
There are three spacious guest rooms, one ensuite and two that share a bathroom. The ceilings are high, and there is a definite feeling of space and light in the homestead. No dinner is available, but a picnic basket may be ordered.

Wilsons at Robe

Victoria Street (P.O. Box 54), Robe, 5274
Tel: (087) 68 2459, A.H. (087) 68 2216
Owner/Contact: Nancy & Terry Johnson
Rooms: s/c cottage
Cost: $95 double, $20 each additional guest

Victoria Cottage is a charmingly restored 4 room stone fisherman's cottage built in 1852. Situated in a fenced cottage garden, with slate floors, open fireplaces and early Australian furniture – equipped with electric blankets, television, video and well fitted out kitchen – this abode is certainly for the discerning traveller who appreciates quality.

The Johnsons also own 'Wilsons at Robe' – an award winning gallery that also provides fine food. The gallery is well laid out and only has quality products. When I was there Anne Mills had some stunning paintings hanging and there were some fine galvanised fish on weathered timber.

Sarah's Cottage

24 Julian Street, West Penola, 5277 (P.O. Box 4)
Tel: (087) 36 3309
Owner/Contact: James & Anne Yates

This whitewashed stone cottage was built in 1872. The pretty cottage garden that surrounds this house, set off by the white picket fence, makes it appealing to the eye as one drives up.

The cosy double bedroom with iron bedstead and the comfortable sitting room with open fireplace are in the original part of the house. At the back, in the extension, a modern timber kitchen and bathroom with spa open out onto a terrace with views over open parklands.

If Sarah's is booked, try Naomi's – they own this one too.

Coonawarra Country Cottages

Mary Street & Helen Street, Coonawarra, 5263 (Box 10B)
Tel: (087) 36 3304 or (087) 36 3220
Owner/Contact: Shirley Skinner

Shirley Skinner is a remarkable woman. I met her manning the Information Centre in Penola – surrounded by chaos with builders invading the building, but she knew where everything was.

She has 4 cottages in Coonawarra – The Skinner Cottage, The Bankhouse, Redman Cottage and Pickers Hut. They cater for 4 9 adults, depending upon your choice of building, with tariffs ranging from an extremely reasonable $50 - $75 for 2, an extra person $20 - $30. This includes breakfast provisions and linen!

The Bankhouse is a clever restoration with open plan kitchen and living area. The romantic bedrooms with half tester beds have ensuite facilities.

Air conditioning, laundry facilities and all that wine on the doorstep to taste – what more could one ask for?

Padthaway Homestead

Padthaway, 5271
Tel: (087) 65 5039 Fax: (087) 65 5097
Contact/Manager: Rosemarie Hayes & Dianne Brown
Cost: $115 per person, $170 single D,B & B

In the nineteenth century Padthaway Estate was prized for its red soil, sunshine and good rainfall.

Today Padthaway Estate offers gracious living in the restored homestead built in 1882. There are six individually decorated bedrooms upstairs, with shared bathrooms. The balcony is accessible to all house guests. Downstairs there is a games room, sun room and drawing room with open fire.

The gardens are worth a leisurely stroll, or for the more energetic there is tennis and croquet.

The original stables house the tasting room and sales – the vineyards are dedicated to Chardonnay and Pinot Noir. Try the Estate labelled Pinot Noir '91 Brut.

COONAWARRA S.A. 5263

Coonawarra Country Cottages, Mary St. & Helen St. (Box 10B)
Tel: (087) 36 3304 or 36 3220 or 36 3251
Owner/Contact: Shirley & Moira Skinner Ⓥ
Rooms: s/c cottages
Cost: From $55 to $80 double, extras $30, children $10
Dinner by arrangement

Koonara Cottage, Tricia Reschke Road
Tel: (087) 36 3267 Fax: (087) 36 3020
Rooms: s/c cottage
Cost: From $50 single/2 nights
No smoking in bedrooms

Ralph's Cottage, Joanna via Coonawarra
Tel: (087) 62 3038 or (018) 838 213 Fax: (087) 62 3394
Rooms: s/c cottage
Cost: From $50 single/2 nights

FRANCES S.A. 5262

St. Aubins Farm Cottage, Danby's Road
Tel: (087) 65 1051 Fax: (087) 65 1001
Rooms: s/c cottage
Cost: From $80 single/2 nights
No smoking in bedrooms

MAITLAND S.A. 5573

Eothen Farmhouse, P.O. Box 205
Tel/Fax: (088) 36 3210
Owner/Contact: Mrs. Rhoda Heinrich
Rooms: s/c house
Cost: From $65 double

MILLICENT S.A. 5280

Heath Park, P.O. Box 303
Tel/Fax: (087) 35 2065
Rooms: 2
Cost: From $95 single
No smoking indoors

MOUNT GAMBIER S.A. 5290

Evelyn Arthur's Homestay, 68 Bay Road
Tel: (087) 25 0511
Owner/Contact: Evelyn & Eric Arthur
Rooms: 2, ensuite
Cost: $95 double, $85 single
Dinner by arrangement • No smoking • No children

"**Mingbool North**", Kirby Road (c/- Box 444)
Tel: (087) 39 8234
Owner/Contact: Jacqueline Kirby
Rooms: 2
Cost: From $70 double, $60 single
Dinner by arrangement • No smoking

NARACOORTE S.A. 5271

Messamurray B & B, Box 20
Tel: (087) 65 2206 Fax: (087) 65 2270
Owner/Contact: Tessa & Richard Levinge
Rooms: 2
Cost: $60 single
Dinner by arrangement • No children

The South East

PADTHAWAY 5271

Padthaway Homestead
Tel: (087) 65 5039 Fax: (087) 65 5097
Contact: Rosemarie Hayes & Dianne Brown
Rooms: 6 Ⓥ
Cost: From $115
Dinner available • No smoking inside • No children

PENOLA S.A. 5277

Miss Thompsons, 35 Arthur Street
Tel/Fax: (087) 37 2250 Mobile: (018) 83 8691
Owner/Contact: Rosemary & Gary Adam
Rooms: S/C cottage
Cost: From double $75 to 8 people $155
Children under 16 free

Moerlong Homestead, Box 258
Tel: (087) 39 3030
Owner/Contact: Graeme & Helene Edwards
Rooms: 1 s/c unit
Cost: $70 double

Naomi's Villa, 20 Riddoch Street (P.O. Box 4)
Tel: (087) 36 3309 Fax: (087) 36 3383
Owner: Anne & James Yates
Rooms: 2, ensuite, separate spa
Cost: $125 double, $30 extra adult, $15 child

Sarah's Cottage, 24 Julian Street, West Penola (P.O. Box 4)
Tel: (087) 36 3309 Fax: (087) 36 3383
Owner/Contact: Anne & James Yates
Rooms: 1, ensuite with spa Ⓥ
Cost: $110 double
No smoking • No children

Ulva Cottage, 14 Bowden Street
Tel/Fax: (087) 37 2250 Mobile: (018) 83 8691
Owner/Contact: Rosemary & Gary Adam
Rooms: S/C cottage
Cost: From double $75 to 8 people $155
Children under 16 free

ROBE S.A. 5276

Grey Masts, 1 Smillie Street
Tel: (087) 68 2303 Ⓥ
Owner/Contact: Raimon Aplin & Andrew Reid
Rooms: 4

Littlecote, 101 Millicent Road (P.O. Box 46)
Tel: (087) 68 2517
Owner/Contact: Mr. & Mrs. J.M. & A.M. Jauncey
Rooms: 1 suite
Cost: $90 single, $100 double
No smoking in rooms ◆ No children

The Criterion Cottage, Bagot Street
Tel: (087) 68 2137
Contact: Mary MacInerney
Rooms: s/c cottage
Cost: From $95 double, $15 extra person

The Lakeside, Main Road
Tel: (087) 68 2042 Fax: (087) 68 2485
Owner/Contact: Mel & Peter Riseley
Rooms: 3
Cost: $95 - $115
No smoking in bedrooms Ⓥ

Wilsons at Robe, Victoria Street (P.O. Box 54),
Tel: (087) 68 2459, A.H. (087) 68 2216
Owner/Contact: Nancy & Terry Johnson
Rooms: s/c cottage
Cost: $95 double, $20 extra person (V)

YAHL S.A. 5291

The Oast House & Cottage, Caroline Headquarters Road
Tel: (087) 24 9536
Rooms: s/c cottage
Cost: From $90 single/2 nights
No smoking indoors

Yorke Peninsula

It looks a bit like a mini-Italy on the map, but this boot-shaped peninsula is just a couple of hours drive from Adelaide. That's all it takes for you to arrive in this quiet, isolated area of the state which owes its claim to fame to the discovery of copper in 1861.

By 1923 the mines had been worked out and the miners from Cornwall gone, but the towns they left behind have retained that strong identity.

The peninsula is known as the Granary of Australia and its barley and wheat are world-renowned.

There are lots of little ports and landing-sites along the east coast, while the west is noted for its safe swimming beaches.

Port Victoria was once the main port of call for sailing-ships carrying grain.

At the boot of the peninsula the Innes National Park has impressive coastal scenery, while Pondalowie Bay is a surfers' dream.

Yorke Peninsula

EDITHBURGH S.A. 5583

Edithburgh House, Edith Street
Tel: (088) 52 6373
Cost: From $120 single/2 nights, including dinner
No children

TROUBRIDGE ISLAND S.A. 5583

Troubridge Island Hideaway, c/o 4 Blanche Street, Edithburgh
Tel: (088) 52 6290
Rooms: s/c lighthouse keeper's cottage
Cost: From $80 single/2 nights

Eyre Peninsula

This rugged coastal region is often referred to as the Peninsula of Parks because almost half the area is reserve or native bushland. But with the bustling cities of Whyalla and Port Lincoln, as well as tourist towns such as Tumby Bay and Cowell, there's more to the region than parklands.

Cowell is one of the world's major sources of jade while Tumby Bay is famous for its fishing and beautiful offshore islands. The region also produces some 10 per cent of Australia's wheat. But it is the natural scenery, particular along the Great Australian Bight, which serves the region best. Towering cliffs, sheltered bays, long sandy beaches and limestone caves are the hallmarks of this area.

It pays to take a trip to the fringes of the Nullarbor Plain and the Gawler Ranges in the far north.

PORT LINCOLN S.A. 5606

"Swanmore Bed & Breakfast", 12 Adelphi Terrace (Box 1630 P.O.)
Tel: (086) 82 2776
Owner/Contact: Eric & Hazel Russell
Rooms: 2, ensuite
Cost: $60 double, $50 single
Dinner by arrangement • No smoking

Willtrees B & B, Lincoln Highway (Box 533)
Tel: (086) 84 3570
Owner/Contact: Margaret Ford
Rooms: 1, ensuite
Cost: $70 double, $40 single
Dinner available • No smoking • No children

Riverland

What hasn't been said about the Mighty Murray!
Its history down the years is the stuff that legends are made of.
One of the longest river systems in the world, the Murray provides a variety of services, from transport to irrigation, along its length.
Apart from being the lifeblood for people along its banks, it is a special attraction in its own right for watersport enthusiasts.
The water is vital to grow fruit and other produce which, in turn, attracts more tourist dollars.
At one stage the Mighty Murray was being compared with the Mississippi as giant paddle steamers used the waters to transport produce and people.
The National Park which bears its name consists of 13,250 hectares and is home to important wildlife such as the rare Murray cod.
Renmark, the region's oldest settlement, is full of history, including the home of irrigation pioneer George Chaffey.

LOXTON S.A. 5333

Nadia Host Farm, Alawoona Road
Tel: (085) 87 4362 Fax: (085) 87 4380
Rooms: 2
Cost: $100 single / 2 nights

Coffin Bay

Finally, a little piece of paradise in South Australia – Coffin Bay. Imagine renting a cottage on a white sandy beach edged with blue, blue water; eating fresh scallops, watching the sun set over the Great Australian Bight.

There is little to do at Coffin Bay – resident population of approximately 100. But there are whales, white pointer sharks, seal colonies, shipwrecks, and keen anglers rave about the fishing – snapper and whiting being the most sought after.

The Yacht Club is open to visitors, and serves lunch and dinner. There are 2 General Stores that are licensed and sell petrol.

This part of the world is somewhere everyone should visit before the tourists/caravan parks move in and ruin the utter peace, beauty and tranquility of this unique area.

Drive - or fly to Port Lincoln and hire a car. John Roger is the man to look out for – he seems to know all of the cottages to rent.